Beyond the
BigFirm

ASPEN PUBLISHERS

Beyond the BigFirm

Profiles of Lawyers Who Want Something More

Alan B. Morrison
Stanford Law School

Diane T. Chin
Stanford Law School

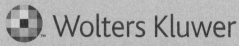

Wolters Kluwer

Law & Business

AUSTIN   BOSTON   CHICAGO   NEW YORK   THE NETHERLANDS

To contact Customer Care, e-mail customer.care@aspenpublishers.com, call 1-800-234-1660, fax 1-800-901-9075, or mail correspondence to:

Aspen Publishers
Attn: Order Department
PO Box 990
Frederick, MD 21705

Printed in the United States of America.

1 2 3 4 5 6 7 8 9 0

ISBN 978-0-7355-6558-6

Library of Congress Cataloging in Publication Data

Morrison, Alan B.
  Beyond the big firm : profiles of lawyers who want something more / Alan B. Morrison, Diane T. Chin.
      p. cm.
    ISBN 978-0-7355-6558-6 (pbk. : alk. paper) 1. Public interest law — Vocational guidance — United States. 2. Practice of law — United States. [1. Lawyers.] I. Chin, Diane T. II. Title.

KF299.P8M67 2007
340.023′73 — dc22

2007005020

About Wolters Kluwer Law & Business

Wolters Kluwer Law & Business is a leading provider of research information and workflow solutions in key specialty areas. The strengths of the individual brands of Aspen Publishers, CCH, Kluwer Law International and Loislaw are aligned within Wolters Kluwer Law & Business to provide comprehensive, in-depth solutions and expert-authored content for the legal, professional and education markets.

CCH was founded in 1913 and has served more than four generations of business professionals and their clients. The CCH products in the Wolters Kluwer Law & Business group are highly regarded electronic and print resources for legal, securities, antitrust and trade regulation, government contracting, banking, pension, payroll, employment and labor, and healthcare reimbursement and compliance professionals.

Aspen Publishers is a leading information provider for attorneys, business professionals and law students. Written by preeminent authorities, Aspen products offer analytical and practical information in a range of specialty practice areas from securities law and intellectual property to mergers and acquisitions and pension/benefits. Aspen's trusted legal education resources provide professors and students with high-quality, up-to-date and effective resources for successful instruction and study in all areas of the law.

Kluwer Law International supplies the global business community with comprehensive English-language international legal information. Legal practitioners, corporate counsel and business executives around the world rely on the Kluwer Law International journals, loose-leafs, books and electronic products for authoritative information in many areas of international legal practice.

Loislaw is a premier provider of digitized legal content to small law firm practitioners of various specializations. Loislaw provides attorneys with the ability to quickly and efficiently find the necessary legal information they need, when and where they need it, by facilitating access to primary law as well as state-specific law, records, forms and treatises.

Wolters Kluwer Law & Business, a unit of Wolters Kluwer, is headquartered in New York and Riverwoods, Illinois. Wolters Kluwer is a leading multinational publisher and information services company.

This book is dedicated to all of the law students and lawyers who have shunned the easy path, and instead chosen a career that is meaningful to them and for the world. It is further dedicated to the thousands who will follow them, hopefully armed with more information about their choices so that they can have careers serving justice and bringing something more to their lives.

Alan B. Morrison & Diane T. Chin

Table of Contents

Foreword — Larry D. Kramer   *xi*

Preface — Alan B. Morrison   *xiii*

Introduction — Kathleen M. Sullivan   *xvii*

**Section 1: Protecting Civil Liberties, Civil Rights,
and the Environment**   **1**

  Civil Liberties & Immigrants Rights — Cecillia Wang   3

  Voting Rights Litigator — Nina Perales   11

  National Origin Discrimination — Deepa Iyer   17

  Women's Rights — Lisalyn Jacobs   27

  Employment Discrimination — Sheila Thomas   37

  Human Rights Abroad — Zama Coursen-Neff   47

  Urban Social Justice Advocate — Ken Zimmerman   55

  Environmental Litigator — Drew Caputo   61

  Environmental Advocate — Doug Heiken   71

Section 2: Direct Service   **79**

  Civil Legal Aid — Kirby Mitchell   81

  Native American Legal Aid — Sylvia Struss   89

  Family Law — Melissa Mager   97

  Immigration Lawyer — Dan Larsson   105

  Solo Practitioner — Joseph Lichtblau   113

  Small-Firm General Litigator — Carlton Reeves   121

  Plaintiff's Toxic Exposure Lawyer — Adam Berger   131

  Plaintiff's Product Defects Lawyer — Stuart Ollanik   141

  Labor Union Lawyer (Private Firm) — Emma Leheny   149

  Labor Union Lawyer (In House) — Ned Burke   159

  University Counsel — Lisa Krim   167

Table of Contents

Section 3: Criminal Law   **175**

    Assistant District Attorney — David O'Keefe   177

    Federal Prosecutor — Donald Cabell   185

    Private Criminal Defense Lawyer — Ed Swanson   193

    Habeas Corpus Specialist — Janice Bergmann   203

Section 4: Other Government Lawyers   **209**

    EEOC Employment Litigator — Raymond Cheung   211

    Federal Civil Appellate Litigator — Alisa Klein   219

    Federal Agency Counsel — Nicola Goren   227

    State Solicitor General — William Thro   237

    Children's Rights Advocate — Kevin Ryan   247

    Senate Committee Counsel — Bob Schiff   257

Section 5: Other Paths to Social Change, Conclusion, and Resources   **267**

    Advocacy by Any Other Name — Three Pursuing Social Change   269

    Conclusion   279

    Resources and Helpful Hints   281

Foreword

By Larry D. Kramer

Richard E. Lang Professor and Dean, Stanford Law School

Stanford Law School has long been committed to promoting public service among its graduates. Stanford pioneered loan forgiveness programs, for instance, and our loan repayment assistance plan (LRAP) remains the most generous in the nation. In recent years, we have worked hard to expand our public service program with the idea that *every* lawyer—no matter what career choice he or she makes—can and should devote part of his or her time to serving the larger community. To that end, we created a new Center for Public Service and Public Interest Law, which has not only given focus to our existing programs and created new synergies but has enlarged what we do to include better career counseling, new curricular offerings, a fellowship training program, and a steady stream of speakers, conferences, and other programs of note.

Stanford Law School has also reorganized and greatly enlarged its clinical program, setting a goal of ensuring that every Stanford law student can and should have a substantial clinical experience before graduating. We recruited Larry Marshall from Northwestern University Law School to become the director and our first Associate Dean for Clinical Education and Public Service. Since arriving at Stanford, Larry has spearheaded the effort to create an innovative clinical program that can serve as a model for other schools. Under this program, we have moved clinics from the periphery to the center of the curriculum. We now offer students a wide range of clinical choices, and, by so doing, give them a palpable sense of the personal satisfaction that comes from using their legal training to help those who have no other access to legal services.

Beyond the Big Firm: Profiles of Lawyers Who Want Something More is another instance of Stanford Law School's commitment to public service and public interest lawyering. We know from experience that law students—not just at Stanford, but everywhere—lack information about the full array of jobs and careers available outside a traditional law firm practice. We know that, beyond generalities and a handful of high-profile positions, students have little sense of just how many ways lawyers serve their communities while finding rewarding professional lives in the law. Like most other law schools, we try as best we can to remedy this deficiency—inviting speakers from different parts of the profession, creating opportunities to network with alumni, sponsoring conferences and programs that bring students and practitioners together, and more. Still, there is only so much we can do, and our efforts at Stanford do nothing to redress the larger problem that students everywhere lack this information.

Alan Morrison, Diane Chin, and the Stanford student-authors of this book have done a tremendous service by creating a vital new source of information and inspiration for young lawyers interested in public service. The thirty-three profiles they have compiled provide basic information about a wide variety of practices and opportunities for lawyers who want to use their degree to pursue a social justice agenda. But they contain much more than just that. These are real stories, about real people, and their profiles offer a window into the real experience of lawyering—a window that should be invaluable to anyone searching for a legal career that is right for them. Not everyone would be equally happy following all, or even most, of these practices. But the sheer number of options is remarkable, and knowing something about them may inspire students to learn more and to think more creatively about their own career choices.

There are countless exciting and useful ways to practice law. And students need to know more about the "something more" that other lawyers have found if they are to make the kinds of choices needed for real career satisfaction. We at Stanford are proud to offer these profiles to assist in that honorable, and vital, endeavor.

Preface

By Alan B. Morrison

There are many reasons why law students go to work at big, traditional law firms — and stay there or move to one of their first cousins. Those firms are the principal recruiters on campus, their salaries are very high, students have large law school loans, and going there is often the path of least resistance.

There is another reason why more lawyers do not go to other jobs: they don't know what else is out there. Of course, every law student knows about prosecutors and public defenders and that there are nonprofit organizations and government agencies that work in a variety of different subject areas. But students' understanding of these other ways to practice law is very limited, and they almost never have a sense of why these other lawyers do what they do or why they like it so much better than the other legal jobs they have held. This book is written to fill that information void.

The idea for the book came into being more than twenty-five years ago when I was on my Sunday morning run in Washington, DC, with Richard Paisner, a lawyer with a strong public interest streak who had become a businessman. His suggestion was to do a series of profiles of lawyers who were doing nontraditional work in order to convey the kinds of opportunities that are out there for those who are willing to explore and perhaps take some risks. I embraced the concept, but bringing it off was a different matter because I didn't have the time (or inclination) to do the interviews and writing myself, and I had no other ideas on how to get them done. Thus, until I arrived at Stanford Law School as a senior lecturer in the fall of 2004, the book lay dormant.

Suddenly, following a discussion about the newly reinvigorated public interest program at Stanford, the answer to the resources question magically appeared: there were 350 first- and second-year students who could do the interviews over the summer and then be around to edit them during the next year. With substantial help from Diane Chin, the director of public interest at the law school and the co-editor of the book, we recruited students (not a hard job) and then found the thirty-three lawyers whose profiles are included. The latter task was made more complicated because our target lawyer was ten to fifteen years out of law school; we had a broad list of types of organizations—in government and out, nonprofit and private, civil and criminal, litigation and nonlitigation—and many subjects to cover. We also wanted, and eventually achieved, broad diversity in geography (fourteen states and the District of Columbia), city size, law school (nineteen schools represented), race, ethnicity, gender, and sexual orientation. And we had to recruit our subjects and train our student interviewers in the very short time before they left for their summer jobs in mid-May 2005.

The chapters have some intended differences, such as what our profilees do, what law schools they attended, and where they live. Some of them knew early on that they wanted to do public interest work of some kind, while others came to that realization much later. Almost no one "planned" a career path that was remotely like the one they followed, and, for many, serendipity got them a job that marked a turning point in their careers.

Almost all of the interviews were done in the summer of 2005, nearly two years before the book was published. Neither the world nor the lawyers we profiled stood still during that time, and we tried to adapt to new job situations and other changes. In one case, a significant portion of a chapter was revised, and in several others we have simply noted at the end that a job change had occurred. All of these new jobs still are nontraditional, and our lawyers could have been profiled in their new positions as well. These changes also make another positive point: within the nontraditional sphere of practice, there are opportunities for movement and a chance to learn new subject areas and develop new skills.

Each chapter is also different because each interviewer brought his or her own perspective and writing style to his or her chapter. Although everyone had my chapter on Sheila Thomas as a model, and everyone was given a number of suggested topics to cover, no two chapters are remotely alike in how the writers approach their subjects and how they weave in the parts of the subjects' lives that brought them to where they are now. We find this refreshing and hope you do also.

Amidst all the differences among these lawyers, two overriding similarities stand out. All of them love their jobs because they fit them, and all of them believe that their work is contributing to society and not just to the clients they represent. Although traditional law firm work is often engaging, not many lawyers at traditional firms would say that they love going to work every day.

There is one other similarity among these lawyers who left traditional law firms: they are much happier now than before. For those who are thinking through their career options, the stories in this book show that it is *not* true that you cannot leave the big firm with the big salary and the big perks and go back to the ideals that brought you to law school in the first place. They also show that nontraditional employers do not view lawyers who have worked for large firms as being eternally beyond redemption. In short, even if you start at a traditional law firm, there is a well-trod path to a different life.

Ideally, every reader will complete every chapter to get a full picture of the rest of the legal world. But we recognize that many readers will be particularly interested in some subjects and not others. Even so, every chapter offers little nuggets of advice on how to find the kind of job you want or identifies what makes that lawyer a happy person. We think each chapter is worth reading even if you have no interest in a particular field of law or a part of the country. And each has a not-so-subliminal message: keep your eyes open because you never know when an opportunity will appear next.

This book is not a how-to-get-a-job manual, but it does contain a chapter with references that may be helpful once you focus your search. That chapter also deals with the major question for many students: can I afford to take the job I love and, if so, how? We have no easy answers, because there are none, but we do have some suggestions. And we also make no promises that your dream job will be available, but we have some ideas about how best to find it. We understand that there are many reasons why students start out at big firms, and many never leave, but we trust that one of those reasons—because you have no idea what else you would like to do if you had a choice—will no longer be true after you read this book.

Introduction

By Kathleen M. Sullivan

Stanley Morrison Professor of Law and
Former Dean, Stanford Law School

Before law school, most of us had a naïve view that all lawyers were courtroom litigators—zealous, elegant, spontaneous, and silver-tongued. It didn't take many weeks of law school to figure out that this was a misleading view. It soon became clear that litigation requires a lot more dogged preparation than it appears to on TV. It became clear too that litigation requires considerable research and writing, not just eloquent sound bites. And it became clear that lawyers do a great many things other than litigation. Lawyers negotiate transactions, start up companies, prepare marriage and estate plans, draft legislation, write executive orders, and advise and counsel both public and private clients on their legal options. Lawyers in our system perform a variety of roles performed by nonlawyers in other systems; as de Tocqueville observed in *Democracy in America*, "When the American people is intoxicated by passion and carried away by the impetuosity of its ideas, it is checked and stopped by the almost invisible influence of its legal counselors."

If law students are quick to recognize the variety of roles that lawyers play, they are often slow to recognize the variety of ways that they may play them. To many aspiring lawyers, legal practice in large private law firms seems the tried and true path to success. And for many it is. Law firms themselves vary considerably in structure, incentives, specialties, and strengths. And many law firms provide richly rewarding careers to those who stay there and valuable training to those who start there and then move on.

But there are also many ways to fashion a fulfilling legal career beyond the traditional law firm. When I was Dean of Stanford Law School, it was my privilege to spend a great deal of time on the road visiting our alumni. Many of them work in traditional law firms, and I was often impressed by the range and quality of their practice. But my travels also took me to meetings with many lawyers who had fashioned very different careers. One traveled to the most troubled spots in the world to monitor and report on human rights violations for Human Rights Watch. Another took on the leadership of the American Civil Liberties Union on the day before 9/11. Yet another took on the chairmanship of Amnesty International. One alumnus, formerly a successful investment banker, became President Bush's chief of staff, while another, formerly a successful company head, became Ambassador to the European Union.

Many of our alumni pursue careers in which they alternate between traditional law firms and public service, as did Warren Christopher, who rose both to chair O'Melveny and Meyers and to serve as President Clinton's Secretary of State. And many of our alumni took an entrepreneurial turn, starting up companies like PayPal or a test-preparation service, and then selling them to larger corporations. Some of our alumni became journalists, featured on CNN or Slate, and one even started a new and successful magazine about Latinas. All of these alumni credited their legal skills with helping them pursue such fascinating nonlegal jobs.

But perhaps most creative of all are those lawyers who invent from within the law, starting or pursuing a new kind of legal practice. A former student of mine at Harvard Law School founded a legal services organization for gay men and lesbians who were discharged from the armed services because of their sexual orientation. Another won a MacArthur award for starting up an organization to represent women who work as maids and other unorganized service providers. Still a third created a new legal services provider for defendants on death row. Co-editor Diane Chin, who we were so fortunate to bring to Stanford Law School as our inaugural Levin public interest and public service director, did a wonderful job bringing many such lawyers to campus to share their experiences.

Among the most inspirational lawyers who have reinvented law practice is none other than the other co-editor of this book: Alan B. Morrison. It was my good fortune to take two courses from Alan when I was a student at Harvard Law School, and his teaching has stayed with me for life. With his impeccable credentials and crisp Navy veteran manner, he could have ascended to the top of any law firm he chose.

But Alan took a different path. Founder of the Public Citizen Litigation Group, he started a new public interest law firm from scratch. Alan spotted issues no one had ever thought of before and made them into new law. Why shouldn't lawyers be allowed to advertise their services, or pharmacists their drug prices? Alan and Public Citizen pioneered the law of commercial speech, reasoning that consumers would benefit from more information, more choice, and lower prices. Why should special interests be able to hijack public policy by exercising one-House vetoes over executive decisions? Alan and Public Citizen established new law on separation of powers, concluding that the more faithfully our original constitutional procedures are followed, the more democratically accountable our government will be. He also found new ways to obtain information from government and new ways to use that information to benefit consumers and the public. In short, Alan blazed whole new paths beyond the traditional law firm and trained a generation of his junior colleagues and students to do likewise.

To go beyond the traditional law firm does not mean going beyond traditional legal education. As Alan often reminded me when I was Dean, students interested in public interest jobs need to take courses in tax, corporations, and accounting as well as evidence, civil rights, and civil procedure. Sometimes the more you innovate in your legal practice, the more you need a legal generalist's full battery of skills. And issues of professional ethics and professional responsibility are as vital for nontraditional as for traditional lawyers. Nor does going beyond the traditional law firm inevitably require a choice between doing good and doing (reasonably) well. Sometimes the most rewarding careers are those that involve elements of risk and adventure and choices that temporarily raise eyebrows among your family and friends.

Nothing can describe the range of nontraditional legal career options better than the individual stories of the lawyers who have taken such paths. The range of options represented in this book is both illustrative and inspiring. Diane and Alan and the students who assisted them in producing this wonderful collection have done a great service for law students and recent law graduates by portraying just how courageous and creative lawyers can be. I am sure that you will greatly enjoy reading about them.

Beyond the
BigFirm

Section 1

Protecting
Civil Liberties,
Civil Rights,
and the Environment

CECILLIA WANG

Civil Liberties & Immigrants Rights

By Diane T. Chin

At many junctures in her impressive career, Cecillia Wang admits she was drawn to becoming what is perceived as a "big-name lawyer." She wanted high-profile cases doing "some big impressive thing." Since graduating from Yale Law School in 1995, Cecillia certainly has done many impressive things and has worked on cases for high-profile clients. Now she knows herself better and realizes that what she "loves most is to make a big difference in a small case" that impacts real lives.

When asked about the one case that makes her realize that she chose the right profession, Cecillia recounts the tale of a criminal defendant she represented six or seven years ago in a losing cause. She does not describe the notorious cases that were in the media on a daily basis, or the litigation that she has helped formulate to protect the rights of immigrants, or *Ali v. Rumsfeld*, the case on behalf of tortured Guantanamo Bay detainees, which at this writing, is currently occupying most of her time. Instead she describes a client who was caught up in bad circumstances and agreed to serve as a drug courier. Although the client readily pled guilty, the case involved a hotly contested sentencing that ended in an extremely unfair prison term. Her client was ultimately deported to the Dominican Republic. She thinks about this client not only because they have stayed in touch, but because of the dignity he brought to the proceedings, what she learned from him about accepting responsibility, and because he always tells Cecillia how much her representation meant to him. When he was in prison, he sent her a Mother's Day card because in his mind Cecillia was a mother to all her clients by bringing them hope and life.

One of the things that strikes you first when you sit across from Cecillia is her ready laugh and her ability to make you feel completely at ease. It is not difficult to imagine her quickly gaining a client's trust or that of opposing counsel, a jury, or a judge. Her personality certainly is an asset inside and outside the courtroom. It is her wisdom, however, gained from hard experiences of alienation and racism, that make you understand how she has succeeded in her career.

Cecillia is a Senior Staff Counsel for the ACLU Immigrants' Rights Project (IRP), where she works on impact cases related to immigration, civil rights, criminal law, and national security. It might seem like a logical course for this daughter of Chinese immigrants to have taken, but there were several paths that she followed before arriving in her California office casually dressed. The office was in a funky downtown area of Oakland, but IRP has since moved into a new, swanky building in San Francisco with the ACLU of Northern California. Cecillia stresses that, while she does have a political and emotional tie to the work in which she is now engaged, it is because she is constantly learning new things and able to exercise her craft with very smart colleagues that makes her work most worthwhile.

Cecillia grew up in Fremont, California, before immigration reform and the "dot com boom" had transformed that part of the Bay Area into a home away from home for tens of thousands of Asian Americans and immigrants. Well into the 1980s, when Cecillia graduated from high school, and even more recently, Asian Americans in this region experienced hate crimes against them—property vandalism, racist graffiti, and physical attacks. What Cecillia remembers about Fremont during the 1970s is that it seemed quintessentially suburban, and was "very, very white."

Like many Asian Americans who confronted racism in a time when the dominant paradigm didn't allow for an understanding of people of color who were not black, Cecillia remembers that the experiences she had were wrong, but she felt confused about how to deal with them. With some chagrin but with a humorous wisdom in her eyes, Cecillia recounts yelling back at fellow students in her public elementary school who had called her an anti-Japanese epithet, "I'm not a nip, I'm a chink!"

She navigated the public schools and found a group of friends who were mainly other Asian Americans similarly forging new ground. It is clear from the way she speaks about it that her childhood and her struggle at the time to understand what felt like a pervasive lack of fairness but that she couldn't clearly name deeply affected her perceptions of American society and hierarchy.

Cecillia's parents, both immigrants from Taiwan who came to the United States to pursue higher education in the 1960s, were typical in their response to her frustrations about racism. Advised by them to "just work harder" and to ignore the taunts, Cecillia excelled in her classes, but as a reporter on her high school newspaper sought to write an exposé on the lack of teacher diversity in the school district. Her journalism teacher discouraged this effort.

As an undergraduate at UC Berkeley, Cecillia found a framework to begin understanding her experiences in Ethnic Studies classes and through student activism. For the first time in her life she says she "felt like [she] could breathe." Cecillia found friends and a community. She entered college thinking she would go on to medical school but had no talent for chemistry. In spite of her love for science, she decided that medical school was not in her future. Instead, she declared a double major in English and Biology and graduated as valedictorian in both.

At UC Berkeley, Cecillia was inspired by the movement for Japanese-American redress and the case seeking to overturn the conviction of Fred Korematsu for his defiance of the Japanese internment orders during World War II. Those efforts and other issues on which she was engaged as a student activist, including as a summer intern at the Asian Law Caucus, led her to think about law school.

Cecillia accepted Yale because she wanted to experience life outside the Bay Area and because Harvard felt too much like Berkeley. Her experiences at law school during the first months of her first year were alienating. Before she found the group of students, professors, and mentors who would help her thrive in law school and the legal profession, she confronted for the first time being middle class in an elite institution. She still recalls with some heat a fellow first-year student in her contracts class belittling her for her confusion about a writ of assumpsit, or the comment of another student that she "must be smart enough if you made it into Yale from a state school."

Though she privately shed some tears, Cecillia also squared her shoulders and determined to do her best. One can imagine that she no longer needed to hear anyone tell her to "just work harder." She naturally fell into the role of a "Berkeley leftie," and spoke a lot in class, challenging assumptions and questioning why there was so little connection between the real world and what was being taught in class.

A few key professors, clinics, and other public interest students helped her find her place at Yale, which she now remembers fondly. She was a student in the Immigration Clinic and Lowenstein Human Rights Clinic, and counts Professors Carroll Lucht, Jean Koh Peters, Harlon Dalton, and now-Dean Harold Koh among her mentors. Her summers were spent externing with San Francisco District Judge Marilyn Hall Patel, who had written the decision overturning Fred Korematsu's criminal conviction some years before, and working in two large firms. What she liked about her summer experiences, though they were very dissimilar workplaces, was her ability to be intellectually engaged in the work.

When asked why she decided to become a judicial clerk on the Ninth Circuit Court of Appeals working for Judge William Norris, Cecillia's response is immediate. "Everyone was doing it." However, she quickly adds that a clerkship "is the best way to start out because it gives you confidence in appearing in court—you know how judges think." She realized during her clerkship that she had learned very little about actual lawyering during law school. She graduated with strong writing abilities, but her clerkships on the Ninth Circuit and then with Justice Harry Blackmun on the U.S. Supreme Court were where she believes she actually learned how to think like a lawyer.

Obviously very bright and academically accomplished, with an already enviable résumé, Cecillia was not certain what she should do for a career. While she was at the Ninth Circuit, she accepted an offer from a firm where she had spent part of her second-year summer of law school. But she felt conflicted about joining the firm. As her Supreme Court clerkship was winding down, a friend from law school, who had been a Skadden Fellow with the ACLU Immigrants' Rights Project, contacted her. The IRP was creating a one-year fellowship and he thought she should apply. Through work at the Lowenstein Clinic, she previously had met Lucas Guttentag, the project's director and arguably one of the best immigration attorneys in the country then and now, and any ideas about becoming an associate at a corporate firm evaporated. In describing the mentor-lawyer who would play an ongoing role in her life and career, Cecillia uses a chess player analogy: "You can just watch him planning the next move, analyzing the whole board, anticipating what will happen."

Cecillia got the fellowship and plunged into a crash course in immigration law and the nuances of a national appellate practice. Painstaking in its selection of cases, the IRP conducts a national evaluation of legal issues prior to filing an action. She learned a tremendous amount from "watching this enormous intellectual machine work" to decide which issues it would push toward the Supreme Court for resolution. It was a world with which she was generally familiar from the other side of the bench during her clerkships. As a practicing lawyer, however, she learned the ins and outs of case evaluation, identifying broad issues that could remedy systemic problems, and continued to strengthen her written advocacy abilities.

But she wanted to get into court and try cases. At the end of her fellowship, Cecillia determined to go to New York. Law firms once again became a viable option, but then another friend had a better idea. Cecillia became a federal public defender in the Southern District of New York.

According to Cecillia, being a federal defender is "the best job in the world. Your clients are anyone and everyone. You are a real lawyer, helping real people everyday. It opens your eyes and prepares you for life." It was in this position where she met her favorite client and in which she says she learned the most.

She carried a docket of cases ranging from drugs and guns to fraud to immigration crimes. Her days were long, usually twelve to thirteen hours a day, and work filled many weekends. Cecillia admits that she became attached to her clients, saying now that the work was "perhaps a little too exciting and emotionally draining." It was hard for her, however, not to make every effort for those clients because often "the system had let them down during their lives and then again in the criminal justice process."

Cecillia reflects that, in this rough and tumble world of criminal defense, and perhaps the entire legal profession, women of color still must "just work harder." Particularly as a trial lawyer, she thinks Asian-American women struggle against stereotype. This operates both in developing one's relationships with clients and inside the court-room. "If you seem earnest or starry-eyed, jurors might assume you've been duped by your more sophisticated, worldly client." Somehow she thinks that it has worked for her, though she is not what they expect from a young, Chinese-American woman lawyer. Still, even now, with all of her experience and success, Cecillia exclaims, "I want more gray hairs! I'm looking for gravitas. I can't wait to be in a courtroom when I look older."

Asked what advice she would give to young women in the field, she observes that she sees young women lawyers who seem to play down their intelligence. She does a mean impersonation of "Valley Girl speak," and asks "why would they think this makes them more effective?" She mentors other young women now, drawing their attention to personality traits that might make them less credible and less professional.

After almost four years in this "best job in the world" in New York, family concerns led Cecilla reluctantly to return to California. She recognized this as an opportunity to recover from "emotional burnout" and, perhaps, to improve her finances. She applied to two firms and accepted a position at Keker & Van Nest.

This proved to be a different kind of lawyering altogether. Highly resourced, in lovely offices in San Francisco, Cecillia worked for a firm with a large profile and for a man with an even larger personality. She said she "clicked" with John Keker and other lawyers at his firm because they are fun and profane and have a trial mentality. She ended up loving her job, as she consistently was learning and being exposed to outstanding lawyers and new experiences, including the glare of the spotlight as she was a team member on cases that held great media interest and presented novel questions of law.

Another phone call would open another door, this time a familiar one. Leaning back in her chair and holding up her hands, Cecillia smiles and says, "Then Lucas calls me out of the blue. He offers me a job to work specifically on criminal law and immigration." She felt incredibly torn. She was financially comfortable for the first time, had fascinating work, and a life that felt like being "a real lawyer." When asked what this meant to her at the time, she laughs again and says, "You know—good cases, getting into court, long hours, no life, fancy hotels, travel, um, long hours and no life."

Cecillia went through an elaborate evaluation process and consulted with friends and examined her budget. She faced a sixty percent pay cut. In a pivotal conversation with Lucas, he asked her the question that would control her decision. "What do you want to do with your life?"

Now, Cecillia says, "ultimately, it has not been much of a sacrifice. I confess to missing my old colleagues and some of the benefits that come with working for wealthy clients, but look at my clients now." It means something to be "really proud to be a lawyer right now." She knows that she has the capacity to do so many things and that she has the freedom to pursue cases because she is part of a well-run organization, working with four other incredibly talented lawyers, student interns, and the IRP's public education staff. She also sometimes pitches in with grant writing. It helps that she is very comfortable with the people she works with, and can be herself. When I spent time at the IRP offices, it was clear that everyone with whom I came into contact felt the same way. There is a very congenial mood within the office. Her office includes toys and art ranging from Jacob Lawrence to Miró as well as boxes and boxes of case files and reports.

This real lawyer also now has a life. At this writing, Cecillia is working on *Ali v. Rumsfeld*, with a team of lawyers seeking to hold the Secretary of Defense and high-ranking Army officers responsible for the widespread abuse of prisoners in Iraq and Afghanistan. This has required her to travel to Jordan to locate witnesses and plaintiffs. Her docket also includes cases challenging long delays in naturalization, discrimination against noncitizens in the criminal justice system, and Freedom of Information Act cases against the Department of Homeland Security.

Cecillia advises students contemplating entering the law and young lawyers to keep their eyes open. "It's just a mistake to allow yourself to feel trapped in any one job." She notes that working at a law firm may have its place, "if it works for your life." Cecillia also reflects that as time has passed, she has watched friends and former classmates leave the law altogether because they were so unhappy being "real lawyers" at "real firms." Only one close friend actually went on to become a law firm partner.

Being a lawyer, Cecillia reminds people: "you can do anything you want," but, she warns, never think that "being a lawyer is everything you are."

NINA PERALES

Voting Rights Litigator

By Soraya Yanar Hanshew

Nina Perales represents duality. She has melded the traditions and expectations of her culture with the demands and frenetic pace of her legal career to be at the same time a dedicated wife and mother and an ardent activist and litigator. To all women who doubt being one and the same, Nina responds loudly: "It can be done!"

According to Nina, the key to harmonizing her traditional roles with those of manager and litigator has been to have passion for each of these roles and for *all* of her life's work. Nina is passionate about every realm of her life. She believes if you love what you do it will become as much a part of you as your family and home. From her background and upbringing to the dual nature of her legal practice, Nina has never hesitated in pursuing what her interests dictate. The result is a life and practice without limits, where cultural traditions and professional ambitions live side by side and the complexity of *who* Nina is becomes exemplified by both her private life and her very public practice of the law.

Nina was born in the Big Apple and considers herself a big-city girl, though she did not live in New York City for long. When Nina was a year old, her parents divorced. Following the divorce, Nina's mother moved with Nina to a quiet, fairly homogeneous Massachusetts suburb where almost all the residents were Caucasian. From that point on, Nina's parents shared custody of Nina and raised her cross-culturally in two vastly different homes—in Massachusetts and in New York City. During the school year, Nina called Massachusetts home. She remembers her time spent in school as academically unchallenging and yet emotionally difficult in that she was almost invariably the only Latina in her class as well as on her block.

However, Nina's mother was progressive and unconventional with regard to Nina's upbringing. When they moved to Massachusetts, Nina's mother, who had been raised as a Catholic, converted to Unitarianism. She made great efforts to expose Nina to nontraditional viewpoints while Nina was living with her. Nina's mother encouraged a worldview with less societal constraints and promoted in her household a paradigm shift where the role of women in society was viewed with a more liberated outlook.

In contrast, when summer arrived, Nina returned to New York City to live with her father, stepmother, and stepsister in their traditional Catholic Puerto Rican household, where family, Catholicism, and ethnic traditions took center stage and were the basis of family life. Nina recalls being constantly surrounded by extended family and ethnic traditions during her summers in New York. Though the city pulsed with energy and brimmed with unconventionality, Nina's upbringing in her father's home was far more traditional than anything she experienced in the Massachusetts suburbs. Regardless, to this day, if you ask Nina where she's from, she will immediately respond, "New York, New York."

Despite her preference for New York City, Nina quickly learned how to meld her differing experiences and existences to complement one another. It is clear that Nina was greatly influenced by this duality of upbringing.

Nina's road toward her extraordinary legal practice began on a unique academic path. When Nina was sixteen, her mother encouraged her to attend Simon's Rock College, a small liberal arts college in Massachusetts that allows students of high school age to begin their collegiate careers early by completing their high school curriculum at the age of sixteen. For Nina, Simon's Rock afforded her the opportunity to leave her racially homogeneous high school in the suburbs, where she felt marginalized by her peers because of both her racial diversity and her intellectual curiosity and ambition. In July following her freshman year Nina turned sixteen; that following September, Nina began college at Simon's Rock.

Immediately upon arriving on campus, Nina felt a sense of belonging and excitement she had never experienced in her earlier academic settings. For the first time in her life, Nina recalls she felt "supported in her difference and applauded in her nerdiness." Today, she credits her time at Simon's Rock for the development of her self-esteem and for creating a deep desire to strive for academic excellence.

After two years at Simon's Rock, Nina's father encouraged her to enroll at Brown University. At the time, Brown was well known for being the place where the Democratic Party's elite sent their children to be educated. Though Nina indicates she fell far short of being part of this group of students, especially with regard to her financial background, Nina was nonetheless one of them. By the time Nina arrived onto the Brown campus, Nina's father was entrenched in politics, having served under the Carter Administration and as Deputy Mayor of New York City. Consequently, not unlike her peers with similarly situated parents, Nina became involved in campus and national politics almost immediately.

Though only eighteen when she arrived at Brown, Nina already felt the need to pursue what she refers to as a "life of service" and soon became involved on campus in urging divestment in South Africa. She chose to major in Women's Studies and participated in groups involved in women's rights. To Nina, this type of political work realized her need to serve others and to do work she felt was "worthwhile." Nina recalls looking at her classmates and realizing "certain people were getting tremendous privileges in society and other people were being denied." She saw that this applied most obviously to the wealthy children of the political elite who traversed the campus in their sports cars, but she also recognized this ultimately applied to her as well. She indicates that only by circumstance and luck was she able to achieve the level of success she's enjoyed, primarily because she believes she was lucky in having the opportunity to be informed regarding her options for education and beyond. Nina believes that there were many similarly gifted students who were not able to pursue a higher education like the one offered at Brown solely because they lacked the information on how to gain access to such an institution. When she realized this, Nina chose to dedicate her time and life to serving those more disadvantaged and less informed than she was. She decided to focus on assisting those individuals society leaves behind. It was this pursuit of service toward the disadvantaged that eventually motivated Nina to study law.

Following graduation from Brown, Nina returned to her beloved New York and attended Columbia Law School. By the time she began law school, it was clear to Nina that her love of law and politics would never be mutually exclusive, and that a life of service was fundamental to her future. She was aware she would have to find a way to combine all of these interests in her future practice. Unfortunately, not unlike her peers in law school, Nina knew generally what she wanted from the law but had no idea how to reach her goal in a practical way. Once again, she claims through circumstance and luck she found her way.

While at Columbia Law School, Nina was approached to work at the Puerto Rican Legal Defense Fund (PRLDF), an organization that had been founded by her father. She was asked to assist on several specific cases, which accelerated as she began her third year in law school. As a result, she was asked by PRLDF to continue her work on these cases during law school and was encouraged to join PRLDF permanently after graduation. PRLDF motivated Nina to pursue a new Skadden Fellowship that was being offered to recent graduates. Nina applied, was awarded the fellowship, and used it to continue her work with PRLDF. Her "life of service" as an attorney began.

During the course of practicing law in New York, Nina met her husband. Nina's husband, also a graduate from Columbia Law School, hailed originally from Texas, and following law school he wanted to return to his home state to practice law. The couple decided to give Texas a try. Nina was offered a position with the Mexican American Legal Defense and Educational Fund (MALDEF) in their San Antonio office and began her work as a voting rights litigator.

Though Nina to this day misses New York City, she admits that serving the underprivileged in Texas is an incredibly satisfying experience. She believes that Texas conservatism provides a fabulous background for efforts to protect the civil rights of minorities, more so than in more liberal states. "The fight is harder fought and better won in Texas." She feels that she could not be in a better place to serve the disadvantaged than where she finds herself now. Nina does, however, admit that nonprofit civil rights work in Texas and elsewhere "is probably one of the lowest-paid sectors of the law. A new attorney might start at $40,000, and top salaries for directors range from $100,000 to $250,000. But that doesn't make the field easy to get into," she warns. "Because our sector is so small, we can be very particular about whom we take in." Nina looks for people with experience as aggressive litigators who, much like herself, demonstrate a commitment to the disadvantaged community. Because her office in San Antonio focuses exclusively on civil rights, litigation on behalf of Latinos in the areas of education, immigration, employment discrimination, and political access, Nina rarely hires recent law school graduates for available positions. But she encourages recent graduates to pursue a practice in this field and notes that though MALDEF has certainly not made her wealthy, she credits her time at MALDEF as being the place where she has been able to meld her interests in politics, law, and a life of service.

Recently, Nina was named Regional Counsel for MALDEF's litigation, advocacy, and public education in Texas, New Mexico, Colorado and six other southern and western states. In addition to managing her office and all regional litigation, Nina herself specializes in voting rights litigation, including redistricting and vote-dilution challenges. She is most famous for her service and participation as lead counsel for Latino plaintiffs in the congressional redistricting in Texas in 2001 and in Texas and Arizona in 2003. As Nina explains it, "Redistricting is the wildest political ride you can ever go on. [Politicians] fight for their lives and to [do in] their enemies—and there's blood everywhere. It's very exciting." For Nina, pursuing a career in voting rights litigation has allowed her to meld her political, academic, and professional interests and passions. As a result, she has been incredibly successful.

Through these redistricting cases Nina has made history. As she sees it, her odyssey with Texas redistricting began in the spring of 2001. At that time the Census Bureau released data affecting redistricting for federal legislative districts in Texas, and the Texas Legislature failed in their task to pass a redistricting plan that reflected population changes in the Latino community. As a result MALDEF filed a case, *Balderas v. Texas*, a malapportionment challenging the map and arguing that it did not adequately protect the interests of Latino voters. Though other parties had filed similar actions prior to MALDEF's, all such actions were dismissed for lack of ripeness. Only MALDEF's case survived.

That summer, the Texas Legislative Redistricting Board enacted plans for the State House and Senate. MALDEF challenged these plans for diluting Latino voting strength as well. Following a change of venue, on October 22, 2001, the trial of the congressional redistricting case began in federal court. The trial resulted in a plan that MALDEF appealed to the U.S. Supreme Court for not meeting the requirements of the federal Voting Rights Act. The plan was affirmed. This was just the beginning of a journey for Nina and MALDEF involving Texas politics, runaway senators and a new host of litigation filed in attempts to protect the Latino majority districts still in existence in Texas.

New redistricting litigation began in response to a congressional map that was drawn in the summer of 2003 by a Republication-led state legislature with great assistance by then Congressman Tom Delay. In spite of a staff-level recommendation that the map not be approved for reducing minority voting strength, senior DOJ officials approved the new districts. The map's focus on altering the borders of one particular district led to MALDEF's representation of Latino community groups to challenge the new map's adoption. The lower courts found in favor of the State of Texas. MALDEF appealed to the US Supreme Court, was granted certiorari, and suddenly Nina found herself preparing for oral argument.

At first, Nina was shocked to learn that the Supreme Court was willing to hear MALDEF's claims of voter dilution. Then she faced the daunting task of simultaneously preparing for oral argument and coordinating the argument with another attorney who represented the Democratic Party in a challenge that had been consolidated with her case, all in a ten week period of time. Because Nina did not want her representation of Latino community interests to be viewed as supportive of one political party, she focused her preparation and arguments strictly on the history of voting rights caselaw, the history of discrimination in voting experienced by

Latinos in Texas, and the voting rights violated by the new map. It was clear from the argument that Nina's strategy used the right tone with the Justices. In June 2006, in a 5-4 ruling, Justice Kennedy wrote the opinion that struck down the Texas map because it violated the voting rights of Latino voters.

From start to finish, Nina has loved her participation in this redistricting madness and reflects that this and other work at MALDEF has allowed her to enjoy the career she wanted. Nina, however, does not see this as her greatest accomplishment. In fact, if asked, Nina will tell you her greatest achievement has been her ability to be an involved wife and mother while attempting to pursue her life as a litigator and advocate. Nina believes in putting family first. She prides herself on the fact that her office truly respects family time and she expects that everyone in her office who is not in trial should be able to go home for dinner. Nina thus encapsulates the dynamic, multifaceted person—first as a brilliant litigator, advocate, and sociopolitical analyst, and second as a dedicated wife, mother, sister, and daughter. To all women who doubt being one and the same, Nina states "It can be done!" All who know Nina can attest to the fact she is doing it, with grace, passion, heart, and courage.

DEEPA IYER

National Origin Discrimination

By Melanie Wachtell

In the seven days following September 11th, there were 645 documented incidents of hate crimes against South Asian Americans in the United States.[1] As one victim described them, "It is the most isolating experience you can go through to be a victim of one of these attacks." Whether isolated by hate-motivated violence or political marginalization, many South Asian Americans and recent immigrants find themselves alienated from the legal system that is supposed to protect their rights. In the nine years since earning her J.D., Deepa Iyer has worked tirelessly to make this legal system more accessible to citizens and noncitizens alike. While she has described many of the steps in her career as "accidental" and has worked for a half-dozen different employers, her sustained commitment to the development of a unified and supportive South Asian American community with a voice in the policy-making arena has been unwavering.

Growing up without much exposure to the legal profession, Deepa did not plan to be a lawyer — or an executive director of a national civil rights organization, for that matter. Her sense of social justice developed long before her interest in the law. Deepa spent her childhood in India and moved with her family to Louisville, Kentucky, when she was twelve. As a young immigrant in a city without a robust South Asian community, Deepa developed a personal understanding of the difficulties facing minorities in a country still struggling with race relations.

When she entered Vanderbilt University as a college freshman, Deepa found the first community with which she could fully identify.

1. Raising Our Voices: South Asian Americans Address Hate, 2002 (documentary video on file with South Asian American Leaders of Tomorrow).

While the school itself was "only beginning to face issues of race and immigration," she remembers that there were partnerships and alliances forming within the minority student body. Deepa created outlets for her interest in minority diversity and equality, helping to form an Indian students association her first year and working to ensure that there were more professors of color and classes that dealt with non-Western experiences.

Although she was politically active in college, Deepa was not similarly excited by her first encounter with the law, which came during the summer after her junior year, when she interned for a trusts and estates attorney. Uninspired by the practice of law as she perceived it, Deepa decided to pursue a bachelor's degree in English. She had a particular interest in the South Asian experience as revealed in literature and applied to a Ph.D. program to study the subject in greater depth. However, wary of the job prospects for academics in her field, Deepa also applied to several law schools. She ultimately opted for the legal track, but considered it a temporary step taken for financial security. She notes: "I thought I could always go back to school later. The J.D. is only three years. So [I thought], 'I'll go and I'll make some money and then I'll go back and enter the Ph.D. [program].'"

Deepa chose Notre Dame Law School, but without, in her words, a "very clear sense of what law school would be like, or what Notre Dame's legal program would offer me." She recalls having not done "enough research, in terms of what the field look[ed] like." As she began classes, like many other law students, she found that in order to succeed in law school, the way she had been "learning and the way [she] had been writing and reading had to change dramatically." Deepa recalls: "I was definitely not prepared for that."

Deepa's somewhat inadvertent decision to attend law school resulted in an experience that, on the whole, she does not remember fondly. "I'm definitely one of those people who can say I didn't enjoy law school. I don't have too many fond memories actually. I have some strong lifelong friends. But it was a challenging experience and I questioned my ability to become a lawyer in the manner that it is traditionally imagined, and mourned the loss of my creativity and originality as I began to learn to think and write as a lawyer." The lack of a strong community was another factor in the isolation that Deepa felt during law school. At the time, Notre Dame lacked a substantial immigrant or minority student body; Deepa says now that she could "probably count the number of minority [law] students on two hands."

Though not a pleasant experience, law school did offer Deepa outlets for her developing sense of social justice. On the academic front, she found an interest in constitutional law, specifically in the use of legal strategies to assist women, people of color, and immigrants. Long dedicated to the values of equal rights, Deepa further developed her commitment to "meaningful access for people who are vulnerable and marginalized," focusing on how she could "use the law to ensure that those individuals have access, not just to the legal system, but to their rights." This included an immigration clinic serving the growing local Latino community.

Deepa became more politicized during her law school years, as she became keenly aware of the power of legal tools to ease the marginalization of vulnerable communities in America. Given her current role as a community leader and legal advocate in the immigrant community, it is tempting to view her law school experience as the period during which she decided that the law would be her way to serve the cause of social justice. While Deepa's commitment to underrepresented communities continued to grow during this time, she recalls that "I can't say that law school crystallized for me the shape that my career would eventually take. It didn't. But law school did start me on the path of understanding the importance of using a social justice framework in approaching the law."

With no clear sense of what she wanted to do upon graduation, Deepa applied for various positions in corporate firms, government litigation departments, and public interest organizations. Law students were tracked toward corporate work or litigation, both within law firm practice. Given her preference for litigation and with minimal information about public interest career options, Deepa accepted an offer to work in the labor and employment division of Ice, Miller, Donadio, and Ryan (now Ice, Miller) in Indianapolis.

She stayed for only ten months. While she had been intrigued by employment law during law school, her real interest was in providing legal help and access to people who needed counsel. At Ice, Miller she found herself representing companies being investigated for employment discrimination. Finding that she was "empathizing more with the plaintiff than . . . with the company," Deepa went through a difficult period during which she was "consumed with doubt," and wondered whether "this was what [she] went to law school for" and "what [she] was supposed to do with her life." Deepa also realized that the corporate culture was not a good fit for her personally, feeling that she would thrive in a more casual work environment. Also, at the time there were not many people of color at the firm, an additional factor contributing to Deepa's sense of unease about the job.

Conflicted over whether to stay and try to change things from within the firm or to leave to pursue a different course, Deepa made "a major decision" to move to Washington, DC, in 1998 and begin her career in the nonprofit sector. At that time there were few role models to whom she could turn for guidance and advice. "I made a gut decision with this move," she notes. "Although I had little experience or knowledge of immigrant rights issues and advocacy, I had a keen sense that the work I would be doing at the nonprofit in DC was closer to what I felt was right for me."

In sharp contrast to the disquiet she felt at the corporate firm, Deepa remembers walking into the Asian American Justice Center's office (formerly the National Asian Pacific American Legal Consortium) in Washington for an interview and "knowing . . . that this was where I needed to be at that point in time." She recalls that she naturally adapted to the nonprofit environment and to the civil rights focus of her work. She was charged with directing three program areas — Census 2000 advocacy, language rights, and voting rights, which gave her a substantial amount of responsibility as a young attorney in a new field. Deepa views her experience as characteristic of the nonprofit world. Describing her love for working at nonprofit organizations, she notes that "[a] nonprofit can allow you the opportunity to take ownership of a program or project and shape it. I've been fortunate to have those experiences." That is exactly what Deepa did at AAJC, where at the age of twenty-five, she engaged with civil rights allies, the White House, and members of Congress, advocating against legislation that would disadvantage Asian Americans and asserting the community's perspective at the policy table.

After two years at AAJC, Deepa sought a position that would add to her experience in active litigation and applied to the Civil Rights Division of the Department of Justice. Deepa was hired as a trial attorney at the Office of Special Counsel for Unfair Immigration Related Employment Practices, where she represented immigrants and citizens who faced employment discrimination. Then-Deputy Assistant Attorney General John Trasvina notes the "unique combination of policy and litigation" experience that Deepa presented as a candidate. According to Trasvina, as a young lawyer Deepa did a "thorough job in terms of motions and research, but where she shines was working in policy issues." The job was a good fit for her, as she was responsible for a full docket of cases, while at the same time charged with educating the community about her department's offerings. Perhaps most important to Deepa, she served as a "point of entry in the government" for people who may not otherwise have had access.

Deepa was acting as this "point of entry" when the September 11th terrorist attacks occurred. Her office was evacuated along with the other government agencies in DC. Living just half a mile from the Pentagon, the "gaping hole" served as a constant reminder to Deepa of the lives lost on that day. At the same time, she was concerned with the emerging "tremendous backlash against the South Asian community." It was at this moment that Deepa was catapulted to the forefront of the anti-backlash efforts at the Department of Justice and in the South Asian American community nationwide. Trasvina recalls that she was "called upon by a lot of different people in the Department after 9/11 to get the message out to protect the civil rights of people in the United States [and] to fight back [against] the urges that had been carried out by some people to commit hate crimes." With three other attorneys, Deepa created the DOJ's Post-9/11 Initiative to Combat Backlash Discrimination, seeking to ensure that hate crimes were being reported, investigated, and prosecuted. During a very intense several weeks, she was receiving reports from people who were victims of discrimination and hate-motivated violence, working with organizational leaders, combing websites, and reading newspaper articles — determined to provide justice for the victims of the 9/11 backlash.

While working full time at the DOJ, Deepa was also serving as the executive producer of a documentary on hate crimes in the South Asian American community, which had been in production long before 9/11. When a Sikh man was killed in Arizona the weekend after September 11th, she quickly realized that the documentary now had increased relevance but needed to be overhauled to reflect the backlash crisis. The final product conveys not only the tragic and unprovoked violence perpetrated against South Asian Americans before and after 9/11, but also Deepa's growing commitment and influence as a spokesperson and legal advocate for the community. Deepa's current career cannot meaningfully be disentangled from the influence of 9/11 and the backlash it incited. She notes: "Since 9/11, things have not really quieted down for me in a lot of ways. I am still sort of reeling from the work we did."

Ultimately, it became evident to Deepa that she had to leave the Department of Justice. She recalls: "It was difficult for me to do outreach into the community and say, 'If you have discrimination complaints, report them to the DOJ,' while at the same time, I was hearing from the community, 'Well, there have been raids by the FBI and the INS. No charges have been filed. We don't know where our family members are. There have been secret hearings.' It was really hard to maintain credibility as a community advocate in the government sector at that time."

Deepa's next job would add another layer of experience for her. She wanted to do work directly in the community and was hired as the legal director for the Asian Pacific American Legal Resource Center (APALRC) in June 2002. A vastly different environment from the Department of Justice, the APALRC start-up organization operated with only four staff members. Here, Deepa found what she was looking for: a local community-based experience. At the APALRC, Deepa set up an infra-structure for a multilingual legal hotline for low-income Asian Americans with limited English proficiency. Deepa was "putting into place policies and processes that had not existed before"—an opportunity intrinsic to the nature of the organization.

Shaeli Agarwala, who volunteered at the APALRC hotline as a law student, recalls the high quality of supervision and informal mentoring provided by Deepa at the time. While Deepa recalls the lack of guidance available to her in pursuing a career in civil rights advocacy, she has actively served as a role model and key mentor to young attorneys like Shaeli, who described Deepa as "exemplary."

In addition to training law students and running the legal hotline, Deepa assumed the role of policy activist, working with other community advocates on a language access bill that was ultimately enacted in the District of Columbia. In only one year, legislation was drafted, hearings and negotiations were held, and the bill was passed, requiring all local DC government agencies to take meaningful steps to provide language assistance in Amharic (an Ethiopian language), Spanish, Korean, Vietnamese, and Chinese. To Deepa, the success of the legislation was "amazing in a sense" given the rapidity with which it came to fruition. She recalls: "It was a wonderful way to see a project evolve [and] to see how much local organizing can make a difference."

Deepa's position at APARLC allowed her to take on a leadership role at a community-based nonprofit and to see a piece of legislation through from its inception. This work rounded out her professional résumé such that by May 2003, when Deepa married and moved to New York City, she had a full array of experiences upon which to draw in pursuing her career.

Once in New York, Deepa did not know what her next step would be, but she eventually started her own company consulting for nonprofits and contributing to reports on equal access issues. Deepa also found time to add the role of educator to her repertoire, teaching courses at Columbia University and Hunter College relating to Asian Americans and law and policy. It was at this point that Deepa felt ready to take on her current role as a leading advocate and organizer in the South Asian American community. As she describes her current position as Executive Director of South Asian American Leaders of Tomorrow (SAALT), "I think that all these years of experiences I've had in various contexts have led me to this point. I couldn't have done this job after law school . . . or before 9/11, or immediately thereafter. I really needed the national and localized experience, and the knowledge of how government and power structures work to help guide [my current organization] in an authentic way that I feel good about on a day to day basis."

Just before taking her current job, Deepa wrote the following in a 2004 working paper published by the Asian/American Center:

> The anti-immigrant and anti-Muslim backlash affected all South Asians in America. It created a crisis which prompted intensive coalition-building efforts and compelled diverse members of the community to adopt a new pan-South Asian identity. The backlash after September 11 is rooted not in a bias against South Asians or Arab Americans only—it stems from biased assumptions regarding religious affiliations, skin color, clothing, and accent. . . . In response, many South Asians, notwithstanding their religious, ethnic, or cultural distinctions, have begun to reconsider their place in America as Asian Americans, as immigrants, and as a united community.[2]

Shortly thereafter, she was asked by the Board of Directors of SAALT, then an all-volunteer nonprofit, to be Executive Director and the organization's first paid employee beginning in the summer of 2004. In accepting the position, Deepa stepped to the forefront of the still nascent effort to organize and galvanize the South Asian American community nationwide.

At present, SAALT is the only staffed South Asian American policy organization focused on civil rights and equal access nationwide. With Deepa at the helm, the organization serves many roles in communities around the country and at the national level, engaging in legislative advocacy and educating South Asian Americans about their rights. Deepa describes a stereotype that currently exists of South Asians as being "highly affluent . . . and well educated," which she believes "masks much of the marginalization in the community based on income, immigration status, and language proficiency." Part of her goal at SAALT is to increase access and involvement by all members of the community. More broadly, it is the mission of SAALT to bring a progressive perspective to policy tables, to highlight the impact of civil rights issues on the community, and to develop coalitions that will strengthen the bonds within the community nationwide.

With 2 million South Asians in the United States, this task for Deepa, the SAALT staff in the Washington, DC area office, and volunteers and board members around the country, is enormous. Deepa describes her experience at SAALT during the first two years of its operations as "a rollercoaster in many ways." While she is not "practicing law in the traditional way," she uses her legal knowledge and legal skills on a daily basis

2. Deepa Iyer, A Time of Crisis, An Opportunity for Unity: South Asians Strive for Social Justice in New York City after September 11. Asian/American Center Working Papers, Queens College (City University of New York), 2004.

in communicating the essence of government policies to community members and aiming to affect legislation and policies to the benefit of South Asian Americans.

As she has always found in the nonprofit world, the greatest advantage is the ability to "make your job your own." She feels "privileged" at SAALT to be able to contribute to the vision of the organization, as opposed to working in an environment where the goals are preset. Moreover, the flexibility of a start-up nonprofit is unparalleled, although there are considerable challenges: There is "always some uncertainty" with regard to funding, and resource concerns are with Deepa "on a daily basis." Every day is hectic, as she tries to "wear many hats" and "juggle a lot of different projects." Given these constraints, Deepa regularly curbs her own expectations with respect to the amount of work SAALT can assume. In her words: "It's been a challenge and a struggle, but also highly rewarding. I've learned a lot about myself and what I'm capable of and what my limits are."

Deepa's commitment to SAALT is rooted in her conviction that collective action and community engagement are the most effective vehicles through which to advance social justice. SAALT is currently facilitating the creation of "working groups" composed of South Asian American community leaders and volunteers in cities around the country, established through day-long "SAALT-Exchange" conferences. SAALT is also engaging in coalition-building at the national policy level with other like-minded civil rights groups and has focused on issues such as comprehensive immigration reform. Deepa notes that a defining moment in her life and career occurred on April 10, 2006, when she had the opportunity to address over 400,000 people at an immigrant rights rally in Washington, DC. "To be able to affirm our community's support and participation in the movement for immigrant rights was an amazing opportunity, and I was very humbled by the experience," notes Deepa now.

Deepa believes that her current undertaking requires all the skills and experience she has developed through her multifaceted career to date. Her ultimate goal is do "something positive for the local community" and not to impose a "top down agenda." The importance of community organizing and local work has been instilled in Deepa over a period of years, through her work with mentors and colleagues who helped her to develop an acute awareness "of the power structures that are in place that many of us are marginalized from, and need to overcome." Working at the national level, she now tries to ensure that she does not erect an independent power structure in the form of SAALT itself, through which the organization would impose an agenda on the South Asian American community. Rather, she focuses on the need to develop local grassroots, community advocates, and local credibility, building trust along the way. Of her winding path to the position of Executive Director at SAALT, she notes: "If I hadn't had the experience of the last eight years, I wouldn't have that [community-based] framework."

Through Deepa's projects at SAALT, a network of South Asian American communities nationwide is steadily emerging—a necessary support system that did not exist for Deepa as a young immigrant in this country. Deepa now stands poised to effect vital change for members of the South Asian American and immigrant communities. Remarkably, this career and the change it has already produced may not have occurred had Deepa not happened upon a law degree, followed her intuitive sense in making career decisions, and been flexible and creative in identifying opportunities to grow and learn.

Deepa hopes that her path will serve as a guide for law students interested in pursuing various paths to achieve their goals: "Much of my legal career has been focused on finding the jobs and experiences through which I can pursue my commitment to social justice. I've had to be flexible and creative in finding these outlets—and as a result, I've made career choices that have been varied and multifaceted, and probably, rather untraditional. Yet, they have also been extremely fulfilling and satisfying—and hopefully, I have been able to contribute a small part to the broader movement for equal rights in this country."

LISALYN JACOBS

Women's Rights

By Laurel Parker

"I've had a Forrest Gumpesque life," Lisalyn Jacobs said. "As clueless as I was, though, I got pointed in the right direction by people who knew far better than I did. My life seems to be littered with fairy godmothers who appear at the right time to point me in the right direction." Consequently, Lisalyn derives great pleasure from talking to law students, college students, and policymakers about her job and her political passions. "Folks did that for me, so I can kind of pay back and pay it forward," she said.

Lisalyn, a first-generation Panamanian American, has a curly mop of hair that makes her look taller than her five feet ten inches. Wearing khakis, flip-flops, and a black and gold t-shirt with a portrait of an African woman, her deep, resonant voice overtakes the room as she props her feet on the radiator and thoughtfully responds to questions. She has an office adorned with social justice posters, paintings from different cultures, ubiquitous post-it notes, and pictures of friends and family. She provides an environment as welcoming as she is: a self-described "de facto office ombudsman," where her co-workers at Legal Momentum in Washington, DC, come to cry on her shoulder as well as discuss the most pressing gender issues of the day.

Lisalyn's commitment to social justice began before she was born. While her mother was pregnant in the summer of 1965, her late father accompanied other Ohio ministers to Mississippi to work on voting rights issues against a "horrible backdrop of violence." Her parents' focus on service informed her upbringing and solidified her commitment to political activism.

Lisalyn grew up in Shaker Heights, Ohio, a suburb of Cleveland, the youngest of three and the daughter of a progressive Episcopal minister and stay-at-home mother. "We weren't really an Air Force family," she laughed, "except that every time we moved it had something to do with my dad's job." In fact, the three children in her family were all born in different places: her brothers, Greg and David, were born in Nicaragua and Nebraska. Because they are twelve and thirteen years older, she said she was always likened to "an only child with three fathers."

After spending her first four and a half years in Ohio, her family moved to Washington, DC, and then to the suburbs of Prince George's County, Maryland. During her second semester in second grade, she became a part of the first group of students in that county to be bussed. "1972 was Prince George's approach to 'all deliberate speed,'" she said dryly.

"I grew up as a somewhat atypical preacher's kid," she said. Her father had been a parish priest for over twenty years, but after moving to DC, he became a chaplain at a psychiatric facility where her mother did volunteer work: arts, crafts, music, and recreational therapy. Lisalyn spent a lot of time accompanying her mother with volunteering and Meals on Wheels, and spent two afternoons a week each summer with her mother on a ward at the psychiatric facility working with patients.

"It's not like I grew up having some kind of fabulous notion of Perry Mason on TV," she said, "but I did have some ideas of saving the world through law. I remember concluding that I wanted to be a lawyer circa the eighth grade," she said. "I'm not sure what happened in eighth grade that was so interesting or compelling—clearly I did not have a particularly broad concept of what one could do with a law degree, so I imagined going to work for a firm because that's all I knew." She smiled. "Turned out to be a very good thing that the law is broader than I could have conceptualized as an eighth grader."

Lisalyn went to Goucher, a women's college outside Baltimore, which became coeducational during her time there. "I had a 'legal bug' by college time," she said, and chose Goucher because it was the only one with a pre-law major. After a year, however, she realized that her plan did not make sense if she decided not to go to law school. Instead, she switched to political science, "not the atypical bent of many law students," she said wryly. She had been fascinated by Oberlin College for years, and after changing her major, decided to spend the latter half of her junior year and first half of her senior year studying at Oberlin. "My lifelong mantra is 'I hate what-ifs,'" she said, "and I didn't want to be in the position of wondering for the rest of my life what would have happened if I went to Oberlin."

"Goucher and Oberlin were as different as night and day," she said. While Goucher was "politically inert—no active Young Republicans, Young Democrats, young anything going on"—Oberlin was the site of sit-ins over disinvestment from South Africa, protests over FBI recruiting, and trudging around Tappan Square with coffins because of U.S. involvement in Central America. This environment gave Lisalyn the opportunity to become politically active, which she did through college radio and an internship with the Democratic National Committee.

After returning to Goucher, Lisalyn wrote a thesis entitled "The Green Revolution: The Impact of Agricultural Technology on Rural Women in Kenya." Her adviser, Dr. Marianne Githens, was, she recalls, the first female awarded a Ph.D. from the London School of Economics. "She saw me as a good, promising student, and her vision was that I would replace her. It was amazing having someone taking that much of an interest in you." However, Lisalyn remained committed to getting a law degree rather than a Ph.D.

Lisalyn's oldest brother, a product of Princeton University and Columbia Law School, also tried to convince her not to go to law school. When that proved unsuccessful, he encouraged her to apply to smaller, less dog-eat-dog, competitive schools. Despite a full scholarship to Emory, Lisalyn decided to go to Stanford. As she was struggling with her decision, Dr. Githens raised an eyebrow and said, "But you got into Stanford. There really isn't any choice, is there?"

"Hindsight being 20/20, I would not have gone straight from college to law school," Lisalyn said. During the summer between college and law school, she worked for Baltimore's Legal Aid Society, which was suing the Department of Social Services for negligence in following up on child abuse accusations in the foster care context. It was there she learned "the cyclical and almost intractable nature of how generations of families ended up as wards of the local Department of Social Services."

Lisalyn began at Stanford without having ever visited Palo Alto. She showed up, two months shy of twenty-two, having never gone to a school more than an hour away from someone in her immediate family, and was greeted by "a tiny room with just a couple of beds and a couple of sinks."

"Law school was where I had my identity crisis," she said. "I had always been a big fish in a little pond, at the top of my high school class, not necessarily working as hard as I might in order to get there. I get to Stanford, where so many people have gone to prep schools, prestigious colleges and universities." She paused. "Stanford may have had full gender integration, but academically, it was an old boys' network. Here I am, haplessly wandering around campus, and other people are chatting about what house they lived in at Harvard. There was a life that had clearly existed for folks about which I knew nothing. There's a whole wheel-and-spoke network way people have of connecting with each other. Having gone to school at Stanford, I am particularly conversant with that network now, but at first, it was difficult.

"Law school marks the beginning of the end of there being a formula for your getting from point A to point B. If you come from a background of privilege, or even if you don't, you walk around with some sort of sense of entitlement: I have these SATs, I have this GPA; therefore, I should get this reward. Law school is the first place that you see the magic wand doesn't necessarily open the door for you. One of my under-grad professors had told me that going into law school is like going into the Marines: they break you down in order to build you up in their image. You rapidly realize that someone is going to be on the top of the pile, and it very well might not be you. You're so used to distinguishing yourself on the basis of intellect, and now you don't know if you can do it. But, ultimately, the shroud of mystification lifts, and you find your way into networks of people who are like-minded and become your friends."

Because the climate at Stanford was political during her time there, with the school endeavoring to make sure all students had one professor of color or one female professor their first year, Lisalyn continued her activism. Chuck Lawrence, Lisalyn's constitutional law professor, became a mentor, as did Jerry Lopez, who taught her "Teaching Self Help and Lay Lawyering" class: "The bewildering weirdness of law school leads you to seek out people like you on some level as mentors, because maybe they can give you some insight into the process."

In addition to working at the Community Law Clinic and as a teaching assistant for an undergraduate civil rights class, Lisalyn was the co-chair of BALSA (Black American Law Student Association) her second year, when the law school was leafleted by the White Aryan Resistance. While the school did have some professors of color, Lisalyn was one of only nine black students in her class and fought to bring in visiting professors of color, including Patricia Williams.

"There was a sense on the part of one and sundry people that because our numbers were so small, we could do more about pressing for social change if we morphed ourselves into one umbrella entity," she said. So she helped start a broader forum called the "Multicultural Council" with all the "usual suspects," such as SLLSA (Stanford Latino Law Students Association) and APILSA (Asian-Pacific Islander Law Student Association), and also the LGBT (Lesbian Gay Bisexual Transgender) and Native American communities. The organization sponsored a National Day of Action to protest the underrepresentation of people of color on the faculty and also the lack of substantive diversity in the curriculum, arguing that students did not have enough of a breadth of options and opportunities for discussion of minority issues in class and that those classes were largely taught by adjunct professors.

"When I was trying to figure out this whole law school thing, I went to my brother's firm," where he worked as a management-side labor lawyer. He had told her that law was a profession filled with people who want to do something else, but see law as a safe profession to pursue. Lisalyn paused, considering this idea. "Five years out of law school, I took a creative writing class, and about half the people were lawyers. So many lawyers really are frustrated something elses. People kept saying, 'I wanted to write the Great American Novel,' 'I wanted to be an actor,' or something else their family wouldn't approve of, or that they would not find lucrative or successful enough. It's a bizarre standard they are using to assess success." She laughed. "I'm not sure how my brother decided to pursue the practice of law," but she smiled as she related that he ultimately gave up his partnership, worked part-time, and went to divinity school, and now works on the staff of the Episcopal Bishop of Massachusetts. "I know a lot of 'recovering lawyers.'"

When she visited her brother's firm, she said, "I thought, this is boring, not compelling at all, not what I would want to do." Between the years she and her brother graduated from law school, 1977 and 1990, she saw an enormous change in the spectrum of what people felt they could do after law school. "He worked for a big law firm in the city — Cleveland — where he had grown up. But for those of us in my generation raised with a social justice core, working at a law firm didn't make sense."

Lisalyn spent her Stanford summers back east. She worked in New York the first summer as a women's rights intern for the Ford Foundation doing research and writing about work-family balance. She worked at a law firm the second summer as an associate for financially "sensible" reasons and to gain the experience it would provide. "A significant number of my colleagues at school were more corporate-focused. I didn't see eking out my existence at some corporate firm, but I couldn't yet get my mind around what it was that I wanted to do."

Lisalyn also spent the fall of her third year in southern Africa, where she studied property division and child custody issues as well as the impact of divorce laws on Zimbabwean women. While in Zimbabwe, a friend saw information about a Georgetown Fellowship, which she applied for and was awarded. "Like my brothers, I 'went home' after finishing school," although her home, Washington, DC, is different from her brothers' childhood home in Cleveland. Lisalyn loves DC because "local politics is national. And once you are in DC for twenty minutes you start meeting the same people you will know for your professional life."

Lisalyn's career path is summed up by a YWCA bracelet she wears: "Eliminating Racism and Empowering Women." "My résumé alternates that way," she said, highlighting the main focuses of her career. "Half the time I'm doing women's rights; half the time I'm doing civil rights." Goucher made her interested in women's studies—only logistics prevented her from getting a minor—and her interest in capital punishment came out of a process paper she wrote in eighth grade. "See, it all goes back to eighth grade!" she said. "Other people were examining how to grow crops, and I was examining the myriad ways one could be put to death. At some point, I took a look in the mirror, either psychologically or literally, and realized that I was a woman of color, so my work has mirrored ways in which I am trying to move the ball forward on either the race or gender front."

Lisalyn's fellowship sought to get women more interested in careers focused on women's public policy issues. During that year, she advocated for women's employment rights before the legislative and administrative branches of government, focusing primarily on the concerns of poor women and women of color. She also counseled victims of sexual discrimination and harassment about their legal options.

After her fellowship, Lisalyn worked at a firm, Howrey & Simon, for four years. She practiced general commercial litigation but continued to do a great deal of *pro bono* work such as housing and employment discrimination, providing assistance and counseling to domestic violence victims, and drafting child custody petitions for clients with AIDS. Lisalyn highlighted the importance for students and young attorneys interested in public interest law to do substantial public interest work early in their careers. "Thousands of people want to leave private practice after a few years, and all the résumés look the same, so people need to make sure their résumés demonstrate commitment to public interest work. Your résumé has to walk the walk; otherwise, you have to rely on the old boys' network," she advised.

"Firms are not particularly friendly places," she said. "Although some people adapt and do perfectly well, they are not very healthy places from an emotional standpoint. Many mothers believe balance to be working before their kids get up and after their kids go to bed in addition to a twelve-hour day. I left in January 1995, and had maybe five good friends working there and all were either in therapy or on antidepressants—and this was *before* Prozac and Zoloft were common. The mentality was, 'I want it all, but nevertheless I have to prioritize my billable hours above other concerns in my life.'"

After firm life, Lisalyn segued into government work at the U.S. Department of Justice. She started in the Office of Policy Development, where she was senior counsel and worked on developing and implementing civil rights and civil justice reform initiatives and policy mandates of the Clinton Administration, including welfare reform, affirmative action,

HIV policy, disability rights, child support, and violence against women initiatives. She also assessed and interviewed candidates for federal judicial nominations and prepared candidates for Senate confirmation hearings. "At Justice, I had a broad portfolio and could never say what a particular day would look like. Invariably, the phone would ring, and something else would come up. For junior associates, law firm life is way more predictable: you do document review for XYZ period of time."

She then worked as the Acting Chief of Staff in the Civil Rights Division, where she oversaw day-to-day operations and revisions to Title IX regulations. "As the Chief of Staff, I could always reasonably expect to have the White House call at 6:00 P.M. Friday afternoon with marching orders for the weekend." She also worked in the Violence Against Women office, where she finalized a comprehensive agenda on domestic violence, stalking, and sexual assault. "Working at Justice turned me into a policy omnivore with rabidly different interests," she said. "I wouldn't last long working on just one issue, which is possible to do in the death penalty world."

After five years at the Justice Department, she decided that she wanted to "hang out a shingle doing policy consulting." Because of the turnover in senior management offices and the changes in the Justice Department, "it became harder for me to get my job done." She worked as a consultant for the ACLU Capital Punishment Project and the National Coalition to Abolish the Death Penalty, the Leadership Conference Education Fund, the Ford Foundation, Global Rights, the Open Society Institute, and the Harvard University Kennedy School of Government.

With all her consulting jobs, she was able to apply her passion and expertise to myriad groups and issues. But by fall 2002, the economy was shakier, and she interviewed with Leslye Orloff, whom she had met years before, who offered her a job at Legal Momentum, the former NOW Legal Defense and Education Fund. Lisalyn found it to be a perfect fit.

The job at Legal Momentum requires her to be their primary lobbyist and legislative strategist. New York City is home to the organization's headquarters, but the DC office works on policy issues. "We don't have a constituency, which can be a negative because we don't have numbers to bring to bear, but it's better to be part of a coalition, and we're knowledgeable about our issues." She works on building coalitions and acts as the media spokesperson on issues from welfare and Violence Against Women Act (VAWA) reauthorizations, to the Federal Marriage Amendment, judicial nominations, and child care, all of which she worked on at the Justice Department. "I get bored relatively easily, but here I get to focus on all the various subparts of my job." She pointed at her desk: "Right now I'm working on welfare, the nomination of John Roberts, and reauthorizing VAWA.

"This job is the first one that has required me to talk about my background as a person of faith to bring the right kind of bona fides to the table. When dealing with conservative groups of people, they can't write me off as some kind of feminist Wiccan. I can testify on Capitol Hill that I am a person of faith, and then in their eyes I have more credibility." She weaves together the issues deftly and passionately. "This administration believes that poor women are poor because they lack husbands. But people don't focus on marriage if they don't know where their next meal is coming from—there's something backward in these priorities. Education, training, and child care are the blocks to getting out of poverty. Studies show that if you help someone become economically self-sufficient, they can get a leg up and then turn their attention to marriage when it's their priority, not the government's."

Lisalyn has also worked in education, teaching graduate gender and international human rights issues classes at George Washington University. "I really liked the teaching," she said. "One thing you learn as a consultant: everything is an opportunity. In DC, everyone knows everyone, and opportunities crop up in all sorts of places. Just because there isn't a job on the table doesn't mean there isn't an opportunity. Get yourself lodged in a place in their brain where they will think of you when something becomes available. I'm extracurricularly overcommitted, but I work very hard at whatever my job is. If you spend enough time in DC, you become Type A," she laughed, "or more Type A than you might otherwise have been inclined to be."

Lisalyn recalled a discussion with Jack Boger—who worked for the NAACP Legal Defense and Education Fund and is now a law professor at the University of North Carolina—about their respective career paths. "People want to know how you did it, but it's not the product of some well thought-out, well-oiled plan. You're crossing a brook, stone by stone, and you kind of go over here sideways for a while." She motioned with her arm. "Something occurs to you, you meander through it, rather than going from point A to point B." She paused. "The real joke is people plan, and God laughs."

"People always look for insight on how I ended up doing what I do, but I staggered about randomly and fortunately ran across and amassed a wonderful group of colleagues and friends who gave me opportunities. It happens to me a lot in life: I meet someone almost randomly who becomes an influence later in my life," readily admitting to her own "'Old Girls' Network.' When I did my Georgetown fellowship at the National Partnership for Women and Families, my supervisor, Claudia

Withers, became a lifelong friend and mentor. We had first met four years earlier at a women and public policy seminar."

"When I went to the White House for International Women's Day and met President Clinton, I felt like Forrest Gump. The whole experience made me wonder how I ever got there. Trying to imagine that my Jamaican-born grandmother would ever have dreamed that her youngest granddaughter would meet the President of the United States, or know the Attorney General well enough to be recognized by name. . . ." Lisalyn struggled for words. "A lot of people thought that I was going to be a minister. It's hard to avoid your family genes, but one does not have to be wearing a collar to be laboring in the vineyard, and you can do just as much social justice work through the law."

SHEILA THOMAS

Employment Discrimination

By Alan B. Morrison

Sheila Thomas is very determined. But you don't get to be a highly regarded, employment discrimination lawyer if you are black, female, poor, and raised in south Texas in the 1960s and 1970s unless you are very determined.

Sheila is now a solo practitioner, working out of her home in the hills of Oakland, California, mainly with other law firms that work on major cases, the biggest of which is a massive gender discrimination class action against Wal-Mart. This arrangement gives her greater flexibility in her schedule and allows her to focus on the big issues for which she is responsible, leaving the day-to-day work to her co-counsel. She also doesn't have a regular job and hence a regular paycheck, but she has the freedom to do what she wants, when she wants.

These are among the trade-offs that Sheila has chosen. She has worked at two public interest law firms, a private civil rights firm, and a prior solo practice. In addition to her determination, Sheila has always seemed to know what she wanted at each point in her legal career, and she has managed to have the kind of job she wanted while handling the kinds of cases that give her great personal satisfaction through her work. That's not easy to do, but then again, Sheila is a very determined woman.

Her story begins in Corpus Christi, Texas, where she was raised by her mother, who earned her living cooking at a university and in health care institutions. Her father was a longshoreman, but her parents were separated. She had two brothers that she tried to keep up with in her youth: "I was rebellious, have always been," says Sheila with a hearty laugh that emerges frequently in conversation. "I was resistant to being treated differently." She was also resistant to being taught cooking by her mother, although she confesses that she now enjoys it. When asked to describe her family's circumstances, she chose "poor," where others might have described a situation with a regularly working parent as "working class" or "lower middle class." But Sheila Thomas does not mince words; she says what's on her mind.

Brown v. Board of Education was decided in 1954, but school segregation did not come quickly to Texas. Sheila was in ninth grade in 1976 when her mother received a call at home from Ms. Jones, one of Sheila's teachers. Ms. Jones, who is white, urged Sheila to enroll in a previously all-white high school, which Sheila did. Ms. Jones was also influential in another way: she encouraged Sheila to attend college outside Texas. For Sheila this was a double reach—going to college and leaving Texas to do so. Her mother had wanted Sheila to be a nurse, an unfulfilled goal that she had had for herself. Being a doctor was "not within the realm" of her mother's ambitions for Sheila: she was concentrating on what the family could afford.

Sheila had no family members who were attorneys, and it was not until some years later that she met her first African-American lawyer. There was no single event, no defining moment that caused her to say, even to herself, that "I need to become a lawyer to overcome . . . injustice."

She got an additional push from Roland Rodriquez, a Corpus Christi resident who actively recruited minority students and helped them through the daunting college admissions process. He did not provide financial assistance but did help as many as nine fortunate students. Sheila was among them, and she went to Yale through his help. Roland's pleasure was less than complete, however, because, according to Sheila, none of his beneficiaries returned to Corpus Christi.

As a result of work, grants, and loans, Sheila made it through Yale. Her decision to be an English major focusing on African-American and women's literature resulted in raising her consciousness about issues important to African Americans and women. At Yale she sensed the need to create a formal bond among those women, which prompted her to start the Black Undergraduate Women's Group.

Looking for work in Corpus Christi during her first college summer, she encountered her initial experience with overt employment discrimination. She applied for a clerical job, but it went to someone else. The person who rejected her told her that, if she could not go back to Yale, she could stay in Texas and go to the local junior college. For Sheila, this translated into "know your place and stay in it." She bagged groceries instead. The next summer she worked at a bank, but by the time that summer was over, she vowed never to return to Texas except to visit, and she never has.

Sheila credits her English major with helping her to be a better writer and to foster her creativity, which is an integral part of her law practice. The first black lawyer she ever met came to Yale on a weekly basis to teach a course on the Harlem Renaissance, which she describes as a cultural rather than legal experience. Through the black pre-law society Sheila met Drew Days, who was teaching at Yale Law School after finishing a term as head of the Civil Rights Division of the Justice Department under President Jimmy Carter. Days was also the first black lawyer to succeed in a way that was a role model for her. Sheila remembers a talk he gave about his experiences, but she didn't need to be convinced to go to law school. She had already decided to do that, as had a number of her friends. She was accepted at two top law schools—Georgetown and the University of Texas—but deferred law school for a year because she needed some time off.

Time off, in Sheila's case, meant time off from school but not from the law. She stayed in New Haven and worked as a paralegal at Wiggin & Dana, probably the city's most respected law firm, whose clients included Yale University. She credits her time at Wiggin & Dana with teaching her the importance of being meticulous and with later giving her a head start in law school, especially in her Civil Procedure course. (Unlike most of her classmates, she had already seen real interrogatories and depositions.) Mostly she found the legal work boring, and her brush with commercial litigation, a patent infringement case, convinced her that her law career would involve helping people, not companies. When it came time to go to law school, she kept her promise to herself and did not return to Texas; she headed to Georgetown Law Center in Washington, DC.

Law school was a necessary step, but not a particularly enjoyable one. Sheila found Georgetown very focused on big firm practice, with too little attention paid to the kind of public interest career that she knew she wanted to pursue. Law school was "too long and needlessly anxiety producing," says Sheila with a laugh that, one suspects, comes much easier now than when she was going through law school. Outside the classroom, Sheila got on the public interest track and stayed there. She worked to help pay her way at a small firm with Paul Reichler and Judy Applebaum, who represented Nicaragua in the 1980s, when the Reagan Administration was trying its best to undermine that country's government.

During her first summer she worked with Joe Sellers of the Washington Lawyers' Committee for Civil Rights, and after her second year she began at the NAACP Legal Defense and Education Fund, where she met three leaders of the civil rights bar—Elaine Jones, Barry Goldstein, and Penda Hair.

Sheila's next job was a direct result of Elaine Jones's advice that a judicial clerkship was a valuable experience that too few African-American law students sought. Sheila acknowledges that she had under-estimated the importance of a clerkship and the mentoring it could bring, especially from the person she refers to as "my judge"—U.S. District Judge U.W. Clemon, a black jurist who sits in Birmingham, Alabama. Her year in Alabama, which she found very different from Texas, provided her with opportunities to observe racism and sexism in a court-room setting. Called to the courtroom one day by a fellow law clerk, she observed what happened when an attorney somehow got an exhibit shown to the jury that the judge had excluded, and Judge Clemon found the excuse so weak that he put the lawyer in jail. The episode epitomized for Sheila the lack of respect that white attorneys generally showed to Judge Clemon by doing things they would never try to do in front of a Caucasian judge. With women the disrespect was more subtle: it manifested itself in ways such as lawyers adding "Esq." only after the names of male attorneys.

She "loved" her year with Judge Clemon and the opportunity to see trials and to observe the response of juries to different approaches, and to talk with the judge about how he saw the cases. But on one thing they disagreed: he thought she should go to a law firm, because she could and because it would enable her to have financial security. She believes that part of this impetus came from the fact that the avenue to a large law firm was not open to him and he wanted her to consider all the options. They disagreed then and "still disagree" about this today.

When her clerkship was over, she returned to Washington and to LDF, as it is known, but this time with a prestigious two-year Skadden Fellowship to pay her modest salary. She continued at LDF for a year after graduating from law school, working on employment discrimination cases, a housing case in which whites and Latinos were able to rent apartments that were unavailable when blacks inquired about them, and legislative work on Capitol Hill. She did very little housing work; instead she worked on voting rights and employment cases. She went to Arkansas with Penda Hair for a redistricting case, with defendant Bill Clinton as a star witness at trial. She also argued *Patterson v. McLean Credit Union,* which was being heard in the Fourth Circuit on remand from the Supreme Court. It would turn out to be her only court of appeals argument, and she won it in a court that is notably unfriendly to civil rights plaintiffs. When her two years were up, she could have stayed on at LDF but found the work there heavily oriented toward DC politics, and the office was becoming more involved in legislation. What she wanted to do was public interest litigation, and to her that meant learning how to litigate big cases. To do this, she moved across the country in October 1991 and became an associate at the Oakland law firm of Saperstein, Goldstein, Demchak & Baller, which mainly handled large-scale employment class actions.

She worked with Barry Goldstein and Guy Saperstein on large class action gender discrimination cases at a time when there were very few other firms handling them. Her first big case was against State Farm Mutual Insurance Company. She was hoping to participate in the damages phase of the case, but, like so many other class actions, it was settled. Her main goal was to learn to feel comfortable litigating large employment class actions from start to finish: how to construct a case, how to get a class certified, and how to get the necessary evidence to prove discrimination. By this time most employers had eliminated blatant gender and racial bias, and so cases had to be proven with statistics. Sheila also came to appreciate how language in statutes matters in the real world in ways that she believes people who work on Capitol Hill fail to realize. From time to time she has thought about going back to Washington and applying what she has learned as a litigator to lobby for better laws, but so far that has yet to come to pass.

Although Sheila speaks fondly of her time at Saperstein, she decided not to stay because she felt that she would be expected to conform to the way that the firm ran its cases, which she saw as doing more or less the same thing every time. She wanted to try out her own ideas. It was not so much that she disagreed with the firm, but she felt she could flourish more by herself. Others asked her to join them, but she demurred, preferring to strike out on her own, which she did for four years starting in April 1996. After she left Saperstein, she continued representing employment discrimination clients, some race and gender cases, and some class actions and individual cases. She had an office but did not have secretarial or paralegal help; when needed, co-counsel supplied it. She worked on some cases on her own, on some as co-counsel, and on some on a contract basis. Except when she was hired to do specific tasks, in all of these cases but one, her fees were contingent on her either winning or obtaining a favorable settlement.

One of the cases that she described from this period involved an African-American man who had worked for years at Chevron. He was not promoted to a job that would have enabled him to stay at the company, and he sued, claiming racial discrimination. He was a "wonderful" employee, but he had a hard case unless other company employees would support him. Surprisingly, one employee told the truth about racial remarks during a videotaped deposition. This broke the case open and produced a settlement. What Sheila saw come out of the lawsuit was not just money, but that once the plaintiff had been vindicated, he was "able to let go of what happened and get on with his life."

After four years on her own, Sheila became director of litigation for the San Francisco public interest law firm Equal Rights Advocates, on whose board she was then serving. ERA had originally done a significant amount of litigation on behalf of women but then had moved into other policy work. Hiring Sheila was supposed to enable the group to take on more litigation work. It was while she was at ERA that Sheila started work on the Wal-Mart gender discrimination class action. Sheila speaks well of her experiences at ERA but concluded that it was not prepared to commit to the kind of litigation program that she envisioned. In short, the fit was not quite what she wanted at that time in her life. In February 2003, after a little less than three years at ERA, she went out on her own again.

In one sense, her work did not change very much because her role in the Wal-Mart case continued, and her assignment as the monitor of an employment discrimination consent decree went with her also. But she was no longer in charge of other lawyers in an office focusing on combating gender discrimination, which freed her to work on voting rights cases and to be a consultant in other litigation, or, as she put it, "to do all this fun stuff." Her job as consent decree monitor brought her back to one part of her practice that she relishes: finding solutions that change the workplace. And, unlike most of her work, monitoring provides a regular salary on a noncontingent basis, although this does not appear to be a significant motivating factor in her enthusiasm for that role.

When asked about what parts of her litigation practice she likes most, Sheila cites the opportunity to be creative in finding solutions that will improve the lives of working people. This involves devising legal strategies, another favorite part of her practice. Much of what employment litigators do is discovery, and Sheila has her own perspective on that process. On the one hand, she dislikes the contentiousness that pervades all discovery — she dislikes arguing all the time. But she "loves to take depositions" and pin witnesses down on their stories and slowly pull together the big picture of what happened and why. She takes very few individual cases because so much of the focus is on a single employee, with the goal of compensating her for her losses rather than on making changes in the workplace. She also acknowledges that the discovery in an individual case also has to be extensive, which is sometimes hard to justify for just one person.

When asked about her favorite case or her best victory, Sheila declines to single out any one. She prefers to look on her work as a series of cases, where the results over time bring about change. Not surprisingly, the Wal-Mart class action, with 1.5 million current employees and 2 million who used to work there, stands high on her list. She began working on the case when she was at ERA because two-thirds of Wal-Mart's employees are women, with less than thirty percent in managerial positions of any kind. In addition to specific claims of discrimination, the case appeals to Sheila because Wal-Mart pays its workers wages that are legal but are not enough to live on.

Sheila's role as part of a team, which has had as many as eighteen lawyers, including five or six senior people like her, is to depose Wal-Mart's division and regional managers, who are some of the highest-level employees in the company. To get a national class certified, plaintiffs had to show that there was a consistency of outcomes that could not be explained as local happenstances. Before a federal judge would be willing to certify a class of this magnitude against a company like Wal-Mart, there had to be evidence, not simply allegations, which meant that very significant discovery had to be completed before the class certification motion could succeed. The trick was to figure out which level of managers were sufficiently high up to know what was going on and be able to speak for the company without being at such a high level that they could profess ignorance or at so low a level that they could only say what happened in their store. The toughest job was to get the employees to tell the whole truth, and Sheila Thomas was assigned a significant part of that task.

So Sheila went to Bentonville, Arkansas, the home of Wal-Mart, which she describes as "not a big place." Sheila's first discovery about those who work at Wal-Mart is that "no one else looks like me." This reference was not just to the male-female divide but to the lack of racial diversity. Sheila notes that the class claims are based only on gender bias, although there are some named class representatives who also have race discrimination claims. She did not expound upon her role in the discovery process, but given the favorable class certification ruling, it must have been significant. Sheila also observes that, if class certification is sustained, settlement seems likely, since that is what happens in most cases of this kind. But, as Sheila recognizes, Wal-Mart is not like everyone else, and so there may be no deal, just litigation.

Sheila is first and foremost a litigating lawyer, but she is very much aware of the nonlawyering skills that help her effectiveness. Even in the class action context, she notes, having a trusting relationship with clients is vital so that she is able to address their concerns by involving them in the decisional process, especially with respect to relief issues. Dealing with clients as individuals becomes even more important when the client is an upper-level employee, where understanding their personal situations and goals is not a luxury but a necessity. When asked about what it takes to do this kind of work, Sheila echoes language heard from many lawyers, such as discipline, perseverance, energy, flexibility, and strategic thinking. But she adds two ideas that are not part of the typical lawyer's lexicon: creativity and dealing with what may appear to be irrational risk taking.

Because Sheila works at home in a variety of different roles on a number of different cases, she has no typical day. Meetings, which used to have a major claim on her time when she was at ERA, play a much-diminished role. She is on the phone much less and uses e-mail much more. She spends relatively little time with the law books now and much more time examining documents and witnesses. Working out of her home office eliminates issues of commuting and what to wear to work. All she needs are a phone, fax machine, and computer. When there are meetings, they are generally at the offices of co-counsel, and when she needs paralegal or other similar help, co-counsel provides them also as part of their arrangement with her.

Being on her own has generally reduced her stress and frustrations, although having to make discovery motions to get what should be readily produced brings them back. Much of her work, including "definitely" the Wal-Mart case, is on a contingent fee basis, which makes it very risky, so she needs some paying clients to keep her going. One of the real pluses for Sheila is that, while many of her weeks are extremely busy, there are times when she can take off in the middle of the day to take care of personal business, and no one tells her she can't. She recalls working much harder when she lived in Washington and during the month before the 2004 elections, but generally she now finds that her work and her personal life are in good balance. Part of this she attributes to the California lifestyle and part to the nature of her practice, which gives her control over her time, which is very important to her. She has become very efficient at what she does and does not have to do many of the time-consuming things that occupy other lawyers. Training young lawyers was very much a part of her work at ERA, but that is no longer the case. She liked the role but found it very time-consuming.

Outside her practice, every other year for the past four years Sheila has taught a course on race relations and civil rights at Golden Gate Law School in San Francisco. Her writings on sexual harassment are directed at practitioners. She was a member of the American Bar Association Commission on Women and is co-chair of the Committee on Civil Rights of the Section of Individual Rights and Responsibilities of the ABA.

Working in the Bay Area has been very important to Sheila's career. She believes that the courts there are more open to discrimination claims than in other parts of the country, although less so now. But even today, cases brought in the Bay Area fare much better than if they are filed in the

Fourth, Fifth or Eleventh Circuits, which compose the states of the Old South. In her view, her kind of practice would also be more challenging in a smaller community, in part because of the greater difficulty in finding co-counsel. The Bay Area and its focus on the outdoors are important to Sheila's personal life, which includes her regular running, which has evolved into her being a marathoner. She loves to read, go to the movies, and spend time with her friends. When asked about whether she has enough leisure time, she seemed pleased to be able to say, "generally yes," and attributes that to the fact that people she knows believe that "there is more to life than working all the time."

Does she have advice for young lawyers just starting out? "Think about what really motivates you," she replied, "what you feel passionately about." If that is what you are doing, it will help you "get through periods when your job is not much fun." Look for work that has meaning, and don't be discouraged about finding a job doing what you really want to do. "I was told this work was hard to get into," but she did it. She was also "told lots of things that turned out not to be true," but she surmounted them so long as you are "clear about what you want to do." And it also helps to have the determination of Sheila.

ZAMA COURSEN-NEFF

Human Rights Abroad

By Tara Heumann

From her office window on the thirty-fourth floor of the Empire State Building, Zama Coursen-Neff has a stunning panoramic view of Chelsea and New Jersey even on a hazy morning. Her small office at Human Rights Watch is decorated with photographs Zama took of children in Israel, India, Malaysia, and Papua New Guinea. Shelves overflow with dozens of vertical files, one for each of Zama's research projects, hand-labeled by country and topic. The modesty of her office belies the importance of her work but reveals the dedication and humility with which Zama approaches every task in her life. She is an attorney, a researcher, a writer, and an advocate; and a voice for women and children who suffer human rights abuses in Asia. Zama has built her inspiring career on a solid foundation of hard work, an open mind, and fearless pursuit of her passion.

Zama was born in Shreveport, Louisiana, in 1971 and lived there until she left for college at seventeen. Her father was a building contractor, and her mother taught school before Zama was born and then stayed home with Zama and her younger brother and sister. Zama is the only lawyer in her family; her brother is completing pharmacology postdoctoral work in San Diego, and her sister is a musician in Johannesburg, South Africa.

When she was very young Zama's interests stood out in her conservative southern town. While many young women in Shreveport became school teachers, Zama didn't think that was for her. At first she imagined being an attorney, only to later reconsider when she learned how most lawyers spend their days. But, more than having any single focus as a child, she had a strong feeling that there was more to life than what she was exposed to in Shreveport. Without realizing it, Zama pushed her borders outward. To her parents' surprise, during her sophomore year in high school, Zama asked for a subscription to Newsweek magazine so that she could read about international affairs. She focused on her Spanish classes and the debating team—activities that seemed to hold both the promise of excitement and journeys to other parts of the world.

With her budding interest in international issues, Zama enrolled at Davidson College in North Carolina. Soon after arriving on campus, she attended a presentation about study abroad in Spain and decided to spend a semester of her sophomore year in Madrid. Madrid was an eye-opening experience. While Zama had carefully planned the trip— including waitressing for a summer at a Cajun restaurant in order to finance the costs—she managed to arrive with only her Louisiana warm weather gear. "I remember being very cold! My researching skills clearly needed more work." In Madrid, Zama improved her Spanish and loved exploring her host country, but what she valued most about her semester there was the unique perspective she gained by viewing her own nation from abroad. "Since I arrived in Madrid in January of 1990, I experienced the Gulf War away from home," she says. "I read about the war entirely through the Spanish press and I didn't realize until I got home how different the coverage had been from what Americans experienced in the United States."

Zama quickly found that study abroad programs were only one way in which Davidson College supported students interested in international work. When she returned from Spain, the college helped connect Zama with Presbyterian Church workers in San Miguel, El Salvador. During the summer between her junior and senior years, Zama assisted a mission worker there by caring for her children, helping with financial record-keeping for a women's artisan collective, and helping lead a study delegation in Guatemala. "It was my first time in a developing country," Zama says, "and I arrived at an extremely interesting time. The war had just ended and the Peace Accords had just been signed."

San Miguel had only a few hours of electricity and running water each day. That trip to El Salvador was Zama's first face-to-face encounter with international crises and the poverty of developing nations. "I felt sorry for the church workers in retrospect," Zama says. "They had to help a completely green American young woman learn how to live in a developing country. They also pushed me to reflect on the role of the United States in the conflict in El Salvador."

When she resumed her studies at Davidson, Zama was already eager to return to Central America. Now a college senior, she needed at least a short-term post-graduation plan. Zama's academic advisor encouraged her to consider law school, but Zama didn't see the law as an avenue to pursue the international development work she had so enjoyed in El Salvador. Zama had completed a weeklong externship shadowing attorneys taking depositions in personal injury cases during one of her winter vacations and had attended a legal career panel on campus. All of the attorneys represented the same bank, Zama remembered, a company with a large presence in North Carolina. "I thought it was pretty boring stuff," Zama admits.

Zama determined that she would work after graduating instead of continuing her education. She learned about Casa de Proyecto Libertad, a nonprofit community organization that defends the rights of immigrants in Southern Texas. That June, Zama moved to Harlingen, Texas, where she spent a year preparing political asylum applications for detained refugee children and counseling the children in preparation for their immigration hearings. Zama also organized some local advocacy programs concerning detention conditions and border patrol abuses against children.

In Harlingen, Zama met attorneys whose work was totally different from what she imagined lawyers did. "It was a complete surprise to me that there were attorneys using the law to do social justice work. I thought maybe I could do that." She was also encouraged by the several female attorneys she met during her year at the border. "I didn't know any women lawyers growing up," Zama recalled. "These were the first female attorneys I really got to know." Zama loved providing direct services but became frustrated with the unjust and chaotic immigration system. "I wanted to work toward systemic legal change."

The following year gave Zama more field experience in international development, this time in Tegucigalpa, Honduras. Paid by the Presbyterian Church, she worked with a development organization translating from Spanish for visiting study groups and with a women's legal aid organization interviewing clients and compiling statistics in a database. "I loved the work," Zama explains, "but the only real skill I had to offer the organizations and the women was English-Spanish interpretation. If I wanted to make a career out of this kind of international work, I needed more tools." Zama filled out law school applications and mailed them from Honduras.

Unsure whether law was the right path for her, Zama resolved only to enroll if she was accepted at a law school that friends professed to enjoy, and so she applied to only three schools. She was rejected by Yale, accepted at Stanford, and was offered a Root-Tilden-Snow public interest scholarship at NYU. The scholarship would cover a substantial portion of Zama's tuition and immerse her in the vibrant public interest law community at NYU. The draw of NYU's strong public interest program and the fact that her soon-to-be husband, whom she had met in El Salvador, had since moved to New York City, made the decision easy. "When I was living in Honduras, Derek and I could only speak twenty minutes every ten days on the phone because it was so expensive. Being in the same city seemed like a luxury." At the end of her year in Tegucigalpa, Zama packed for New York. Manhattan was an instant fit, and Zama quickly found support among the NYU public interest students and faculty.

Though Zama entered NYU in the fall of 1995 with a well-developed interest in international issues, she found herself finishing her second year without having taken any courses in international law. She learned that the NYU Center for International Studies had a one-year fellowship program that combined rigorous classes with scholarly research and writing. "At the interview, the director told me frankly that I had the least amount of foundational coursework of any applicant. I assumed I had blown my chances of ever getting back into international work. Getting accepted was a total surprise. And I was immediately terrified of not having that coursework!" The fellowship required Zama to take numerous courses in international law during her final year at NYU. On top of that, she couldn't resist signing up for the school's dynamic criminal defense clinic. "I was taking classes that met at the same time," Zama remembers. "Each week I had to figure out which class I would skip." The program also required each participant to write a law journal note and present it at a conference. The research for the note turned out to be the most rigorous academic project Zama had ever undertaken. Entire days disappeared as she studied in the law library stacks. "It was like being in a pie-eating contest," Zama says with a smile. "The pie is great, but you're shoving it down your throat as fast as you can. Law school taught me to take a huge amount of information and digest it really quickly."

Zama supplemented her NYU course work with internships during both the summers and the academic year. In August before her first year of law school, Zama had worked as an asylum paralegal at the Central American Refugee Center (CARECEN) in Hempstead, New York. In the spring semester of her first year and throughout the summer, Zama interned at the Vera Institute of Justice in the Appearance Assistance Program. In addition to researching newly passed immigration laws and developing a training program for new staff members, Zama got to see how an organization like Vera works. From that internship, she also gained exposure to innovative ways to reform government systems.

During her second year at NYU, Zama further pursued her interest in immigrants' rights by interning at the Lawyers Committee for Human Rights (now Human Rights First) in its Asylum Program, where she interviewed people seeking representation for the asylum hearing process. Wanting to deepen her legal research and writing skills, Zama went on to intern at the ACLU's immigrants' rights program that summer.

These internships gave her invaluable experience for her current work at Human Rights Watch.

Reflecting on her law school experience eight years after graduation, Zama is glad she went to NYU. "I didn't exactly enjoy being in law school, but NYU was really the best case scenario," Zama says honestly. "Those three years gave me the tools to do something that I really love, to do work that I never would have imagined possible before law school. And I met some amazing people who have become great friends and colleagues." For Zama, the opportunity to work in an organization like Human Rights Watch made the rigors of law school worthwhile.

Several of Zama's professors and fellow students encouraged her to apply for a clerkship after graduation. But Zama was eager to begin working, and a clerkship sounded too much like a fourth year of law school. She kept an open mind about clerking, however, and through discussions with faculty, she came to believe that the skills she would gain in a clerkship would be useful and that she might be able to find a judge with a strong commitment to public interest. Ultimately she applied for and accepted a clerkship with Magistrate Judge James Francis in the Southern District of New York. "It was a year of excellent training," Zama says.

Determined to pursue her interest in human rights, Zama began to research employment opportunities in the field. She had learned about Human Rights Watch during her year at the Mexican border and thought the organization would be a good fit for her. "I thought that the work they did really made a difference," Zama says. Human Rights Watch offered a competitive one-year fellowship program designed for newcomers in the field of international human rights. Zama applied for and was accepted as a Furman Fellow immediately following her clerkship. "It was my dream job," Zama remembers, "but there was a catch." They wanted her to relocate to Washington, DC. "My husband had a great job in New York doing information management at the Vera Institute," Zama explains, "and I wouldn't live apart from him."

Much to Zama's delight, Human Rights Watch was willing to place her in the New York office in the Asia Division. Though Zama's background was exclusively in Latin American affairs, she was prepared to learn about a new region of the world in order to work at Human Rights Watch. "Finding a full time job in human rights is very difficult," Zama explained. "I was lucky to get the job not having any experience in Asia at all."

As a Fellow, Zama monitored human rights developments in Malaysia, researching repressive laws and writing a report on Burmese refugees. Zama felt that Human Rights Watch was a good fit for her personally and professionally, but her Fellowship only lasted one year, and she had to be prepared to start a new job in the fall. She conducted a thorough job search during the winter and spring, applying for a wide range of jobs. "My intern told me, 'Don't close your own doors,' and I took it to heart. I applied for things I knew were a real stretch, and I got rejected from some jobs. But I also got my first choice — a permanent position in the Children's Rights Division at Human Rights Watch."

Seven years after that first professional journey to Asia, Zama also counts among her work destinations Afghanistan, El Salvador, India, Sri Lanka, Indonesia, Israel, and Papua New Guinea. She is now a Senior Researcher in the Children's Division, where her job is to document and expose human rights violations and to promote a series of policy recommendations to governments, diplomats, and agencies. Much of Zama's time is spent conducting field research and preparing written reports of her findings, but public speaking, media campaigning, and advocating with government officials are also integral to her work.

Zama is responsible for the organization and completion of her research projects, from identifying what issues to tackle to using the finished research to create pressure for change in policy and practice. Zama determines the length of her research trips (usually three to five weeks) and arranges her own interviews with victims, agency workers, government officials, diplomats, and others with firsthand information. However, documentary evidence that corroborates or contextualizes an issue is also important. "Our work is only as good as our word — credibility is key, so you can never overstate or rely on an emotional reaction to anecdotal stories."

Though Zama's research projects all share a similar trajectory, each day's tasks are different. Zama is currently finishing a report on attacks on schools in southern Afghanistan and planning a second research and advocacy trip on police violence in Papua New Guinea. She is also monitoring developments in India related to past reports on child labor and HIV/AIDS and doing as much follow-up advocacy as possible. When she is not traveling, her days in the office are spent mostly writing at her computer, talking on the phone, and corresponding via e-mail. Though her research and writing are largely done independently or in a team of two, there are opportunities for collaboration when her reports go through the internal review process.

Zama usually works six days a week, five in the office and one at home. It's a rare weekend, she says, when she doesn't have at least three to six hours of work she wants to finish. She arrives at her office at around 9:15 and stays until 7:00 or 8:00 most evenings. She also gets another hour and a half of reading of press clips done on her commute to and from her Brooklyn apartment. "Public interest doesn't mean you work less," Zama says with a smile. Researchers' salaries at Human Rights Watch range from about $45,000 to $65,000. "I couldn't be doing this without the Root Fellowship or without NYU's loan forgiveness program," Zama explains.

Zama is happy not only with her individual responsibilities at HRW, but also with the other members of the Children's Rights Division. "I really admire the people with whom I work," Zama says, "and I know I'm fortunate to be able to say that." The Division is currently directed by Lois Whitman, who brings knowledge and experience from her work in Turkey, Ireland, and Jamaica and from practicing law, including at the New York City Commission on Human Rights. In addition to Zama, the children's rights team includes four other researchers, each specializing in a different region: two advocates and two assistants.

Like a law firm job, work could easily consume Zama's entire life, and she actively sets aside time to spend with her family and pursue other interests. Zama likes to run in Brooklyn's Prospect Park, has participated in the New York Marathon, and serves on the board of her condominium association. She and her husband enjoy hiking and camping, and they often use their limited vacation time to visit their families in Seattle and Louisiana. Zama also volunteers time to provide *pro bono* legal services for immigrants. This lets her practice her Spanish and enjoy somewhat more immediate results than she usually sees from her daily work.

Zama is pleased with her job at Human Rights Watch because she feels like she is always learning. "This job is why I went to law school," Zama says. "I usually get up in the morning eager to get started." In 2002, Zama made her first trip to Afghanistan to research the lives of women and girls in western Afghanistan after the fall of the Taliban. "There wasn't much information available about what was really going on in Herat. When we got there, we saw that people were afraid. Torture in detention was a routine practice, there was no freedom of expression, the media was totally controlled, women's rights activists were being punished, and women who didn't wear burkas or who tried to drive were being arrested."

In 2003, Zama went back again with the organization's Afghanistan researcher to look at violations in the south and southeast. On her last day in the country, Zama received an unexpected visit from a woman whose story she will never forget. "She was active in the women's department of the rural area where she lived," Zama explains, "and had held workshops for women on the most basic rights, like the right to leave their homes." On International Women's Day, she had organized a public meeting. For the first time for them, women stood up and read poems in public. A friend of one of the women who spoke out told Zama what happened next. The night after the meeting, gunmen from a local militia broke into the home of one of the women, tied up her and her husband, looted their home, and warned her never to talk about women's rights again. The gunmen then traveled to her sister's home. The sister hid in the outhouse with her infant child for two hours until the gunmen left. An anonymous letter was later sent to the woman, threatening to kill her and her family.

After relating this story, the friend asked Zama, "If a woman's hands and feet are tied, what can she do?" The clear implication, Zama thinks, was that the victim had also been raped. After telling Zama all of this, the friend continued, "As long as I have blood in my body, I'll continue to fight for women's rights." To Zama, this woman "wasn't a victim, but she needed backup."

It is these testimonials that motivate Zama during the time she spends in New York turning stories of suffering into a mandate for action for the international community. After she has collected previously undocumented evidence of abuse, Zama feels a responsibility to the people she interviews. "In each country I may have face-to-face conversations with some thirty to sixty victims. They may show me scars. They may not have ever told anyone else what happened to them. After I corroborate their stories, my job is to turn their experiences into a report from which all readers draw the same unavoidable conclusion: that the abuse has to stop."

Every day, Zama uses her skills and energy to improve the lives of those who suffer the gravest indignities. A combination of planning, sacrifice, fellowships, and making a few mistakes here and there have made it possible for her to do the work that she loves. "You need to make sure that you can finance law school so you have the option to do something other than work at a firm, and you need to have enough experiences to know what that other thing is," Zama advises. "You don't go through those three years of law school to do something that makes you miserable." Above all, Zama notes, "a law degree is a powerful tool that you can wield to do work that is both meaningful and fun."

KEN ZIMMERMAN

Urban Social Justice
Advocate

By Piper L. Bringhurst

Nothing about Ken Zimmerman gives away his impressive legal background. Ken has a Harvard degree and is a graduate of Yale Law School. Ken is also the founding Executive Director of the New Jersey Institute for Social Justice (NJISJ), which he lovingly refers to as a "social justice think and do tank." Before moving to Newark to accept this position in October 1999, he had been Deputy Assistant Secretary for Enforcement and Programs at the U.S. Department of Housing and Urban Development and a senior trial attorney in the Civil Rights Division of the U.S. Department of Justice.

The NJISJ is an urban advocacy and research organization working on diverse projects ranging from prisoner reentry programs to the creation of jobs in major construction projects, and from litigation aimed at stopping predatory lending practices to advocating alternatives to drivers' license suspensions because such suspensions act as barriers to employment. After finishing college, Ken worked at a community action organization and spent time teaching English in the Israeli Peace Corps.

Ken had always been interested in politics. He began to think about going to law school while he was still in college, and he knew that he liked to write and debate. His decision became final while he was interning at the Connecticut Department of Environmental Protection. On a particularly difficult issue, the solution to which was unclear, Ken recalls someone saying "the lawyers will end up determining what we're going to do." Although he says he now has a more "honest" view about this, he nevertheless wanted to become a lawyer to "get things done."

While in law school, which he at first disliked, Ken also obtained a Masters of Urban Planning at MIT. He believed that the legal perspective was too limited, and he wanted to combine approaches and bring disciplines together to solve social problems. Tied to his interest in urban communities is Ken's overarching interest in people. Despite all his successes and achievements, helping people to grow is what he does on a grand scale. He is sincerely fascinated by individuals, their stories, and learning what they need to succeed.

When Ken was approached to found NJISJ, accepting the opportunity to head it would mean moving his family from Washington to New Jersey. But the organization was a place where Ken felt he could truly realize what it meant to be a public interest lawyer as he translated the experience he had gained into practical solutions for the problems of urban residents. Powerful as these considerations were, however, the hard question was whether the opportunity made sense for his family. Ken and his wife did not make the decision to move until they could manage the transition process effectively for their young children. Ken cautions that family considerations can be just as powerful as any others, and he urges law students and young attorneys to "pay attention" to family concerns as "entirely legitimate."

Ken describes his experience founding NJISJ as not without challenges. He began in a donated office in a suburban location and "spent the first six months getting lost." Although the organization began with Ken as its only member, it currently has a staff of sixteen.

Ken's first priority is to help an organization already working on an issue to be more effective. He was inspired to take this job because it would allow him to exemplify what he believes progressive lawyering should be: wielding technical expertise in a variety of areas locally, combined with an awareness of developments in the national arena. His goal on coming to NJISJ was to get to know the issues of urban Newark well, thereby allowing him to enhance community efforts.

One challenge he faced was simply the time it took to get to know the community. He spent six months to a year overcoming "a very appropriate skepticism" about him as an outsider who had come in to fix the community's problems. His style and concern helped surmount this obstacle, and he also built a staff that reflected Newark's diverse viewpoints. He also says he benefited from being a newcomer in other ways. For example, his lack of involvement in local history allowed him to be viewed as a neutral party in contentious and longstanding community debates.

Ken is particularly proud of his involvement in the recent allocation of $8.5 billion for the building of new schools in New Jersey. As a result of a New Jersey Supreme Court decision, the state undertook the largest public works program in its history. Ken gathered the local school districts, the construction trade unions, and local advocates and community groups and created a construction training program to enable recent high school graduates to become union members. To date, over 175 Newark residents have become union members, the program has moved from a privately funded pilot program to a publicly supported model, and the State has now committed up to $20 million to replicate the program throughout New Jersey.

Ken is clear that the program's success involved both recognizing a moment of political opportunity and taking the time to build sufficient relationships that allow people to trust each other and work together. While the issue of maximizing the number of local residents who work on major public construction projects is always a hot-button issue, by working to understand the complicated interests of the parties, consistently promoting a vision of what could succeed, and forging relationships between individuals, Ken was able to overcome these challenges and now counts the program as one of NJISJ's major early successes.

Lasting social change must be rooted in the community and that takes time. You must get others in the community to buy into your project. Ken has mastered this approach, and it allows his organization to take on diverse projects that are unified by a single goal: challenging the barriers that prevent individuals and the community from reaching their potential. To make this happen, Ken uses research, creation of demonstration programs, and public education and mobilization, as well as more pointed advocacy. Ken characterizes himself as a litigator, but recognizes that litigation, while an exceedingly powerful tool, is also extraordinarily blunt. While Ken notes a number of NJISJ's litigation successes, such as the first appellate court decision in the country that recognized that predatory lending could violate federal and state civil rights laws, he emphasizes that litigation must be used strategically and that a public interest advocate must explore many avenues to achieve solutions.

Ken believes there are two important aspects to being a public interest lawyer: (1) being an activist and (2) being a problem solver — skills that make him successful that were cultivated in law school. In Ken's work, it is important to identify the source of a problem, the reasons that it has not been solved before, whom you need to get involved to solve the problem, and what constituencies' interests must be understood and supported in order to maintain solutions over the long run. These are the kinds of skills that an aspiring public interest attorney should strive to develop. Ken also notes that bringing a unique background of interdisciplinary skills helps too. Of the four lawyers on his staff, three have other advanced degrees. Though this may show that "the organization provides a home for those who can't decide what they want to do when they grow up," it is also true that being a successful urban advocate requires the blending of a variety of different approaches and perspectives.

One of the things that Ken loves about his job is that there is no typical day. He jokes that because he has the "attention span of a nursery schooler," he enjoys bouncing from one activity to another. At the end of the day, however, all of his work "turns on people," and he says "that is what it's really all about." Although he enjoys writing and doing other legal tasks, the work has to be grounded in people for it to be worthwhile to him.

Ken says that his daily activities break down into three general categories: (1) he does extensive work outside the organization, such as public speaking (he recently gave the graduation speech at the Drug Court commencement ceremony for the Essex County Courts), legislative testimony and meetings, and working with funders and other groups; (2) he handles tasks that traditionally come with running a business, and here he points out that public interest organizations are often in need of good, sound management; and (3) he does substantive work such as program development and design and legal strategizing. Though Ken enjoys his work, he is frustrated by things that are out of his control. For example, when NJISJ sets up a way for a group to advance its own interests and benefit the greater community at the same time but the group doesn't take advantage of it, Ken is discouraged. But he acknowledges that NJISJ is a small organization and that this at times limits its utility. Ken feels he has really succeeded when the other people he involves in a project are viewed as the project's effective and successful leaders. He wants to take talented people and put them into positions where they can succeed. In turn, his greatest frustrations come from feeling like he is an obstacle to getting something done.

When asked to elaborate on what he finds most rewarding, he tells about the individuals that he has seen succeed through NJISJ's initiatives. He glows as he recounts the story of the first-ever female African-American to be admitted to the Steamfitter's Union. Ken says that connecting to the humanity of what is happening is the thing that is most significant about his work. This means not just the individuals who are helped by the change he creates, but also the people he finds who share his values. Ken revels in finding people in unexpected places who are willing to help in his efforts. His goal is to get them involved.

It is clear, though unsaid, that Ken's confidence and inner peace come largely from living in accordance with his values and trying to be the kind of person he admires. He does the things he thinks are good and right and strives to cause the change he wishes to see in the world. He is supported by a community of like-minded people who share his values, and this provides immense satisfaction. His career as a public interest lawyer contributes to the reason he is so content. He believes this has provided deeper and more diverse experiences than he could have found in the private sector, but he is not a crusader who thinks that law firms and the attorneys who work in them are evil. Rather, Ken urges that "people can do a variety of things"—people can be very valuable in the private sector and can support many worthwhile causes. This, too, is consistent with Ken's overwhelming enthusiasm that each individual should thrive and flourish.

Public interest work, Ken argues, is a richer experience than private sector work in every way but one—monetarily. Lawyers get a lot more responsibility and far more interesting and diverse assignments in the public sector. But Ken believes people have entirely valid reasons for doing other things and urges that one is not going to sell out simply by spending some time at a corporate firm. Deciding to go with a financially more stable career may be an appropriate decision, particularly for a person worrying about caring for a family. It is dangerous to demonize people for making such a choice, although fair to examine if they commit themselves to *pro bono* or otherwise support public interest causes. But Ken feels lucky never to have had to go the big firm route himself. He and his wife are both attorneys in the public interest field and they have three children. Despite the challenges, they have made it work, and one can see that Ken is a remarkably contented man because of it.

Ken loved his positions at the Justice Department and at HUD, but he now has much more control and flexibility to design his own schedule and partake in family events. If necessary, he can leave to make his daughter's soccer game or his son's parent-teacher conference. Ken has made it a priority to create a culture in his organization that supports people in their private lives as well as in their careers. But knowing about Ken's intense respect and sincere concern for the individual, one would expect nothing less. Ken positively lights up when he talks about his family, and it is evident that this excitement is not just for his own family, but for his colleagues' families as well.

Although Ken knew he wanted to be a public interest lawyer, his career has been far from planned out in advance. He has been practicing for almost twenty years, but he never could have predicted that he would be doing what he does now. He worries that some students just start on the corporate trail because they can't find any other path. Ken encourages people to acknowledge the "unknown" aspect of a public interest career but to also realize that there is a fundamental richness in the potential opportunities one can find. He believes that once one gets started, the full breadth of possibilities begins to emerge. Furthermore, consistent with the character of a true altruist and humanitarian, Ken urges students to "follow their hearts." The best way for one to do that is to be sustained and enriched by one's daily activities. Ken has done that, and he provides an extraordinary role model for all those who hope to love what they do.

Editors' Note: After this profile was completed, Ken was offered the position as Chief Counsel to the Governor of New Jersey, which he accepted.

DREW CAPUTO

Environmental Litigator

By Salena Copeland

After we won the first round of litigation [in an offshore drilling case], I told the press something like "We think it's a really bad idea to drill more oil wells in valuable and fragile California coastland." That showed up in the LA Times. The next day, Rush Limbaugh attacked me by name on his radio show. I have a friend who listens to Limbaugh so he knows what the right-wingers are thinking. Rush Limbaugh said, "Environmental whacko Andrew Caputo says," and then he read my quote and said, "So, where are we going to drill? Can we drill on the East Coast? Can we drill in Alaska?" My friend called me up right after Rush attacked me. I saw that as a sign I was doing the right thing, if Rush Limbaugh was attacking me by name. I got serious environmental street cred for a few weeks after that happened. You know you're doing the right thing when Rush Limbaugh's going after you by name.

The case that got Drew Caputo labeled an "environmental wacko" involved offshore oil leases. Drew counts the first round of litigation in this case a big victory—street cred aside—because Natural Resources Defense Council, joined by the State of California, argued successfully that the federal government should not be able to extend leases during the offshore leasing moratorium. Drew and NRDC first got involved in 1999, and in the summer of 2005 the battle against the federal government still was not over. Although NRDC prevailed in the district court in 2001 and later in the 9th Circuit, the Bush Administration had been trying to "fix the legal violations that the court had identified in the successful litigation." This gave NRDC reason to sue again over the problems with the new proposals to extend the leases.

Drew's persistence and passion in the offshore drilling case is part of the territory of working in environmental law. Drew is currently a senior attorney at Natural Resources Defense Council, where he's been for over twelve years and where he's worked before and after being labeled an environmental wacko. Drew's entire legal career has been in environmental law. Since he graduated from Yale Law School in 1990, he has worked for the Sierra Club Legal Defense Fund (now Earthjustice) and NRDC.

Growing up in a "middle middle class" town in southern New Jersey, an area not exactly known for its great outdoors and open spaces, Drew had a typical childhood—working parents, Boy Scouts, beach vacations. His path to environmental law and his passion for preserving the environment is made all the more interesting because of his East Coast origins.

Although Drew did not know that he would eventually go into environmental law, he has been committed to advocacy since adolescence. He claims that was because he was argumentative as a child. His interest as a boy in advocacy and history led him to an interest in the law. In high school he started thinking about becoming a lawyer because, as he says, "a lot of politically and historically important figures were lawyers. Heroes like Thurgood Marshall got things done with the law."

Because he loved history so much as a child, Drew chose it as his major at Brown University, where he had many opportunities to hone his advocacy skills. During the nuclear arms race, he spoke with senior citizens about spending on nuclear weapons when the resources might have been used elsewhere, and he worked to educate students about nuclear weapons. He also worked on the Free South Africa Movement. However, his participation on a budget committee gave him the best opportunity to actually bring about change. Brown had a committee that made recommendations about the budget to the board of trustees, the Brown Corporation. The budget committee gave students the chance to have real input on university spending. Drew worked to increase resources for financial aid, hoping to make Brown "need-blind" so that students would be admitted on their merits, not on their parents' ability to pay.

During his last summer as an undergraduate, Drew had his first legal internship and his first glimpse into politics. He interned for the late Massachusetts Congressman Gerry Studds, who represented Cape Cod, Nantucket, and Martha's Vineyard. Drew had always been interested in public policy and politics, but his internship taught him how politics really worked. He remembers, "When they call a vote [in the House chambers]—on CSPAN, you don't see this—all the buzzers on Capitol Hill go off. All the congressmen and congresswomen come in the doors. The committee chairmen on both sides, they stand by the door as all the members come through, and they give a thumbs up or a thumbs down. People coming in the door have no idea what the vote is about because they've been in a committee meeting or something.

That's how politics is done in the real world. You have this idea of thoughtful analysis, but it's thumbs up/thumbs down."

Even after his observation on the lack of thoughtful analysis in making law, Drew still wanted to be a lawyer. His professors at Brown helped Drew continue his interest. While an undergraduate, Drew took a class called "The Politics of Legal Systems," which was taught by a political science professor who also had a law degree. Drew says that the class was not pre-law in any sense, but it was on how the legal system functions. "I loved that . . . taking a step back and looking at how the legal system operates from a cultural and political perspective. Law isn't just about enforcing a contract; law is a social course, for better or for worse." Drew benefited from Brown's serious scholar-professors and from studying with the "leading lights in History." His thesis advisor was James Patterson, who has since written a volume of the Oxford History of the United States.

Drew's love of Brown's academic culture led him to choose Yale Law School, which he saw as the "Brown of law schools" because it deemphasized grades and encouraged nontraditional paths. "You don't have to get on the tried-and-true path of private partnership in order to have a satisfying and significant career." Drew knew he wanted to go into public interest law and did not want to be a private firm lawyer, so choosing a school that encouraged a nontraditional path was right for him. But that did not mean that he would enjoy law school. In fact, he did *not* like law school. He explains, "A large part of that was me."

What he liked so much about Brown—lots of different people from different backgrounds, interested in different topics, and doing different things—was absent in law school. "Law school attracts a lot of people who are similar and who by definition in the first year are studying the exact same curriculum." Drew thinks he would have benefited from taking a year off before law school instead of going straight through in order to get more perspective on the real world. The other aspect of law school that frustrated him was that law school is very theoretical, and Drew is a practical thinker. He wanted to be an advocate, specifically a public interest advocate, and he felt that that was not what law school was about. Despite Yale's nontraditional culture, Drew felt that the most valued Yale graduate was someone who did an appellate clerkship and immediately went into teaching.

Although Drew missed the diversity of Brown and was not enjoying law school, he had many law professors who left lasting impressions. Drew Days, later the Solicitor General under President Clinton, taught Drew's Federal Jurisdiction class. He was intimidated by Days because Days was so smart and had been a civil rights litigator before going into teaching. Drew remembers that Days was a "tremendous" professor. Another professor who affected Drew is Michael Ponsor, who taught Pre-Trial Civil Litigation. In that class, Ponsor walked the students through the whole litigation process. He was a federal magistrate judge at the time and would use the cases before him to have the students write answers to complaints, draft complaints from factual narratives, and file dispositive motions. After that, they would argue to the bench—Professor/Judge Ponsor.

The nonacademic life at Yale was also influential on Drew. He was active on Moot Court, arguing a case involving preemptory jury challenges based on race in civil trials. He was also tangentially involved in the Environmental Law Society, which put on a conference in his 2L year that helped solidify his choice to practice environmental law.

Before he attended the "20 Years of Environmental Law" conference, Drew spent his first summer as an intern for Sierra Club Legal Defense Fund. Drew had never really spent time in the west because he was an East Coast guy, so he wanted to spend a summer out west. One day he went into the career services office and saw a handout from the SCLDF Denver office. Handwritten at the top was "Summer Job still available." Drew called and was hired—his first foray into environmental law.

He loved everything about that first summer job. He was bored in law school because he could not get "jazzed" about abstract legal issues. At SCLDF, he was dealing with complicated legal issues in areas he found important—endangered species and wild areas. He was hungry for the ability to use law in the service of something he really cared about—a theme that is prevalent in his life. This contrasted with his second summer job at a private firm in Boston. Although he loved the people there and it was a firm serious about *pro bono* work, he knew it wasn't for him. He rejected the offer for post-grad employment quickly because he was afraid that in a weak moment in his public interest job search, he might take the firm job out of fear.

In deciding to work in public interest immediately after law school, Drew took a different path than many of his colleagues. He remembers that everyone else in his class applied for clerkships, and he didn't even apply. Now, Drew views the decision not to work in a judicial clerkship as a mistake. "You learn a lot about what is good and bad about advocacy by watching advocates for a year in a district court and getting the insight that a good judge can provide to you." But because Drew saw a clerkship as another year of law school, something he wanted to avoid, he went straight to a position with the Sierra Club Legal Defense Fund.

Drew's first job after graduation was not quite fellowship and not quite a partner-track associate position. SCLDF did not hire anyone straight out of law school for a permanent position as a staff attorney. Drew started as a two-year associate attorney in SCLDF's Denver office. Attorneys in that position were expected to leave after two years, and most did. But not Drew. After the two years, SCLDF created a position for him, and he worked as a "project attorney" for an additional year.

SCLDF's way of teaching new attorneys how to litigate is Drew's ideal model. He describes what he sees as the three models as the Big Firm Model, the Justice Department Model, and the SCLDF's model. "In the Big Firm Model, as I understand it, they have mini-classes or seminars. I've never worked in a firm, so I don't even know if that's right, but that's how they do it. And even if they don't [do it that way], they put their associates in and tell them to do discovery requests. The Justice Department Model is where you walk in the door, they shake your hand, they hand you twenty cases and tell you to run all draft documents through your supervisor, and 'Good luck!'" Drew thinks that those learning litigation in the Justice Department Model can really wallow because the litigation process is not intuitive and new attorneys really need more help. The SCLDF model is working closely with another skilled litigator or several skilled litigators. New attorneys get to learn hands on, but in a graduated way as their abilities improve. "You learn by doing, but not in the sink or swim way of the Justice Department. I got lucky."

Drew loved everything about working at SCLDF, just as he loved his summer position there. He cared about the issues they worked on—the docket was almost exclusively federal court litigation, heavy on endangered species, public land protection, and river protection—and he loved working in Colorado. On weekends, he would spend a lot of time hiking and camping in the Rockies. "It was fun for me to be able to spend time in the same areas I was trying to protect in the work day." One of his cases involved an effort to protect some proposed wilderness areas in Colorado, New Mexico, Nevada, and Utah. So he drove to Southern Colorado and climbed a 14,000 peak, which was inside one of the wilderness areas. He was suing the first Bush Administration about its unwillingness to protect the area and was able to spend a three-day weekend there. It meant a lot to Drew that he was protecting these spaces; "I loved that they were in a part of the country that I was living in and had grown to love."

From a skills standpoint, Drew benefited from choosing a public interest job over a big firm job. He found himself arguing motions, even dispositive motions, before he was even a year and a half out of law school. He calls that a "really fabulous experience." Before he left SCLDF, he was cross-examining witnesses in evidentiary hearings and had delivered a closing argument in a successful preliminary injunction hearing.

Choosing SCLDF gave him another great opportunity. In his 1L summer job there, he'd worked closely with a lawyer named Doug

Honnold, who Drew sees as his first and most important mentor. Honnold was a major factor in Drew's decision to work at SCLDF after graduation. Drew admired Honnold's passion for trying to protect wild places from bad government policy. Honnold has since moved to the (now Earthjustice) Montana office, and Drew still calls him to work through legal issues.

A major case Drew worked on involved a timber sale outside of Yellowstone National Park after the famous fires. The Forest Service had decided they wanted to start "salvage logging," which is logging burned trees. The Forest Service justified this decision by saying that the trees would "go to waste" otherwise, but burned trees are really valuable wildlife habitat for owls and other birds. They were also cutting "green timber," living trees. SCLDF saw the salvage logging of burned trees as a way for the Forest Service to get into many areas they would have had difficulty logging otherwise because of their value as habitats for many animals, including endangered species. It was the first case Drew worked on as an attorney, and he lost. "We had what I thought was a really persuasive case with fire experts explaining that fire is a natural part of the forest life cycle — it doesn't mean that the forest is ruined when a fire comes through." Drew was heartbroken over the loss. He visited the area he had been working so hard to protect, and it had just been clear-cut. Although this early loss was devastating, it makes his subsequent victories all the more important.

After working in litigation for three years, Drew wanted to take a different approach. He knew litigation does not always solve the problem or end the dispute. Environmental laws are almost all procedural and process-oriented. Drew illustrates this by explaining, "Say the Forest Service wanted to clear-cut and log the entire state of Oregon to turn it into a parking lot — putting aside the Endangered Species Act, which is one of the rare environmental laws that has a substantive limit on what people can do. As long as they wrote an environmental impact statement that said, 'We're going to clear cut the whole state, and it's going to have a horrible environmental impact. All the wildlife habitat is going to be gone, and there is going to be no place for the rain run-off to go — because it's all asphalt — so there's going to be a lot of flooding . . . ' As long as they disclose all that stuff, the law would allow them to do it." The decision about whether or not to log, whether a dam can be built, or whether or not a species gets protected, is in most part a political decision. Drew worked in an office that did environmental litigation "as well or better than anyone in the country," but that is all that SCLDF did.

Drew was looking for something he calls "integrated advocacy" — the ability to attack a problem from every angle. "If there is a legal vulnerability, we can file a lawsuit. If it's the type of issue that really needs more attention in the public mind, then we can try to get more media attention on it by issuing a report or by holding a news conference. If things are moving politically, we have an opportunity to influence good legislation or stop bad legislation." Many environmental issues also need good scientists.

Drew found that integrated advocacy with Natural Resources Defense Council. Working for NRDC also allowed him to move back East to Washington, DC, to be closer to his family and friends. NRDC allows room for more strategy in a changing political environment. Drew clarifies, "It's important to know how the political process reacts to public interest environmental lawsuits—particularly since the change in Congress in the wake of the '94 elections. In the old days, the worst thing that could happen to your lawsuit was that you filed it and you lost it. Now, the worst thing is that you file your lawsuit, win it, and Congress amends the law in a reaction to your legal victory."

Drew's litigation docket at NRDC is similar to what he had at SCLDF. He almost always sues the federal government and rarely goes to trial. Drew explains that a major part of his work is getting information into the paper administrative record that an agency must compile in the course of making a decision that NRDC is challenging. The agency gets deference in many cases, and it is important in framing the cases that NRDC presents the issues in such as way that they are clear and understandable. The Justice Department says, "You should just defer to us, your honor," and if the case is complicated, the judge may be tempted to just throw up her hands and say, "Too complicated. I'm deferring to the expert agency." Drew works to simplify complicated legal and scientific issues to persuade the judge to rule in NRDC's favor. To help him, Drew uses NRDC's on-staff scientists and outside referral scientists. In Drew's San Francisco office, he teams with two scientist/policy people to identify environmental concerns.

As a Senior Attorney at NRDC, Drew works in many coalition efforts. He is not just representing NRDC in many of his cases; he's also representing other environmental groups. In some of these cases, he has co-counsel, and in others, he just checks in with the other counsel while leading the case. All of his work is part of a broader mandate.

There is no pressure for Drew to bill hours. NRDC's mandate is to protect the environment, not make money. This distinguishes NRDC from many firms. Drew works fewer hours than he would if he were to work at a private firm, but he still works nights and weekends when a brief is due. However, he is always happy to work extra because he cares about the work he is doing. He does not get the financial reward that he would in a private firm, but that is not why he went into environmental law. At NRDC, Drew gets to bring the cases that his team thinks are the most important cases for protecting the environment. "It's an incredible gift, an incredible privilege, to be able to work on the things that seem the most important in terms of protecting the resources." He never loses sight of the fact that to him it is a "privilege" to do this kind of important work.

Remembering the privilege of protecting the environment is important when Drew loses. His job is to serve the client and give it his best shot, but when he loses, it is really hard. It is hard for him to leave the case at the office because he is so entwined with the result he hopes to get. He explains how he feels when he loses, "It's personally debilitating because it's depressing. A certain amount of losing goes with the turf here." At those times, he thinks of how nice it would be to be a private firm lawyer who is not as emotionally tied to the cases. Losses are hard for Drew.

Victories, like the one that labeled him an environmental wacko, help make up for the losses. Drew has been working with scientists at NRDC in coastal and river policy, fighting offshore oil drilling, protecting under-water wildlife habitat, and helping to set lower catch levels for fisheries.

Choosing a nontraditional path has allowed Drew many opportunities that those in private firms do not have. Drew has taught for Stanford University in its Stanford in Washington Program. He has published articles on environmental law, testified before Congress, and served on a number of committees while in Washington, DC. Drew says that there is "tremendous gravitational pull" to go work at a private firm. He has a message for those who are still deciding: "Pretty much everyone I know who did something different [from a private firm] is happy. You should fight to get the job that speaks to you. They got jobs that were rewarding. The first job is the hardest to get. If it's not perfect, you can have the opportunity to get another job later. Be flexible."

Drew's flexibility, his passion for environmental law, and his commitment to integrated advocacy at NRDC carried him to San Francisco, and he is in the West to stay. "I worked really hard to get here, so I'm not leaving. The outdoor environment is phenomenal. And my little girl, Julia, is a California girl."

Early in 2006, Drew made the difficult decision to leave NRDC after thirteen years, to join the U.S. Attorney's Office in San Francisco as a criminal prosecutor. He did so for two main reasons. First, he wanted to branch out substantively, to deal with legal issues and areas of the law that he'd had no exposure to in his many years of specialized practice as a public interest environmental litigator. Second, he wanted to get trial experience. Public interest environmental lawsuits against government agencies almost never go to trial and instead are decided on the basis of the paper record the defendant agency compiles in the course of making the decision challenged by the environmental plaintiffs. Even in the district court, public interest environmental litigation is akin to appellate litigation, since the parties largely are working off a paper record established below (in this case, the paper record established before the agency). To get trial skills, Drew felt he needed to leave NRDC and go to a place that focuses on trials. Drew is excited about his new job, which he calls "public service, just in a different way than I did it at NRDC." Still, it was very hard for him to leave NRDC. He says "I loved working for such a long time to protect the environment, and I cherish every minute of every workday I spent at NRDC trying to make the world a better place for our children and our children's children."

DOUG HEIKEN

Environmental Advocate

By Kathryne TafollaYoung

Weekday mornings at nine, Willamette Street is an easy bustle of offices, banks, and cafés, of brick and wood buildings two and three stories high, with the names of local businesses stenciled in bright paint. Dogged traditionalism and a vibrant counterculture coexist comfortably in downtown Eugene, and dark slacks and a briefcase are conspicuously out of place. Next comes Morning Glory, a café with hardwood floors and yellow walls, its mismatched tables spilling onto the sidewalk, then Red Agave, a trendier bistro with signs advertising organic Oregon beef. Even a local can walk down Willamette Street a dozen times without noticing the metal door wedged between the two restaurants. Its sole marker is a street number painted shakily on the glass above. Halfway up the door, someone has duct-taped a pale green index card. "BUZZER," it reads in ball-point scrawl. With a slight push, the door opens, revealing plywood patches hammered unartfully above the railing.

At the top of a creaky wooden stairway, beyond a workroom of folding chairs and dilapidated carpet, is the Eugene field office of the Oregon Natural Resources Council (ONRC), the organization where Doug Heiken has worked for environmental justice for the past ten years. In these modest quarters, immeasurably different from a conventional law firm, Doug has filed appeals, influenced members of Congress, monitored timber sales, and mobilized volunteers. His approach to his work is as determinedly independent as his confines. He is wearing a short-sleeve shirt, jeans, and Birkenstocks. Is this his usual work attire? "No," Doug explains, chuckling; today he is dressed up. The brown sports coat hanging near the window is "strictly for the media," he says with an infectious wide smile.

Voted "Most Individual" in high school, Doug has proven his classmates' prediction sound, as he has forged an enviably varied path for himself in environmental law. "This kind of work is something new all the time—I love that about it," Doug says, the excitement palpable in his voice. "Wildlife surveys one day, water pollution the next, and watch dogging timber sales the day after that."

Growing up in suburban southeast Portland, Doug never dreamed of the law. His father owned a small business; his mother was a homemaker. While both had gone to college, no one in Doug's family had ever attended law school—nor did Doug's father admire the profession—a fact that, while Doug was young, dampened his attraction to it. Instead, he spent his free time camping, fishing, hiking, and taking as many art and science courses as he could. A self-described "jack of all trades," Doug experimented with half a dozen majors as a University of Oregon undergraduate, including Economics, Geology, Engineering, and International Studies. Finally concluding that he needed a solution-oriented career, he settled on Planning, Public Policy, and Management, which integrated his devotion to science with his budding interest in politics—an intrigue that led him to a senior-year internship in the office of state legislator Bill Bradbury, who is now Oregon's Secretary of State.

"That was a very formative experience for me, working in the legislature, seeing how laws were made," Doug says. Twenty years later, his eyes still brighten as he relates his first exposure to politics. "I started to learn the importance of an 'and' or an 'or' or an 'if.' You can have a knockdown, drag-out fight about one word. It's amazing." One of Doug's main projects that year was estimating the environmental impact of a proposed nuclear waste site near Oregon's Columbia River. He researched for months and outlined the situation for Bradbury one morning as they drove to a press conference: with the river so close by, the nuclear waste would seep into the water and spread lethal toxins throughout the state. Bradbury was so impressed with Doug's work that before they reached their destination, Doug had helped the legislator write a speech publicly opposing the waste site—and the plans for the site were soon abandoned. The experience, Doug says, rendered his long days in the library suddenly potent. "I had such a clear connection with the work I had done," he explains. "It was great watching it all come together."

And yet, Doug didn't head directly for a life in law or politics. It was the 1980s, and with the country in the midst of recession, job opportunities for a Public Policy Management graduate were scarce. After his internship with Bradbury's office, Doug headed home to Portland and worked in an ice cream shop until he had saved enough money to buy an old Econoline van. He piled his worldly possessions in the back and drove to San Francisco to look for work. For months, he slept on the floor of a friend's warehouse and labored at a silk-screening shop, printing T-shirts for tourists. But even though Doug wasn't chasing the law, it seemed to be chasing him: he connected with a temp agency, which paired him with a large corporate law firm in San Francisco, which soon hired him as a full-time paralegal.

It's difficult to imagine a world less suited to Doug than being involved in corporate law. His easy manner seems more apropos of beachcombing than working at a big law firm. "It was a pretty hierarchical environment for me. If I'd have gotten stuck in that kind of work, I don't know how I would have survived." As a paralegal, Doug wasn't directly involved in the firm's litigation. But throughout his time there, he was acutely aware of the causes his support role furthered — defending tobacco and asbestos companies against health-related lawsuits. "I worked with a bunch of neat people," Doug says. "But the moral content was extremely low. It just felt bad. I wasn't longing to be one of the attorneys."

Three years later, Doug decided he'd had enough of the law firm, and — a true Oregonian at heart — enough of California. He wrote to Bill Bradbury, who had become state senate majority leader, and asked if he had work available. Bradbury invited him back, and Doug repacked his Econoline and drove north. For one full legislative session, he worked as a policy and budget analyst, still unsure where his career would lead. That same year Doug reconnected with an old high school friend, who was fresh out of law school and working as an appellate clerk. When he heard about Doug's experience in a law firm and the state legislature, he ordered an LSAT form, plopped it in front of Doug, and told him to fill it out. "We bet beer on whether I'd do better than him on the LSAT — one for each point," Doug recalls with a smile. "I won seven beers."

Still unsure that a life in the law was for him, Doug applied to only one school, his alma mater. At 27, he was older and more experienced than many of the students in his first-year class, but this did little to calm his first-year nerves. The curriculum appealed to him, but the "bizarre intensity" of law school testing did not. After the first round of finals was over, Doug relaxed considerably. He maintained strong grades but spent many afternoons hiking with his future wife — who was also a first-year law student. During his second and third years, Doug followed the same jack-of-all-trades pattern he had as an undergraduate, ignoring recommended courses in favor of those that interested him. He successfully petitioned the university to let him take classes outside the law school, where he dabbled in hydrology, geographic information systems, and the history of the American West.

For a short time, Doug considered returning to big law firm life with a law degree and even spent a winter break at his old firm in San Francisco. "I kind of got sucked into that assembly line for a while," he says. "During that brief time in law school when everyone is interested in big firms, I was following the mold." But for Doug, the impulse didn't last long. After taking a Public Lands course, he became intrigued with timber, grazing, oil and gas, and water law. He signed up as a volunteer for—auspiciously—the Oregon Natural Resources Council, now called Oregon Wild. Doug's advisor there, Wendell Wood, put him to work on the "yew tree" problem.

"I was completely immersed in the project," Doug recalls fondly, plucking his glasses from his nose and wiping them with the front of his shirt. A yew, he explains, is a big, stubby hulk of a tree whose bark contains cancer-fighting agents. But stripping its bark kills even the hardiest centenarian yew, and so Doug's challenge was to convince the pharmacological world to use its needles instead, which contain a lower concentration of the agent. While more expensive, the needle-made version is just as potent, and spares the tree's life. Doug's final project was published by the Oregon Law Review. Spanning more than seventy pages, the article describes the cultural history of the yew, technological alternatives to bark-stripping, and the legal implications of possible approaches. "It was the best training I could have received," Doug says.

After law school, most of his friends went to work at law firms, but Doug had already fallen hard for policy work. "You see so many people who do three to five years in a firm before they do something interesting. I decided to skip that three to five years and go straight to something interesting." Ever the individualist, Doug discovered that the bar exam wasn't required for the administrative and policy work he wanted to do—and never took the exam. While this means that Doug is not a lawyer, he stresses that his law school training was crucial for his work.

After graduation, Doug called Tom and Audrey Simmons, a couple he had met at the legislature. Together, the Simmonses had founded Water-Watch, a Portland-based nonprofit focused on combating the overappropriation of Oregon streams and rivers. They were opening a field office in Eugene, and Doug signed on to help them start it.

Having exited law school with plenty of loans, Doug acknowledges that surviving on a public interest salary is no cakewalk. "All along the way, money was a sacrifice," he says. "But it's doable." He explains that many young lawyers who try to transition into public interest work after a few years at a firm eventually have a harder time financially than those who start out in public interest. "Many firm lawyers get used to a lifestyle too expensive to be supported by the wages at nonprofits," he says.

While Doug enjoyed his work at WaterWatch, it came to an end when a new executive director wanted to consolidate operations in Portland. By then, Doug's wife was working at a local plaintiff's-side firm, and they'd bought a house in downtown Eugene. Neither wanted to move. Doug's experience landed him a job at Forest Service Employees for Environmental Ethics, a nonprofit that represents the interests of progressive Forest Service workers. There, Doug crafted a "whistleblower's handbook" to help employees who wanted to speak out against agency practices be able to maneuver through the legal gauntlet without getting fired.

Although Doug enjoyed the work, he embraced the chance to return to ONRC when a position opened at its Eugene field office. Several years and a few jobs later, he was finally back at the nonprofit that had given him his start in environmental law.

As Doug tells the story, the cycle seems almost implausibly perfect: even his office evinces a distinct equilibrium. One wall is filled entirely with old filing cabinets. An index card is taped to each drawer. "Grazing," reads one of them. "Mollusks," reads another. "Litigation." "Yew." "Landslides." Mounds of legal and scientific research perch precariously atop the cabinets. More files are stacked on the desk, partly obscuring the paneled window that overlooks Willamette Street. The wall above Doug's computer is covered with topographical maps of Oregon. A plush Smokey the Bear sits on Doug's computer, a home brewer's manual is on a table near the door, and there are several photographs of Doug's eleven-year-old daughter. Every pile of paper, every map, every file, seems an aspect of some grand and deliberate plan. Doug smiles at this observation, then laughs it off. "I just know where to find everything," he says simply. Yet, clearly it is more than that, and Doug's smile belies his knowledge of this: he has chosen the best of both worlds, bringing his laid-back, individualist style to serious work about which he is passionate. After ten years at the ONRC, the job fits Doug like a glove.

On any given day, Doug might hike into a forest to do field research, hold a press conference, meet with Earthjustice attorneys handling an ONRC case, or testify in front of the state legislature. The sheer variety of his daily work is Doug's favorite part of the job. He lists a few projects in which his office is currently involved: defending the Northwest Forest Plan and old-growth forests from political winds; challenging the discharge of polluted water into the upper Klamath River; suing the Fish and Wildlife Service to protect species such as lynx and lamprey under the Endangered Species Act; watchdogging over half of Oregon's 260 annual timber sales through site-scoping, researching, and commenting on prospective environmental impact; lobbying the Oregon legislature about biomass utilization; challenging Forest Service decisions to sell public forests without taking public comment; working against the Administration's decision to repeal the National Forest Roadless Area Conservation Rule — and this is just the beginning.

For each project, extensive media work is key. One of Doug's biggest challenges is combating the public's image about environmentalists. "There's this huge conception that we're all the same," he says. The "extremist" image of environmentalists has been a barrier to winning lawsuits — and to winning public support. "People see one realm of environmentalism that turns them off, and then they don't want to get involved," he explains. In reality, environmental groups encompass a wide spectrum of political goals and practical strategies, they differ in many ways, and they often disagree with one another. He wishes that more people would "understand that not all conservation groups are the same."

In his current role, Doug's political background serves him well: a nuanced understanding of state and federal government mechanics is important to environmental legal practice. One of Doug's greatest frustrations is the prevalence of administrative law — which can shift drastically on an executive whim. Doug shakes his head as he speaks of this and frowns for only the second time in two hours. "The Roadless Rule is a perfect example," he says. In 2001, after eighteen months of work among environmental groups nationwide, the Roadless Area Conservation Rule was designed to protect fifty-eight million acres. It was based on two million public comments and six hundred hearings. Then, just a few years later, "the Bush Administration pulled the plug on it — without hearings, without public comments, without preparing an Environmental Impact Statement." Congressional riders — small changes tucked into larger bills — are another political obstacle. Doug describes the endless frustration of getting legislation passed, testifying before a legislature, and drafting countless documents — only to have a single, swift signature erase the efforts. "Environmental work," he tells me, "is a constant battle."

As demanding as Doug's job is, the ONRC's relaxed atmosphere helps diffuse the stress. Doug is careful not to replicate the hierarchies he saw during his brush with law firm life — a fairly easy task, since the Eugene office has a staff of only three. He explains that, while they each have specific duties, these are fluid. "Anyone can ask anyone to do anything else," he says. "Whether it's taking out the garbage, fixing the coffee machine, or meeting with the governor." Unfortunately, the traditional law firm's typically posh confines aren't replicated either. Doug's second-floor room is hot in the summer and cold in the winter, and it lacks the small luxuries of even a government office. Yet the old building holds an undeniable charm. Once a candy warehouse, it was bought and refurbished by the owners of a vegetable co-op on the floor below and is now home to a dozen community groups besides the ONRC, including a wetlands restoration group, an election reform nonprofit, a printers' guild, and several human rights advocacy groups. At any given time, something interesting is always in motion, Doug says. Though the groups are not formally linked, a central bulletin board and casual hallway conversations help create a progressive community.

Limited resources also translate into a temptation to work long hours. Doug advises, "You have to have skill at handling your projects. Some things get done well, and other things just get done." Yet Doug maintains that balancing his work life, family life, and outside interests has not been a struggle. The ONRC's Eugene office is a five-minute bike ride or a twenty-minute walk from Doug's house, and he limits himself to forty hours a week at the office. Additionally, each week, he spends about ten hours at home reading to keep abreast of legal and scientific developments. Because his personal passions relate closely to his legal work, Doug has found that his hobbies and his work tend to energize one another, which he touts as a significant benefit in many types of public interest work.

Certainly, acquiring a job like Doug's is no easy task, especially straight out of law school. But Doug emphasizes that a little enterprising can make it possible. "A great way into environmental work is volunteering," he explains. "If you're a known quantity, you're way ahead of the competition. It's much better than just looking good on paper." Because environmental lawyers for nonprofit organizations often have more work than they can handle, they're willing to dole out interesting projects — if a student can nab ten minutes of their time. According to Doug, interns who require a lot of supervision or aren't self-motivated tend to fall through the cracks.

Doug acknowledges that environmental legal work isn't for everyone. A strong streak of individualism is every bit as critical as strong writing skills, creativity, and the ability to subsist on small wages. He also acknowledges that the risk-averse nature of many law students prevents them from considering the jobs that might ultimately prove most fulfilling. But for those who can handle its challenges, public interest work is a reward in itself. Doug smiles as he says this, then seems suddenly distracted by thought. He glances past his stacks of files, through his ivy-lined window, and onto the bustle of Willamette Street. Without a doubt, this dogged individualist has just started planning his next fight.

Section2

Direct Service

KIRBY MITCHELL

Civil Legal Aid

By Adair Ford

Kirby Mitchell did not have a childhood dream of becoming a heroic advocate fighting for equal justice. He did not intend to become a leader in the public interest field, a legal aid attorney, or even a lawyer. But his fascination with the mechanisms of social order led him to become all three. Now he serves as the managing attorney for an office of the South Carolina Centers for Equal Justice largely because, as he puts it, he "wanted a job where he could make a living while being curious about the world."

Kirby grew up in Whitinsville, a Massachusetts mill town. His father was an insurance claims adjuster; his mother was an English teacher and active community volunteer. Kirby sees his career as an amalgamation of his father's analytical policy interests and his mother's practical perspective on helping those around her, but he never considered the legal profession when he was growing up.

Kirby admits making his decision about going to Furman University based on his visit to the lush green campus and his romanticized view of the South. While there, he developed an interest in economics and majored in the subject, but, like many liberal arts students with broad interests, he didn't find a calling in any particular career. He might have been a journalist or businessman had it not been for Dr. Judy Bainbridge, one of Kirby's professors and advisors at Furman. During his junior year she suggested he take the LSAT. He did extremely well on the test and began wondering if law might be a career he could excel in and enjoy.

Kirby met the director of Greenville's Legal Aid office, Robert Jenkins, who decided to take Kirby on as a VISTA volunteer (Volunteer In Service to America). Kirby managed the agency's volunteers, assisted attorneys in the office, and helped with special projects. Kirby's experience at Legal

Aid provided the exposure he needed to feel confident he wanted to go to law school, but he wasn't ready to go just yet. Kirby had studied in London and Brussels during his senior year at Furman, and the experience left him craving more time abroad. It was an exhilarating rush for him: he was very curious about how societies function and how individuals navigate societal processes. Kirby used the connections of his sister, a German professor, to land a job teaching English in the Czech Republic. He was the first American teacher at Maticni Gymnazium in Ostrava, where he designed and taught English conversation classes. Kirby's weekend role as a basketball player for a club team landed him local fame in the sports section of nearby newspapers. Kirby intended his time in the Czech Republic to be a nine month stint, but a relaxed life of teaching conversational English and getting paid to play basketball, interspersed with trips around the continent, was not so easy to leave. During holidays, he traveled all over Europe. After two years there, however, it was time to return to the States and embark on his next learning experience: law school.

In 1993, Kirby enrolled at the University of Georgia School of Law. The first year of law school was lackluster: its competitive nature and the constant anxiety it produced disappointed him. The focused training of law school didn't fit his nature the way his liberal arts undergraduate education had.

During his second and third years, however, he discovered how law could affect people's lives. He worked part-time at a law office handling various civil and criminal matters and participated in the university's legal aid clinic. The clinic gave Kirby the opportunity to help people navigate the legal system. Kirby worked at legal aid his first two summers of law school, which solidified his interest in legal aid and confirmed his desire to work in the field.

After law school, Kirby joined a law office as one of only two attorneys in a small town about fifteen miles from Greenville. The general practice fit Kirby's generalist nature well. He was able to handle a variety of different types of cases and was not expected to specialize. He worked on real estate cases, estate administration and planning, and what Kirby terms "everyday litigation."

Kirby enjoyed private practice. He had never intended to practice corporate law, but he also did not leave law school with the goal of becoming a public interest lawyer. He wanted to be part of a legal organization where client interaction was key and where he could serve each individual.

But Kirby was still drawn to legal aid and decided to return to Greenville, where he had been in VISTA. He was familiar with the organization from his earlier experience, and it offered a number of attributes Kirby valued highly in a job. He wanted the opportunity to work with people on a daily basis and to deal with policy issues that have implications for society.

As a staff attorney, Kirby handled a heavy and varied caseload. He worked on bankruptcy, foreclosure, social security disability and landlord-tenant cases, among others. The difficulties he now faces as a legal aid attorney are not "tricky or cutting-edge legal issues but practical, pragmatic problems of litigating with no money: how to get information without being able to afford depositions or how to help clients that don't have the money to pay for court fees." Attorneys must appreciate their client's situation and show compassion but not pity. He naturally exhibits such a demeanor and, as a result, has excellent rapport with his clients.

Even though many of his cases are what Kirby calls "bread and butter"—those that don't involve the intricacies of a law or move the law forward on a particular topic—he notes that he only finds the work boring if he doesn't take the time to really talk to the clients. Among other things, Kirby has learned how to run a meth lab. If you find a clerkship boring, Kirby recommends trying out legal aid.

Kirby enjoyed his position as staff attorney and had no management ambitions. Reflecting on the position of managing attorney, Kirby remarked, "It's not what I had in mind for my career." But Kirby's leadership ability, grasp of the essence of legal aid services and skills as a lawyer made him a perfect candidate for the job, and in January 2000, after only a year and a half as staff attorney, Kirby was offered the position of managing attorney for the Greenville and Anderson offices of Legal Services.

The position suits Kirby well. He still retains a full caseload and sees clients on a daily basis but also gets to direct the organization as a whole. He's responsible for determining which cases the office accepts and rejects, ensuring grant money is used wisely, and training new attorneys. A typical day involves a relatively quick hearing in court, making a number of phone calls to clients, meeting with his staff to determine which new cases the office should take on, and conferring with the resources development staff. Kirby estimates that he spends approximately fifty percent of his time on managerial duties and the other fifty percent performing the direct legal services he so enjoys.

One of Kirby's principal responsibilities is the triage of cases. The disheartening quality of this task bogs down many legal services organizations; choosing among deserving clients is never easy, and turning someone away is even more difficult. But Kirby handles triage in an efficient and professional manner. As he says, "You have to knock it out and get back to work, back to the people you can help."

Every Thursday morning, all of the attorneys meet to discuss what each case will require, the cases' pros and cons, and the attorneys' current caseloads. Each week the office sees cases involving domestic abuse, family court, housing, special needs adoption, consumer law, and social security disability. The office can handle only about half of the cases and must think strategically about which ones to take.

Part of this strategy involves rejecting the more marketable cases. At times, a particularly sympathetic client with a very strong case comes in, and Kirby's instinctive reaction is what any attorney's would be: take the case and look forward to winning. However, these appealing cases are the ones that can be easily referred, and therefore should be. As Kirby points out, "I have no interest in taking cases from the private bar." There are plenty of cases private practitioners are unwilling to take, so if a member of the private bar is willing to take a case because it's a fee-generating case or because it is a particularly sympathetic *pro bono* case, Kirby is happy to pass it on. Kirby's goal is to go into court with clients who would otherwise be forced to go on their own, and this goal guides him in case selection.

Kirby must also address the particular caseloads of his staff. Several of his staff attorneys are funded by specific grants, and these grants have restrictions on the type of casework the attorney may perform. For example, one attorney is funded by a Victims of Criminal Acts grant, which is intended to help victims of criminal activity with the civil side of their cases. This attorney might help a client obtain a restraining order against a battering spouse. But the grant also has specific restrictions, such as that the attorney may not help a client file for divorce. Because members of his staff are restricted in the work they may do based on their funding source, whether a particular case falls into one of these categories is a factor in whether the office may accept that case. Ensuring that these grant monies are spent on cases that the funding organization intended is key to continuing that stream of income and an important aspect of Kirby's job.

Often grantmakers want to meet the actual attorneys who receive their money and hear firsthand whether their money is well spent. Kirby is often the person they meet. He attends and participates in presentations by funding organizations such as the United Way. He also works closely with the resource development staff to communicate the services that he and his staff provide to the community. Kirby has a critical responsibility to ensure that Legal Services' financial supporters are happy with how their contribution is used.

Another of Kirby's mission-critical responsibilities is training new lawyers. Young attorneys in the office receive on-the-job training and have responsibility immediately. There is very little formal training before attorneys are handed a caseload. They observe Kirby in court a few times and then go to court themselves. They do, however, have the ongoing support of all the other attorneys in the office. The interaction with other lawyers, new and experienced, is the "best part" for Kirby. Attorneys regularly discuss ongoing cases, brainstorm solutions, and support each other in difficult cases. They vet each other's strategies in ongoing cases, discuss how to deal with difficult clients, and tell funny war stories. They allow their collective experience to benefit each of them.

This collaborative environment helps maintain a high morale in the office, one of Kirby's top priorities. He points out how easy it is for a legal services office to fall into a "woe is us" mentality, dwelling on unfortunate outcomes in clients' lives. He believes that attorneys help support each other by talking about the disappointing cases, such as when a battered woman returns to her batterer, but that focusing on these cases too much is detrimental for the organization. He stresses the importance of "being seen by clients, funders, and each other as a positive energy." The attorneys need to recognize they're making a difference in the lives of people, convey this to funders, and be an ongoing source of hope for clients.

The Greenville office of the South Carolina Centers for Equal Justice (a 2002 name change from Legal Services) has a special source of hope and positive energy: its office manager. She was a client of the office seven years ago. A victim of kidnapping, she was on welfare and involved in an abusive relationship. After her case was closed, she went back to school, received a Habitat for Humanity house, and accepted a job at the Greenville office. During her time there, she has received three promotions and has excelled at her job. She is a daily reminder of the contributions legal services makes to long-term differences in people's lives. With the look of someone who counts himself as blessed, Kirby remarks, "It's so important that she is here."

However, the attorneys at the South Carolina Centers for Equal Justice don't always get to see the impact of their work. In fact, in most instances no news is good news. As Kirby explains, "When we don't hear from them, that's a good thing. They're probably doing well and are at least not requiring our services." Another sign of success is when clients do return but don't qualify for services due to their income. Though it's difficult to turn these former clients away, their increased income signals positive changes in their lives, changes to which Kirby's team contributed.

Kirby makes a point to remember the significance of these instances when the reality sets in that they are rare. He voices his toughest frustration at legal aid, "Even if we do brilliant work for our clients, most of them will still be poor." At one point, Kirby recognized that tax refunds are the biggest transfer of wealth in the country and his clients were simply not exercising their right to obtain the largest financial help the government can offer. Often clients simply lack the education or sophistication to file tax returns properly and receive all the benefits to which they're entitled. the Executive Director of the South Carolina Centers for Equal Justice learned of IRS grants to help low-income people return to good standing with the agency, and Kirby jumped on the opportunity. The Centers for Equal Justice received an IRS grant, and Kirby launched a state-wide Low-Income Taxpayer Clinic. The clinic advises clients about tax laws designed to help low-income taxpayers with issues such as the Earned Income Tax Credit, provisions on school loan debt, and Innocent Spouse Relief. When clients take advantage of such provisions, they often find that instead of owing the federal government money, they are actually entitled to a refund. Kirby says, "It's just the best feeling when a client receives a $3,000 refund." Kirby finds the role of Supervisor of South Carolina's Low-Income Taxpayer Clinic constantly rewarding.

As managing attorney, Kirby gets to pick his cases, which allows him to keep a varied caseload that fits his generalist nature and to control how the organization's money is spent, an important element in Kirby's job satisfaction. Everyone in the office works 37.5 hours per week (though the attorneys usually put in a few more hours) and receives very generous holidays and vacation time. Because the organization recognizes it cannot pay what a private firm can, it provides attorneys with ample time to devote to family, friends, and community.

Kirby runs marathons, volunteers in the community, and is active in local nonprofits. He volunteers annually at Furman's collegiate Mock Trial tournament, does volunteer mediation, and even had time to travel to Sao Paulo, Brazil, as a member of Rotary International's Group Study Exchange Team. He raised $4,600 for the American Liver Foundation through its Boston Marathon Run, was on the Board of Directors for the Greenville Cultural Exchange Center (an African-American museum and cultural center), and has been Chairman of the Board of Directors for the Clubhouse Gang, Inc., since 2001. Taking a leadership role in this organization that assists low-income children through after-school tutoring and life skills training has allowed Kirby yet another opportunity to change lives one at a time.

He feels that these opportunities to be involved with nonprofits in a leadership capacity are largely due to his current job. Nonprofits tend to want attorneys on their board of directors, but most attorneys are too busy to become involved with nonprofits. According to Kirby, nonprofits also tend to be more comfortable asking legal aid attorneys to serve on their boards, assuming that legal aid attorneys will be more sympathetic to nonprofit causes. Having a forty-hour workweek provides Kirby time to accept these requests and be involved in the community.

Being involved with the community is also a reason Kirby chooses to work in Greenville rather than metropolitan areas such as Atlanta or DC. With a population of 58,000, Greenville is a medium-sized town, and the county, with 350,000 residents, is large enough to support international businesses like BMW, Hitachi, and Michelin, but small enough that Kirby might run into former clients at the grocery store. In a community of this size, Kirby says, "You can really feel the ripples of your work spread. . . ." Problems in Greenville seem manageable.

The working in a community of this size is also different because attorneys specialize less. Kirby particularly likes this aspect of working in Greenville. He is not a housing lawyer or a tax lawyer. He can delve into a number of different issues every day. He enjoys seeing completely different situations involving various elements of the law. Kirby explains that it doesn't make sense for legal aid offices in non-metropolitan areas of the South to work on cases that might make new law. Too many people exist who can't make use of the laws already in place. The biggest priority is to ensure that people are not forced to go to court alone.

This focus on individuals fits Kirby's personal philosophies well. Many people try to help the poor in what he terms "passive" ways. Kirby finds it much more fulfilling to actually meet people and help them face-to-face. He views himself not as an advocate of the poor but as an advocate for individuals who happen to be poor. To Kirby his job is not about political and social change, but about providing help to the core of society, and the legal system only works if everyone has access. He finds it remarkable that his job could ever be viewed as controversial and that movements exist to do away with legal aid. Kirby has never been politically active. He's just a damn good attorney helping ordinary people with everyday problems. In doing so, he has become a leader among his peers, one of Greenville Magazine's "Best & Brightest 35 & Under," and an unexpected hero to countless Greenville residents.

SYLVIA STRUSS

Native American
Legal Aid

By Henry Huang

During a day-long seminar at a hotel in Flagstaff, Arizona, Sylvia Struss leads sessions on discovery tools for civil litigation and conducts a mock trial with student advocates. The students are not lawyers; they are Tribal Court Advocates, who represent clients in Navajo Tribal Courts. Sylvia is an Anglo-American from Massachusetts. Everyone else is Native American.

Sylvia works for DNA People's Legal Services, a nonprofit law firm that serves primarily Indian populations. For most of her years with DNA, she has assisted low-income clients in domestic violence and consumer protection cases. Sylvia's experience is unique: the laws and customs of the Navajo Nation differ greatly from those of the regular U.S. legal system. This chapter is not just about a nontraditional job with low pay and no cubicles — it is also about a nontraditional life story and path into the legal profession.

Sylvia grew up in Hingham, Massachusetts, where her father sexually abused her and taught her that women were dumb and worthless and never amounted to anything. She testified against her father in court when she was just fifteen. Sylvia endured these wrenching experiences and has put them behind her, saying "I've given up thinking of myself as a victim." Her spirituality has helped her deal with her past. Today, she comes across as positive, active, and energetic.

Even during her early, troubled childhood, Sylvia resolved to become a lawyer. While she had entertained dreams of becoming a veterinarian, her first serious professional goal was to be a court reporter. Her father had given her a typewriter when she was nine or ten so that she could type insurance business letters for him, and before long, she became a masterful typist—at one point, the fastest in Massachusetts. Eventually, her ambition shifted from simply recording courtroom proceedings to participating in them. Also, her father's abuse had influenced her to disprove his misogynist views of women by seeking a powerful profession— one where she could change people's lives for the better.

Sylvia fled Hingham after high school for urban Boston. While taking college classes, she found a job in the MIT's Patent Office, where she handled professors' inventions and research grants and contracts. She jumped at the opportunity to take a job at Harvard and also enrolled at the Harvard Extension School, graduating *cum laude*. But despite her achievements as an undergraduate, Sylvia is absolutely clear about one thing: college was just a necessary stepping stone to law school.

She also created Harvard's Trademark Licensing Program, which solved the problem of retailers selling unlicensed Harvard merchandise, but never seriously considered patent or trademark law as a profession because of its desk-centered lifestyle. She had also started her own slip-cover business—making enough to earn $15,000 a year.

Sylvia initially applied to law schools in 1992 (her list included Harvard and Suffolk) and received not a single acceptance. She admits to some puzzlement: while her LSAT scores were slightly below average, she felt that her experience and training bolstered her case. She decided that she was simply not meant to start law school at that particular time. Resolving to uncover the reasons for the rejections, she harried Suffolk's admissions officers, insisting that she would reapply endlessly until they let her in. (Harvard refused to talk to her.) In the interim, she continued her slip-cover business and volunteered at MCI Framingham, a women's prison, where she counseled inmates and taught physical fitness classes.

The next time Sylvia applied to law schools, she got accepted. She chose Northeastern for its co-op program, which places students in term-time jobs for school credit. During one of her first classes, her professor demonstrated a client interview by essentially simply telling the "client" what he wanted to hear. Appalled, she came close to demanding a tuition refund two weeks into the semester. A friend's forceful intervention convinced her instead to talk to Northeastern's career services office.

When Sylvia described her experiences and desire for client-oriented work, her counselor suggested Big Mountain Legal Services, which served Native Americans and which would eventually lead her to the Navajo Nation. Within a month after starting at Northeastern, she had lined up a co-op job in Utah for the fall of her second year.

What classes would be most interesting to a lawyer precommitted to a public interest profession? Surprisingly, Sylvia found her Contracts course refreshing, due to her professor's method of giving students cases involving slavery contracts, which forced the students to consider the fundamental moral problems of legal obligations while learning black-letter law. Her most useful class, she says, was Civil Procedure. "You don't get it at the time," she observes, but it all makes sense and becomes extremely important in practice; indeed, it is now the focus of her lectures to the Tribal Court Advocates in Flagstaff.

The most satisfying courses for Sylvia were clinics, due to the invaluable hands-on litigation experience they offered. What's noticeably absent from Sylvia's memories of law school are the usual issues for most students: competing for grades, worrying about law review, and stressing over callback interviews at New York law firms.

When the time came for her internship with DNA, Sylvia drove cross-country to the Utah desert, to the Navajo reservation that DNA served. The nearest grocery store was miles away, she recalls, but to Sylvia the desert was a personal paradise: "I fell in love with the land," and the work fit her legal aspirations. She went to work on Social Security benefits and domestic violence matters.

Sylvia's time at Mexican Hat also affected deeply her personal life. During her college years, she admits to having used illicit substances. But while she said it was a "wonderful escape" at the time, she recognized the drugs' dangerousness and went clean after finishing at Harvard in 1992 (she boasts of completing law school without alcohol, drugs, caffeine, or sugar!).

Soon after her stay in Utah, she went to Colorado to attend her first Rainbow Gathering — a colorful mix of the environmentally minded, where she camped out on federal lands to celebrate, among other things, the Native Americans' respect for the land. There Sylvia found a deep spiritual connection to Indian teachings and a similarity between her life and the Native Americans' misery at the hands of the government. "Their 'father' had abused them and done as much as possible to put them down." Yet, she says, "their spirit was going to live." To Sylvia the gathering was a unique experience that persuaded her that she had discovered her calling and convinced her to return to the reservation full-time after law school.

During her remaining semesters at Northeastern, she tried other legal services jobs, but after graduating, she made her way back to Arizona, to accept a full-time position with DNA on the Navajo reservation. She gave birth to twins in Flagstaff but lived on the reservation, working with victims of domestic violence and practicing almost exclusively before the Tribal Courts. Nine years later, Sylvia has found that practicing Native-American law is a unique experience.

Sylvia's job with DNA People's Legal Services sounds like most public interest or legal services positions: In her trailer office she conducts client intakes, and serves indigent populations. But working as an attorney in the Navajo Nation is especially nontraditional because the law, both substantively and procedurally, requires a different perspective on culture and tradition. Because the Indian reservations are "sovereign" but "dependent" their laws differ from state laws.

During the training session at the Radisson, the instructors devote the morning's first lecture to jurisdiction. Jurisdiction, Sylvia notes, is always first and foremost on DNA advocates' minds. It is often tricky to determine where to file a case: in Navajo court, at another reservation, or in a state court. The answer depends on whether non-Indians are involved in the case and—in Sylvia's domestic violence cases—where the children involved live.

Once they establish jurisdiction, Indian lawyers face other unique legal issues. The Full Faith and Credit Clause of the U.S. Constitution presents a special problem because, simply put, the tribes do not have to follow the doctrine. Because Native Americans were not parties to the Constitution, their courts do not adopt all constitutional doctrines. This creates a problem for Sylvia in child custody cases. While forty-eight states have laws that require local officials to enforce child support decrees issued by other states' courts, the tribes do not. Thus, enforcing child custody against a parent who moves to another territory can be difficult.

But perhaps the most significant difference in tribal practice is the role of tradition and custom. Indeed, tradition is a large reason why Sylvia's job is "nontraditional." Sylvia feels that the Tribal Courts are much more flexible and equitable than other courts. Where a state court judge awards only temporary custody in a divorce proceeding, tribal courts also award temporary child support and alimony. Tribal judges respect Navajo values that stress "harmony"—a word Sylvia uses repeatedly to describe the Navajos' philosophy. This sometimes requires lawyers to invoke age-old custom and tradition that harkens back to Navajo stories of creation. "It's almost like practicing law back in the time of John Locke," she muses. "You're trying to decide, 'what is our law? How did we do this?'"

Because of the relative scarcity of Navajo case law, attorneys like Sylvia can make equitable arguments that invoke Indian history. In *Smith v. Yazza*, a case before the Navajo Supreme Court, Sylvia convinced the court to rule her way not just by citing codes but by analogizing the facts to traditional Navajo methods of resolving disputes. Practicing in Tribal Court therefore provides much more flexibility and creativity than in state courts: "It's an awesome place to practice law, because you really feel like you're making a difference in people's lives."

Outside the courtrooms, dealing with Navajo Nation clients also requires a touch of cultural sensitivity. She once encountered a client seeking Social Security benefits who related his story by starting with a snake bite suffered years ago as a child—a particularly bad omen for Navajos—eventually leading to his current legal woes. Mediation, known as "Peacemaking," is even more fluid. In Peacemaking, family members of the opposing sides replace the lawyers in a negotiation process that often takes far longer than other mediation procedures but produces more successful and lasting settlements.

Practicing with DNA People's Legal Services also provides an unusual opportunity: the chance to write laws. While many legal services groups are restricted from lobbying legislatures as conditions of their funding, DNA is permitted to participate in the Navajo Tribal Council's legislative process. For example, DNA drafted the domestic abuse and consumer protection acts for the Navajo Nation and has considerable say as to how the laws should apply, and to whom.

The socioeconomic dynamics of the Navajo population also ensure that DNA sees a unique ratio of cases. Sylvia sees very few housing cases, for example, because the reservation has only one landlord—the Navajo Housing Authority—and most outside lenders will not give mortgages to Native Americans because it is very difficult to foreclose on reservation property. Instead, Sylvia's caseload includes domestic violence, employment issues, and a plethora of consumer protection problems, where disreputable retailers have "Navajo Appreciation Days" but actually bilk Natives through unreasonably high interest rates and down payments.

A few years ago, Sylvia finally moved to Flagstaff, mostly so her twins could attend regular schools. Since then, she finds herself more often in Arizona courts than in Tribal Courts. "I do miss being on the reservation and practicing in Tribal Court." But if she has had to sacrifice some of her regular domestic violence work in the Indian courts, she takes on greater responsibility by managing grants for DNA, recruiting attorneys for their Volunteer Lawyer Program, and proposing new initiatives—such as expanding DNA services to help the Northern Arizona gay and lesbian community. She also receives calls from other advocates seeking advice on domestic violence cases. But when asked if she'll take on a high-level administrative role with DNA, Sylvia says that she works best when doing individualized client work. Her "average" day consists of client interviews, negotiated settlements, and visits to court—and probably always will.

Throughout a day of training presentations and role-playing exercises at the Flagstaff Radisson, Sylvia is one of only two non-Native faces in the meeting room. Yet, if this might seem incongruous on the surface, her identity doesn't present itself as a problem during the day; if anything, the members of the various tribes in the small audience treat her presence and advice with evident respect.

Respect is of obvious importance to lawyers, but is especially vital to public interest lawyers seeking to help a client base of a different racial, cultural, and socioeconomic background. While Sylvia is a Caucasian single mother who hails from coastal Massachusetts, her clients are dark-skinned, low-income residents of Indian reservations in the Southwest. This contrast raises the question of barriers: how do differences in race, language, and education affect her practice?

Overall, Sylvia feels that these barriers are low, or at least readily surmountable. For Sylvia, being white made her a minority in Mexican Hat, Utah, and Chinlé, Arizona, but her status was not necessarily a problem. She has observed that Native clients tended to trust white lawyers more than Native advocates due to stereotypes about education and competence. In fact, the Tribal Court Advocates whom Sylvia trains will have a harder time with credibility than she does, despite sharing a common heritage with their clients. Most important, Sylvia gained credibility by living on the reservation and staying with DNA for nine years; most lawyers work for only three years before moving on to other positions. She cites humility and her management experience from working in Harvard's Trademark Licensing Program as helpful. Bearing twins soon after moving to Chinlé was also a boon, as Navajos believe twins are sacred.

As to the language barrier, Sylvia also encountered minimal difficulty. The barrier certainly exists: twenty percent of her clients spoke only Navajo, and she has regularly argued in courtrooms where she was the only person unable to speak the language. While she felt no pressure to learn Navajo, she insists that, like travelers to foreign countries, a little sincere effort to pick up bits and pieces goes a long way. She also explains the term "born for," which the Tribal Court Advocates use to introduce themselves during the training: in the matrilineal Navajo culture, a member introduces himself by stating his mother's clan and his father's clan, which he is "born for" (Sylvia herself is English and born for the Germans). Yet, before the audience at the Radisson, she is quick to point out that if a white lawyer is the only non-Navajo speaker in the courtroom, he has no right to request that the trial proceed in English. Translators can and should be a valuable resource in such circumstances.

Have there been occasional negative experiences with cultural barriers? Sylvia mentions one time when she went to vote, and a Navajo woman yelled at her to go back to where she came from. But such outbursts are rare, she insists.

Instead of focusing on these barriers, Sylvia offers some ethnographic accounts of the cultural benefits of living and working on the reservation. Such proximity allows her to witness Navajo customs to a certain degree (non-Navajos still cannot view certain ceremonies). She recounts, for example, her experience with the squaw dance, apparently an artistic gathering performed to cleanse a Navajo who has just ended a relationship with a non-Navajo. By stuffing a lock of the non-Navajo's hair into a bullet and firing it off, Navajos believe they can bring bad tidings (of varying severity) to an outsider. Sylvia was once asked to donate her hair for a squaw dance by a Navajo colleague who knew less about the ceremony than she did.

Sylvia's description of her surroundings leaves no doubt that her job is accessible to anyone willing to learn new customs. Sylvia relates an influential experience she had during her first fall in Mexican Hat: an elderly Navajo woman whom she had helped said to her, "Thank you, my daughter—for you are my daughter, even though you're white." That, perhaps, best summarizes her experience as a non-Navajo living and working among Natives.

If working for DNA is nontraditional, it is like all other public interest jobs in one major respect: trade-offs. Like many lawyers who choose their passions over their pocketbooks, Sylvia is not rich, but she finds her rewards in helping people on a day-to-day basis.

The economics of her situation are not easy, but they are very manageable. Because of her Harvard job and slipcover business, Sylvia luckily has no outstanding college debt. Law school, however, was an entirely different and expensive proposition. "I intentionally went into denial," Sylvia laughs. She chose to ignore the lurking debt burden to pursue her dream, banking that by doing what she loved, the money would follow. To a large degree, her bet has paid off: DNA, the Arizona State Bar, and Northeastern Law School have all granted her substantial debt forgiveness.

However, Sylvia has not been immune to lifestyle changes. When she started in Chinlé, she earned only $23,000, but rent was extremely cheap on the reservation. After having two children, however, and moving to semi-suburban Flagstaff, she faces a higher cost of living. Her salary is now a respectable $43,000. She still drives an ancient yellow Volvo but now has her own home and enough money to give her family a reasonably comfortable life. Her two eight-year-old twins, Elizabeth and Emilio, scamper happily around and after they leave, her cats take their place. Her house is cozy, busy, and half-renovated—the staircase and upstairs are still unfinished, partly because Sylvia is doing most of the work by hand herself.

When asked to "sell" her job to future lawyers, Sylvia stresses the pioneering qualities of her work but also the realities of life in the desert Southwest. Newcomers to the reservation will confront a new environment and must be prepared for the unexpected. And because DNA serves clients in four states, lots of traveling and solitude are commonplace—she revealed that she was visiting Santa Fe and Farmington, New Mexico and Window Rock, Arizona, all in one week. As a result, most lawyers who leave DNA depart for more *comfort*, not necessarily more *money*.

Sylvia acknowledges that she has considered other options from time to time. Big firms in big cities never enter the equation, but she is receptive to the possibility of working for other charitable organizations. As someone who enjoys variety in work and life, she remains open to other paths beyond the law. When asked what she'll be doing in another forty-two years, she said it wouldn't be surprising to find her building homes with Habitat for Humanity.

But in the end, Sylvia found and followed a special spiritual connection with Native-American ideals, combining her early personal experiences with her professional goals. By melding these with a willingness to travel and explore new places, she found the perfect place for herself and her family while also finding a professional niche in the law. If there is such a thing as a nontraditional path in life and law, Sylvia has followed it.

MELISSA MAGER

Family Law

By Megan Nelson

The practice of family law is Melissa Mager's self-professed third career. However, it was sailboats, not a legal career, that brought Melissa to Seattle, Washington. At the time of her move to the Pacific Northwest, she had no intention of becoming an attorney, but it was law school and her legal career that allowed her to move from election cycle job searches. She was tired of looking for a new job every time one of her bosses decided not to run for reelection, so she enrolled in a law school night program while working full-time for the Oklahoma governor. She graduated after three and a half years at the age of forty.

Born in Oklahoma City, Melissa moved away at age eighteen to attend college in Washington, DC. Neither of her parents was a lawyer; her mother did not finish college, her father had a degree in international relations and joined the Marines during World War II soon after graduating from Yale. When the war ended, Melissa says that her father "just wanted to return to Oklahoma and work in his family's mortgage banking business." However, he encouraged her to go away to college at a time when most fathers might have engaged in a lot more oversight of their daughters.

Melissa attended Mount Vernon Junior College, a small two-year women's college that has since been combined with George Washington University. Mount Vernon directed its students into one of two fields of study, fine arts or political science, and utilized the Capitol's resources in supplying students with internships at the Smithsonian, the National Gallery of Art, offices of legislators, or administrative agencies. In her selection of classes, Melissa attempted to avoid politics: "Without the benefit of 20/20 hindsight, I, of course, was in fine arts, which I loved." Washington's vast amount of art, furniture collections, and architecture, provided an entire city as Melissa's workshop. After completing her two years at Mount Vernon, she went back home and enrolled at the University of Oklahoma, where she graduated in 1972 with a degree in art history. Based on her contacts from her previous internships with the National Portrait Gallery and Mount Vernon, Melissa decided she had a better chance of getting a job in Washington.

She returned to DC and got her first job as a part-time secretary in a new law office. While technically this was her first exposure to the practice of law, Melissa admits she never considered it as such. Her employers were three young male attorneys from New York straight out of law school whose practice consisted primarily of criminal defense. Their office was strategically located at Seventh and F Streets, between the federal courthouse and the office of a bail bondsman. Melissa describes her first job as strictly secretarial — she typed pleadings, with emphasis on the word "typing," given the absence of computers — and it was a "gas for a kid from Oklahoma."

She worked in the office for two years, during which her self-described wonderful and undemanding employers allowed her the opportunity to focus on her true passion: sailboat racing, an avocation she acquired at summer camp in Minnesota. The Chesapeake Bay was near her office, and she met people with sailboats. She joined a crew that raced every weekend and competed in a sailing circuit that included Long Island Sound and San Francisco.

In 1974, Melissa decided to apply for the receptionist position of Oklahoma Senator Henry Bellmon. Senator Bellmon chose to staff his DC office with Oklahoma citizens but had a hard time keeping employees because they did not enjoy living in Washington. Melissa was offered the job upon assuring the Senator that she loved living in the District. She started working the very day President Nixon resigned from office. With very little knowledge about switchboard operation, Melissa's switchboard lit up as she fielded phone calls from distraught Oklahoma constituents who believed that the Nixon's resignation surely meant imminent invasion by the U.S.S.R.

After a year or two of working as a receptionist, Melissa became a legislative assistant in Senator Bellmon's office, where she covered housing, banking, urban and veterans' affairs, and the law of the sea. Most of the other legislative assistants attended Georgetown, George Washington, or American University law schools. She was often asked by the Senator, "don't you want to go to law school?" Melissa claims her response was always "no." She loved working in Washington; and at that time she met every president elected during her lifetime except for Harry S. Truman and was exposed to the likes of Anwar Sadat and Menachem Begin. Melissa had everything she wanted and couldn't imagine going back to school.

Then Senator Bellmon decided to retire in 1981 and, despite opportunities on the Hill, Melissa made her second decision to desert the political arena and to leave Washington. She had already decided she did not want to grow old in the District. She took a year off and drove around the United States looking for a new place to call home. Her sole requirement: "any place with water." Melissa began in Oklahoma; she went west to Colorado and skied at Vail with friends; stopped over in a Las Vegas Motel 6; drove to California; flew to Kauai and back to Monterey, California. She traveled up the Oregon coast to the Washington Peninsula and came into Seattle by crossing Puget Sound on a ferry. Despite the slight drizzle, Melissa found Seattle amazing. Within a couple weeks she was sailing and had joined a volleyball team. In Melissa's own words: "Seattle welcomed me."

After three or four months in Seattle, Melissa really needed an income. She did not want to go back into the world of politics or think about job security from election to election. However, Melissa knew very few people in Seattle. Therefore, when she was offered a staff assistant position with Washington State's Speaker of the House, she took the job. State legislative work paralleled that of the federal legislature— appropriations cycles, program funding—but she was no longer "rubbing shoulders with the likes of Ted Kennedy." Her views were also more liberal than those of her new boss. When she was asked to write a letter outlining the Speaker's opinion regarding abortion funding, a laughing Melissa says the draft letter came back with the comment, "This is not quite the Speaker's position. Could you tone it down some?" When the legislative session ended, Melissa did not want to continue making the 140-mile round trip between Seattle and Olympia every day, and the Speaker was retiring to become a partner in an architecture firm.

Melissa left politics behind for the third time to take a marketing position in the Speaker's new architecture firm, John Graham & Company. Graham was responsible for many of the buildings in Seattle, including the Space Needle. She worked at the firm for four years, primarily drafting project proposals. Near the end of her tenure, however, the firm was bought by a Nebraska company and the office's atmosphere became disharmonious. Frustrated with her job, Melissa received word in 1986 from her former boss, Henry Bellmon, that he was running for governor of Oklahoma again, so she went to Oklahoma to assist with his campaign. Bellmon won the gubernatorial election and offered Melissa a position on his staff as the Economic Development Liaison. She struggled with her decision to reenter the political realm: it had taken her so long to move back up after being right at the crest with a good salary in Washington, DC; she had eaten through her retirement funds during her year of cross-country traveling; and she had recently bought a house in Seattle.

Despite her initial hesitation, Melissa decided to go to Oklahoma for a year and happily quit her marketing job in Seattle. In only a short period of time, Melissa realized that she was not going to be able to walk away from the job in a year. Oklahoma was absolutely devastated by the Penn Square Bank failure, which took down Seafirst Bank as well as many other good banks; consequently it was difficult to find money in Oklahoma for development. This realization forced Melissa to have a conversation with herself. She refused to return to Seattle in four years (Governor Bellmon had committed to serving only one term) and be forced to endure the question, "Well sure, honey, we would love to give you a job but can you type?"

More education was Melissa's solution, and because many of her fellow staffers were attorneys and because of the large role the law played in the governor's office, she chose law school. Prior to her decision, she spoke with the governor's past press secretary, who had become the governor's counsel, about whether law school was the right decision. He told Melissa, "anyone who can tackle the bond industry as the governor's Economic Development Liaison can handle law school." That comment confirmed her decision.

Melissa had to attend school at night. Luckily, Oklahoma City University had a very good night school just three miles away from the governor's office in which Melissa enrolled in September 1986. The average age of students in the night school was thirty-five. Because the bottom had dropped out of Oklahoma's oil and banking industries, a lot of people were redesigning themselves and going back to school. Melissa and her fellow law students took learning the law seriously, but, as she describes it, "we didn't take some of the grief that law professors put you through seriously. It was difficult to humiliate people via the Socratic method [who] had previously had lucrative careers."

Melissa graduated from law school in December 1990 with no area of emphasis but never envisioned herself at a large law firm. She thought she was most likely to get back into legislative work, given her political background. She also thought Native-American law might present some good opportunities in the Seattle legal market. Given her position with the governor, Melissa was also interested in banking law. Looking back, she wishes she had taken commercial paper or tax-related classes, because they would have been beneficial to her later family law career.

Melissa's favorite memory of law school was working with two professors to write a law review article detailing the history of Oklahoma's initiative process from statehood to the present day. The article coincided with Governor Bellmon's initiative campaign to amend the state constitution. (Melissa describes Oklahoma as having a very populist ilk.) Melissa did not participate in any law school extracurricular activities, given the demands of her full-time job, which included traveling to Hong Kong, Shanghai, Tokyo, and Jakarta to start Oklahoma economic development offices.

Using her political connections, she got the Oklahoma Attorney General and the Chief Justice of the Oklahoma Supreme Court to speak at her night school commencement. Soon after, she packed up and drove back to Seattle—just in time to start the bar review course. Even after taking the bar exam, Melissa admits to not really knowing what type of law she wanted to practice. She chose not to apply to any large law firms. Melissa felt that not only would a large firm not be a good fit, but that large law offices would be extremely hesitant to hire a forty-year-old woman. Instead, she began applying to small, insurance-based firms—without much success.

Applying her political know-how, Melissa decided to pursue a judicial clerkship. She contacted an old political connection from the state legislature who had moved on to be the administrator of the Court's Office. She knew whom the governor was appointing as new superior court judges. The next time the governor made a judicial appointment, with the inside scoop Melissa was the first person to contact newly appointed Judge Charles Mertel, and with her résumé in hand, she got the clerkship. For the next two years, Melissa worked in King County Superior Court's civil division. She loved her exposure to the courts' various actors. The court frequently heard big personal injury cases, which required juries. She learned a lot just watching the trial attorneys and began showing her own talents to the Seattle bar. Melissa noted who were the good and who were the bad litigators, and, as a result, learned which attorneys she thought she would want to work with. She began sending her résumé to those attorneys. Cynthia Whittaker was one of them.

Whitaker, a family law practitioner, was in front of Judge Mertel three times while Melissa was his clerk. Melissa was impressed with Whitaker's trial advocacy skills: two of the three cases Melissa witnessed went beyond the ordinary division of property disputes and contained some nasty child abuse aspects. Whitaker, however, already had an associate and was not interested in acquiring another but offered to make phone calls for Melissa on her behalf. In 1994, Melissa had to call Whitaker's office to arrange a hearing date and asked for her associate. Whitaker's receptionist informed her that the associate was no longer working there, and Melissa, seizing the opportunity, asked to submit a résumé. The receptionist laughed. "Funny you should ask; this morning Cynthia asked me to contact you."

Melissa became Whitaker's new associate in August 1994. During Melissa's interview, she admitted not knowing whether she wanted to be a trial attorney. Whitaker accepted her hesitation with the caveat: "I don't care whether or not you want to do trials, but it is a motion-driven calendar. We are in court all the time." Melissa was hired despite her knowing little about the family law calendar. King County, Washington, the area in which she practices, has completely idiosyncratic courtroom procedures and rules. Despite her limited knowledge, Melissa began acquiring her own clients. It did not take her long to realize that family law practitioners would greatly benefit from having a Masters in Social Work and that her clients, men and women alike, were coming to her during the most vulnerable times of their lives. Melissa explains that her clients enter the office not knowing if they are going to be able to stay in their houses, have enough money to live on, or be able to see their children. Even if the client is the spouse that is ready to move on, dissolution has a huge impact on them.

During her twelve-year family law career, Melissa has had child support trials, but has yet to have experienced handling a full dissolution trial. "It is by choice," she explains.

> I have looked at it many ways. I know that I am in a [firm] with one of the most esteemed family law trial attorneys. At 43 years old, I have looked at this career as my last career; and not something that I wanted to be hard-charging, get to the top of the heap, make partner in the first two years type of thing. I had already been there. I wanted to get into a practice that would see me through the next ten to twelve years; that I could feel comfortable in and build a little world in.

While Melissa admits to wanting to retire comfortably, she describes the practice of family law as a field "few will get rich in." Family law practitioners may only charge by the hour; there are no contingency fees. It is simply the billable hours, Melissa notes, that allow the attorneys to make a good living. Family law cases do not generate million dollar fees. Melissa herself works approximately nine hours a day. She also admits to working many Sundays.

In spite of her hours and field of practice, in the middle of her family law career Melissa married an engineer in 1999 who loves his job and puts in almost the same number of hours she does. When asked about balance, she explains that because she chose to marry past her "child bearing" years, she has not had to worry about children-related issues. Neither Whitaker nor Melissa's other associate have children. Melissa believes individuals who really want to make their families a priority choose a type of law that involves virtually no trial work. She also describes her husband as having a bit of nerve to marry a divorce attorney. But Melissa can rarely bring her work home or talk about her cases with her husband because many of the cases involve parties who are politicians or business bigwigs.

The practice of family law is dependent on client referrals. Melissa describes herself as lucky to be working with Whitaker, who, after working in family law for thirty years, is a rainmaker. Referrals also come from other attorneys and judges. "No one," Melissa explains, "calls you out of the phone book." Family law is very client-driven and oriented. It can be scholarly but doesn't involve jury trial work. It is also difficult to practice exclusively in a small town without a large population base. The clients' attorneys all practice right where they live, and the practitioners want their clients close by to facilitate their presence at motions and for meetings.

When asked about a highlight of her family law career, Melissa cannot name just one. Each year she has a favorite client. But she acknowledges that the cases she settles in which she is able to get a really good deal for her clients are some of her greatest successes. For example, Melissa describes "where a woman has been a stay-at-home mom and the marriage ends and the husband has been controlling and tells his wife, 'you cannot stay in the house.' Watching the empowerment that the law can provide" is very gratifying. Melissa is able to settle approximately eighty percent of her cases, which she observes is satisfying for all parties. She describes her career choice: "Family law really suits me. I have been fortunate to have landed on my feet many times. I don't think there would be any other type of law that I would rather practice. You work in tax law, business law, property law and sometimes even criminal law. You feel like you are making a difference with your clients; you are always leaving them in a better place than when they came to you."

Seattle's family law practice is a small world, a world, Melissa says, in which most lawyers know each other, work together, and pick up the phone to work out agreements with opposing counsel for required orders. She concludes her description: "it is the way I like to practice law very much." Most family law attorneys are solo practitioners or work in very small teams. Melissa, in the Law Offices of Cynthia Whitaker, works with Whitaker and one other associate. Melissa's office is located right down the street from the courthouse, which is a benefit for a practice that revolves around motions. She shares the space with a small group of attorneys who have come together to spread the cost of administrative support and research-related expenses.

Family law as described by Melissa is perfect for attorneys who do not like the idea of massive litigation; it is practiced primarily by motion. For example, the parties have filed a petition for dissolution and the client needs temporary financial support. The clients may have one or two income streams, and there are children that need time with both parents. If you cannot reach an agreement with opposing counsel beforehand, you go into court and move for temporary orders. These orders may dictate actions ranging from control of bank account withdrawals to mandatory health insurance coverage or how custody will be handled until the case moves forward. The recommended orders are presented in writing and then the attorney has five to ten minutes to plead the case, depending on how much the judge or commissioner wants to hear.

What makes a good family law practitioner? Melissa believes an attorney well-suited for family law is able to define himself or herself as such during the first meeting with a client. The client's vulnerabilities, emotions, and insecurities have to be addressed from the beginning. By the time the client's marriage is dissolved, the client should have the strength and confidence to move on. For example, a fifty-five-year-old woman may walk into the office having been a homemaker for thirty-five years and now her husband wants a divorce. She is frantic and dis-traught, and is seeking quick answers to dramatic questions about what she will be able to do with the rest of her life and how she will be able to live. Family law practitioners have to balance their compassionate side with an ability to take over, providing structure, calmness, and a frame-work to get through the panic. The family law attorney provides leader-ship and guidance and referrals to programs if necessary.

When forced to describe a drawback of family law, Melissa notes the frustration associated with not being able to do everything for one's cli-ents, as well as being forced to witness the inhumanity and emotional abuse that people inflict on each other and their children. Due at least in part to the emotions involved, there are also more malpractice actions filed against family law attorneys than against any other type of attorney. Family law practitioners, Melissa explains, have to be very vigilant and make sure clients understand all their moves and all the rules. They must be interested and engaged with human problems, and willing to step into human dramas.

Melissa's experiences and her examples show how rewarding that human connection can be for an attorney who tries to help her clients find smooth sailing out of stormy conditions.

DAN LARSSON

Immigration Lawyer

By Nathaniel Garrett

In the lobby of Dan Larsson's office a neon American flag glows brightly atop a wooden bookcase. In the corner, beside a rack of magazines, the Larsson Immigration Group has placed an overflowing box of toys. At first glance, both items seem out of place in a law office, and yet they serve as obvious reminders of the unique nature of immigration law. As immigrants looking to live, work, or marry in the United States, Dan's clients often arrive confused, desperate to make a life for themselves and their children. And like the neon flag in the lobby, many are looking to Dan as a bright symbol of possibility, with hopes that he will be able to help them through the increasingly complicated procedures required to become U.S. citizens. In immigration law the stakes are high for lawyers and for their clients and families. As Dan puts it, "immigration law is like a medical procedure. Because what's at stake? Your life."

Like his clients, Dan himself came to America as an immigrant. Born in 1962 in Nyköping, Sweden, which is approximately sixty miles south of Stockholm, Dan's sojourns abroad started when he was a young child. Because of Sweden's generous vacation policies, Dan and his family enjoyed numerous opportunities to travel across Europe and frequently ventured into Germany to visit his mother's side of the family. Through travel in Poland and the former East Germany, Dan was exposed to international politics at a young age. He remembers well the experience of being searched by soldiers while passing through the Iron Curtain. "I think that's what got me interested in politics and law," explains Dan.

The idea of visiting America was first planted in Dan while swimming competitively in high school. Many of his teammates spent time in the United States as exchange students and came back with fond memories. "I liked traveling through Europe," says Dan, "so I thought that would be an interesting thing to do." In 1979, when Dan was seventeen, he came to Whitefish, Montana, to spend a year as an exchange student, where he was exposed to America and to American football. A successful athlete at home, Dan caught on to the game quickly and earned a spot as the starting kicker on the team that would go on to win the state championship.

With plans to attend college in the states, Dan returned to Sweden to finish high school and serve a required year in the national military. Ever the traveler, Dan was shipped north to the Arctic Circle to serve as a Swedish mountain ranger. When his time was up, Dan immediately began shopping for schools in the United States. As Dan readily admits, there were things about Sweden that he would eventually miss. "Growing up in Sweden, it's a neutral country. The population as a whole is a lot more knowledgeable about politics and the world. That makes it easier to see both sides of an issue."

Nevertheless, Dan was ambitious and anxious to return to America. World-savvy but anxious for some level of support during college, Dan thought about either returning to Montana to be near those he had known during his year of high school or venturing further west to the University of Oregon, close to a family that had hosted his sister as an exchange student. At the time, Eugene, Oregon, was known as a marathoner's city. For Dan, who had moved on to long-distance running, that factor tipped the balance. An old friend from his high school days in Montana was the starting center for the Ducks football team and even tried to convince Dan to walk onto the team. But by then, Dan's interests were changing, as he moved away from competitive sports.

"I did well in college, but I actually started to do more and more of what my hobby was, which was music," says Dan. Singing lead and playing the bass for "Secret Agent," Dan dedicated himself to the band throughout college and even made a go of it for two years after graduating. The band enjoyed some success in making a compilation of Oregon's best rock songs. Ironically, however, Dan's competitive spirit resurfaced, and the athlete who could measure success on the field grew increasingly uncomfortable with the elusive nature of success in the music industry.

"There are lots of extremely good and talented musicians that never go anywhere, and unlike being a sprinter or a runner, you have to be talented, but there is a clear winner when you get to the finish line. With music, as with the arts, you can be very good and you may still starve," explains Dan.

In search of a profession that would reward the hard work he was willing to put in, Dan moved back to Sweden with plans to save money for law school. "I've always been interested in the world," says Dan. "Even while playing music, I never just partied, I kept up with world news and politics."

In 1991, Dan enrolled at Seattle University School of Law. His interest in world politics and diplomacy drew him to a class on immigration and into an immigration clinic, but throughout law school, Dan was still convinced that he would practice international corporate law. After getting involved with the Swedish-American Chamber of Commerce during school and meeting an attorney at Seattle's then-largest law firm, Bogle & Gates, Dan took a job with the firm his first summer to practice in their international business group. In many ways, Dan enjoyed the experience but perceptively recognized the ups and downs. "It was a big firm with a lot of resources, and they wine and dine you as an intern but then they work you to death."

In his second summer, Dan decided to try a Seattle firm of a more manageable size. At Mullavey, Prout, Grenley & Foe, he worked with approximately twenty attorneys on corporate cases and got his first taste of immigration law. Dan accepted a job with Mullavey, Prout after law school and soon got a look at something not taught in school, "the economics of how firms work." To keep the firm financially sound, Dan was expected to bill heavy hours, but he was also not being handed enough clients. That forced Dan to find his own clients, a good experience for a lawyer with thoughts lurking about opening his own firm.

Besides the billables and the stress of finding his own clients, there were other things that bothered Dan about his day-to-day practice. For one thing, Dan had less flexibility in choosing the cases he was allowed to work on. For another, Dan found his experience with corporate litigation unpleasant. "I really didn't enjoy working against other lawyers. The U.S. system is an adversarial system. You find out fairly quickly that it doesn't really matter what is right and what the truth is. It's more a question of how much money can you afford? Of course, you still need the facts and the law on your side but that doesn't mean you're going to win."

For the athlete and former musician who had expected to find due reward in the courts of law, such a realization must have been frustrating. The combination of Dan's frustration and the increasing realization that he was effectively generating his own clients without enjoying the financial or professional rewards of his footwork helped Dan make a pivotal decision: he decided to open his own firm in Seattle and to try a field of law that appealed to him more than commercial litigation.

Although Dan suggests that he "stumbled" into the practice of immigration law, the decision makes perfect sense in retrospect. After all, by working with immigrants who hoped to live and work in America, Dan realized he could "stay involved in international business and to some extent litigation in a different way, and actually be helping people."

Dan also found the daily practice much more amenable to his personality. "In general litigation, you start out with people who are angry to begin with, either because they are a certain somebody or because they are being sued. It's just not a very pleasant thing. And it depends upon what kind of person you are, but I didn't find it very fun to do. And in immigration law, our adversary is the U.S. government, which doesn't always mean that it's going to be adversarial. You represent people, foreign nationals that want to come here to work, live, marry, whatever the case may be. Your clients in immigration are happy to have your help. So you don't start out with angry people." Dan also found it easier to work with other attorneys because all private immigration lawyers are on the same side. "As immigration lawyers, you help each other out. It's a very collegial area of the law." And in a melding of his professional and personal life, Dan himself became a U.S. citizen in 2003.

Since 1996, Dan has been his own boss. He continues to seek new business, but now no one else profits from his efforts. And the work increasingly finds him. "If you have knowledge and you communicate and have good customer service, then you have good results. There's really nothing magic about it."

Dan's firm now represents immigrants from all over the world and has handled cases in almost fifteen states. As a lawyer in a field that changes constantly, Dan notes that "it's a very rewarding thing, and it's very challenging. And it doesn't get boring." Perhaps what makes the role so interesting is the critical role that Dan plays in the lives of his clients. In addition to being a lawyer, "you have to be a social worker," says Dan. The complexity and consequences of the immigration system are so daunting that in some cases, it may be better not to explain too much. Instead of getting bogged down in minutia, Dan tries to fight for his clients in the courtroom and support them in their daily lives.

"I have to try to convince people that I know what I'm doing," said Dan. It is important to constantly remind them, "you have the law on your side. Go through the process and you should be successful."

Fortunately, it worked out that way for one of Dan's recent clients, a Ukrainian immigrant named Inessa who was looking to make a life for herself and her thirteen-year-old son in Oregon. Inessa moved there in the spring of 2000 on a three-month visa and planned to marry a man who lived in Medford, Oregon. Before the wedding could take place, however, both parties changed their minds and the wedding was called off. Just months later, she met Steve Polk, a cook in a Russian restaurant in Medford. The two married and she applied for legal status shortly thereafter. The couple figured she eventually would receive a green card, which would allow her to stay.

Meanwhile, the couple moved on with their new lives, buying a home and the Russian restaurant, with plans to run it together. Unfortunately for the Polks, federal regulations required that Inessa return to the Ukraine after her original marriage plans were canceled and then reapply from her country of origin through the visa process. And so Inessa and her son were sent back to Odessa while the government processed her new visa.

For nearly a year, they struggled to get by in Odessa. She had trouble finding a job in the slumping economy, and her son missed a year of school in the states. While in Odessa, Inessa admitted to an Oregon paper, "I'm so upset and depressed—my son is very upset. I did nothing wrong. I just want to be over there with Steve. It's everything like dream for me with him. I can't believe this happened so quick to us."

At the same time, Steve Polk lost nearly $40,000 on the costs associated with Inessa's deportation and her absence from the restaurant. Eventually, through Dan's work on her behalf, the Polks were reunited. Steve told the local paper that, despite the challenge, they would move on. "We are both young and strong and we don't give up," he said. "We are going to recover from this and move forward."

Along with the success stories, there are increasing challenges for Dan. Undoubtedly, 9/11 has affected everyone, but, at least professionally, it has impacted immigration lawyers disproportionately. Congress has increased restrictions on immigration, and that means additional complications for those looking to make a life in the United States. It can also mean undergoing experiences that are likely to shake an immigrant's faith in the American legal system.

"Over the last couple years unfortunately, after 9/11, it's become very challenging. The government has taken an increasingly narrow look at the law and how to deal with things," says Dan. "There has been a big erosion of due process after 9/11. And we see it more than just about anyone else because it's very difficult to fight the U.S. government. And if they don't give you access to people, there is not much you can do about it."

Despite the challenges, Dan does not give the impression that he would rather be doing anything else. In fact, says Dan, it is more important today than ever to make sure that there is somebody protecting the constitutional and due process rights of immigrants. "It's rewarding to get somebody here, for a family to be able to stay here."

Today, Dan oversees an office that includes support staff: another attorney who came to Dan after spending years helping Microsoft employees through the immigration process and his wife, a nonpracticing attorney who manages the firm's operations. In 2002, Dan and his wife moved the firm to Bend, Oregon, a town of just under 60,000, and a three-hour drive southeast of Portland. Bend is too small to justify an immigration practice like Dan's, and he finds himself traveling frequently to support a client base that primarily resides elsewhere.

The advantages and disadvantages of running such a small but flexible office are obvious. On the one hand, says Dan, "the downside of running a small firm by yourself is that when you go on vacation, you don't make any money. But at the same time, if you want to take half a day off to go skiing, you don't have to ask for anyone's permission." For someone constantly frustrated by the lack of correlation between effort and results, there is an important additional benefit to running one's own law firm. "Whatever you put in is what will come back out."

For Dan, running his own small operation in a field of law that appeals to him personally and politically makes perfect sense. But in a way, that is the only lesson Dan draws from his professional path. Not that working in a big firm or doing corporate litigation is bad per se; it was simply not the right fit for him. In fact, says Dan, he hopes that law students will work in a big firm if that appeals to their personality and to their professional dreams. "It is good to try different things. I'm glad that I got the experience of working in a big firm. I'm glad I got to work in a smaller firm. I didn't realize that I was going to be an immigration lawyer in a small town when I went to law school. You just don't quite know; it's good to get as many experiences as you can, and you'll figure out what your passion is."

At the same time, it is clear that Dan has trouble understanding why lawyers would stay in a job that fails to make them happy. "Like with any job, whatever you choose to do, you need to be passionate about what you're doing. If you find a firm, is it fun? If it's not fun, it's not worth it."

In all probability, the idea of starting one's own firm is attractive to many lawyers and law students. But for many, the prospect seems terribly risky, fraught with the potential for failure and financial struggle. Interestingly, for Dan that is a backward way of looking at the enterprise. After all, says Dan, no one is ever going to look after your professional career like you will. As proof, Dan points to the fate of Bogle & Gates, the firm that he summered with after his first year of law school and once the largest firm in Seattle. A merger was proposed, and the firm split when some lawyers were in favor of the move and some opposed. Many young lawyers were left behind.

"The reality is just because you have a job at a big firm doesn't mean you can keep it," says Dan. "The only person you can count on is yourself." At some point, says Dan, "I realized that if I wanted to take control of my own destiny, [I] can do that by starting [my] own firm."

No one would argue with the fact that Dan has taken control of his destiny. Like everything else about his career, the choice to move to

Bend, a city with a small-town feel, was a deliberate choice. To Dan, the motivating factor was not just that he and his wife had grown up in smaller towns and that Bend offered a ten-minute commute and nearby skiing. More important was the birth of his son. "Especially after we had our son, living in the big city, being professionals is hard," explains Dan. "Once we realized that what we do, we didn't have to be in the city to do it, we started to look for a smaller town. Bend is a better place for our son to grow up."

The combination of working for himself and in a smaller town allows Dan to take time off to go to his son's school functions and be a more present father, something he clearly takes seriously. "It's my time and I can decide what to do with it. If I miss work, I'll make it up another time."

When one examines Dan's life in its entirety, the line between his own story and that of his clients begins to blur. Like all of his clients, Dan himself is an immigrant drawn to the opportunities that America offers. Like many of them, he is willing to work hard and make precarious choices to ensure that his children are safe and given even greater opportunities. As an emigrant from big-firm work and big-city living, Dan continues to fight for other immigrants, and it seems that he at least has finally found home.

JOSEPH LICHTBLAU

Solo Practitioner

By Erica Blachman

At 5:30 P.M. on a Tuesday evening, Joseph Lichtblau has just ended a call with opposing counsel on a foreclosure and bankruptcy case, but his mind remains on the case well after he hangs up the telephone. For Joseph, this case is not only a challenging entry into a new body of law—the complex Truth in Lending Act—it is also a fascinating human story. Settling down in a small conference room within his shared office space, Joseph conveys his client's story with ease and sincerity, emphasizing the unique circumstances facing his client. The story is intriguing indeed, as it entails a business favor gone awry among friends, human error, and the potential for substantial economic loss to Joseph's client. As one issue leads to another, it soon becomes apparent that Joseph's fascination with this story is not unusual. In fact, Joseph loves that there is "always a human side" to each case that he handles.

Joseph is not only interested in learning the story behind a case, but also in figuring out how he can best help his client resolve the matter. Joseph likes that, as a solo practitioner, he is able to develop close relationships with his clients. In particular, he enjoys giving his clients "good solid advice" and often finds himself offering as much "life advice" as "legal advice." Although he is a litigator, Joseph reveals that common sense often leads him to advise clients *not* to sue in a particular situation. Joseph laughs quietly as he recounts the number of times that he has asked a client, "Do you really want to sue your employer?" or "Do you really want to sue your landlord?" It is likely that this honest and straightforward nature is what draws clients to Joseph. Aware that giving good advice makes a difference, Joseph notes that a particular client has repeatedly turned to him largely because "he likes my advice." In addition to finding this advice-giving role not only personally satisfying but good for business,

Joseph also considers it an obligation that attorneys have to those who live in their communities.

Joseph's intrigue with the human side of cases does not detract from his deep interest in the legal issues at stake in each case. Joseph admits that bankruptcy in general, and the Truth in Lending Act in particular, are new areas of law for him, yet that did not stop him from taking this case when it came through his door. In fact, the freedom to explore different areas of law — and even to periodically "reinvent" himself — is one aspect of solo practice that Joseph especially values. In Joseph's mind, "switching gears" to an area that interests him "makes not just what you are doing creative, it makes your life more creative." Joseph explains that the case that he just described has piqued his interest in bankruptcy law and has prompted him to consider actively pursuing similar cases in the future.

Tackling a new area of law is not something that Joseph takes lightly. He shares stories of attorneys who have attempted transactions that are too complicated for their limited knowledge of the area and recounts the troubles that have resulted for those attorneys and their clients alike. Thus, whenever he confronts a case that involves an area of law with which he is not familiar, Joseph clearly tells his client that this is a new venture for him but assures the client that he will do the best job he can possibly do. He then spends many hours researching and seeking advice from other attorneys who have specialized in that area of law. Joseph explains that such research and networking skills — both of which he has developed throughout his legal career — are critical to any solo practitioner's success.

Joseph was methodical about developing his skills throughout law school and in his early years of practice, but not with the intent of becoming a solo practitioner. In fact, law school itself was not even part of his plan until several years after he earned his undergraduate degree in 1982 from Tufts University in the Greater Boston area. After college, Joseph held jobs in several different locations and industries, including landscaping work in Colorado, before he eventually returned to Boston. While Joseph does not cite any of these early jobs as influencing his decision to attend law school, he does point out that using the expression "time off" to describe a student's life between undergraduate and law school is a misnomer. For most students, including Joseph and the vast majority of his future law school classmates at Northeastern University School of Law, the years between college and law school were filled with hard work in the "real world" that provided invaluable learning experiences.

Joseph did not grow up among lawyers, but he does believe that his family and friends influenced his eventual decision to go to law school. Joseph grew up in Englewood, New Jersey, where his father was a surgeon and his mother was a psychologist and a playwright. Having come from a professional family background and having displayed a love of philosophy and a knack for arguing, law school became the natural suggestion offered to Joseph as he pondered his career options. Even once he decided to go to law school at the age of twenty-seven, the question of which law school to attend remained unanswered. His decision to attend Northeastern was shaped largely by his experience at the school's open house, where Joseph was impressed by the presentation and the personal attention the current dean gave him. Joseph was also attracted to Northeastern's unique Cooperative Legal Education Program (Co-op) because he figured that it would be useful, an assumption that has been confirmed repeatedly throughout Joseph's career.

Unlike many attorneys, Joseph unequivocally states that he loved law school. Although he had found minimal inspiration in his prior schooling, Joseph considered the law school environment to be refreshing because the students were treated as adults. Joseph was invigorated by the realization that he was preparing to enter a profession that was steeped in history and governed by its own ethical and cultural codes. Even as a law student, Joseph was motivated by the human side of law and recognized the great responsibility that he would bear as an attorney, when "people will be coming to you with serious issues." This commitment to serving clients and upholding the integrity of the legal profession has not dwindled over the years; it remains ever-present in the manner in which he conducts his practice.

In the classroom, Joseph found himself most engaged by litigation-oriented courses such as Civil Procedure and Evidence. To feed this growing interest, Joseph participated in four co-ops, each of which exposed him to different aspects of a litigation practice. Joseph's first co-op was at the U.S. Attorney's office in Boston, where he sat at a small desk inside the office of one Assistant U.S. Attorney. Joseph capitalized on this close proximity by carefully observing and learning from his supervising attorney and by actively seeking feedback and critiques of his own writing. Joseph emphasizes that although submitting one's writing for criticism by others requires a thick skin, it is the only way in which a law student will truly learn to "sound like a lawyer" in his or her writing.

In Joseph's next co-op, he served as a clerk to Justice Shirley Abrahamson on the Wisconsin Supreme Court. Joseph recalls that this experience was a real "eye opener" because it allowed him to see "how everything happens." In fact, Joseph found this clerkship to be so worthwhile that he pursued two additional clerkships immediately after law school—first as a clerk for the Massachusetts Superior Court and then at the Massachusetts Appeals Court. Joseph considered each of his clerkships to be extremely valuable, and he now espouses a clerkship as one of the most important experiences a law student or young attorney can have in building a career. Having observed how judges responded in a variety of cases and circumstances, Joseph feels confident that he can generally predict what a judge will do in a given situation. Being able to convey such predictions to clients has made a difference in his practice, especially given that, as a solo practitioner, his practice depends largely on his relationships with clients.

In particular, Joseph's year as a clerk for the Massachusetts Superior Court prepared him for his current role as a solo practitioner in Massachusetts. As a clerk, Joseph traveled throughout the state, working in many different courthouses and meeting many judges. In his practice today, Joseph often finds himself in these same courtrooms, even before some of the same judges for whom he once worked. This experience not only gives Joseph's clients confidence in his knowledge of a particular court; it also helps him to understand and adjust to the culture of each particular court in which he practices.

In addition to his clerkship experiences, Joseph worked in four small and medium-size law firms before becoming a solo practitioner. Joseph credits his law firm experience — in two firms as a law student in the co-op program and in two firms as an associate attorney — with developing his research skills and providing him with practical lessons that have proved invaluable. For example, Joseph has incorporated several lessons about discovery that he learned at these firms into his personal philosophy for solo practice. Joseph dubs this philosophy "Tai Chi law," though he admits that he is not certain whether it is an accurate metaphor. The point, Joseph explains, is that a solo practitioner (and small firms, for that matter) must do more with less.

As an associate attorney at small firms, Joseph learned how to conduct discovery when one does not have the resources to "scorch the earth." A small firm or solo practitioner simply cannot review thousands of boxes of documents; rather, the attorney must manage to get the most important information "with just a few sheets of paper." Joseph distinctly remembers valuable advice offered by a senior attorney at one of his previous firms. The attorney explained to Joseph that the "purpose of discovery is not getting the smoking gun . . . because you won't get the smoking gun." Instead, the attorney explained, the goal is "finding out what they don't have." Joseph gleaned a similar lesson about depositions when a senior partner completely rejected the list of eighteen people that Joseph had suggested for deposing. The senior partner simply stated, "We will not be taking any depositions in this case." The firm won the case — without taking any depositions. From this experience, Joseph learned that if you already know the "worst evidence" against your case, you are likely to waste your time deposing individuals who will just add to the pile of evidence against your position. Joseph admits that he has occasionally strayed from these lessons and from his "Tai Chi law" approach and has found himself overloaded with documents or depositions. In general, however, Joseph has found his do-less-with-more method has been a critical factor in his success as a solo practitioner.

In addition to these practical lessons, Joseph valued his time at law firms for the lifelong mentors he met. Joseph characterized both of his law firm co-ops as "research jobs" but noted that he regularly interacted with partners and associate attorneys. At each of these co-ops and at the firms where he was an associate attorney, Joseph repeatedly sought out "smart people," whom he asked for interesting and challenging assignments as well as tough criticism of his own work. Joseph notes that he was lucky to come "under the wing of very brilliant mentors" at each firm and throughout his career, and states that it would have been very difficult to have succeeded as a solo practitioner had he not first learned the trade from these experienced individuals.

In fact, Joseph relied significantly on these mentors and his previous firms when he first struck out on his own. The first year can be quite challenging, explains Joseph. This is especially true if, like most new solo practitioners, you do not bring a host of clients with you. Fortunately for Joseph, his old firm sent some clients and cases his way; even so, very little money was made in his first year of solo practice. Joseph had planned for this circumstance, because he knew that many solo practitioners actually run a loss in their first year. It does get easier each year, Joseph explains, because "if you're good," the clients will come. How they come to you, however, is not always clear-cut.

Joseph admits that, when he first started, his marketing plan was as simple as "getting an office and opening it." Although his business-oriented friends reprimanded Joseph for having such an undeveloped business plan, Joseph found that, over time, he was able to generate enough clients to build a successful practice. Joseph explains that some clients have found him through the Yellow Pages or referral guides, but emphasizes that he has received a significant percentage of his clients networking with other attorneys.

Given the importance of networking, the location of Joseph's office was perhaps the best decision that Joseph made in his first year of practice. Leasing a small space in a downtown Boston building filled almost entirely by small law firms, other solo practitioners, or various legal service agencies, Joseph was perfectly positioned to pick up business at any moment. Conversations in the elevator or in the hallways have, on countless occasions, resulted in Joseph's receiving a case from another attorney. For example, Joseph's office neighbors, many of whom are real estate transaction attorneys, are more than happy to pass along cases that require litigation. These referred cases have enabled Joseph to establish his real estate litigation practice. Joseph does, however, add a word of caution regarding referrals. Solo practitioners, he states, must be "ready to sort through a lot of bad cases" that other lawyers are eager to sell, and they must be careful not to take on an unsavory situation "that you don't want to get mixed up in." While every attorney should be protective of his or her reputation, a solo practitioner must be especially so, as his or her entire business rests upon name recognition and personal reputation.

Though not taking away from the importance of networking, Joseph readily admits that there is also a great deal of chance in how a solo practitioner acquires clients. With a smile on his face, Joseph explains that he believes one of his best clients came to him through error. He thinks that this client had lost a sheet of paper that contained the name of an attorney in Boston who had been recommended to him. The client then, Joseph believes, looked in the Yellow Pages and found his name, thinking that it was the name that had been written on the paper. Such is life as a solo practitioner, remarks Joseph.

Of course, when Joseph was a new solo practitioner eager for clients, he could not be too choosy about which types of cases he handled. Joseph recalls that his first case challenged the inclusion of a twelve-year-old boy within the scope of a new sex offender registration law in Massachusetts. After this case, Joseph represented several other individuals challenging the registration act and eventually built a reputation as an expert on such cases. At the same time, Joseph was developing a successful practice in employment law, landlord and tenant law, and real estate litigation. Joseph has found it very important to have experience on this short list of practice areas, so that he is always able to respond quickly when asked what he "does" as a solo practitioner. Yet, as he previously explained, he is grateful that he is able to alter these practice areas as his interests shift. Joseph no longer handles sex offender registration act cases and is currently considering the addition of bankruptcy to his practice areas.

While extolling the virtues of the freedom to explore different areas of law, Joseph cautions against the belief that solo practice grants an attorney unlimited choices. A common misperception is that solo practitioners have absolute freedom to work when they want, and can take off for the beach if they like. Joseph explains that solo practitioners, especially those who litigate, often find themselves without unlimited freedom. Clients demand attention, and litigation entails observing strict court deadlines;

in addition, a solo practitioner does not have anyone to whom he can pass off the work if he goes on vacation. At the same time, however, Joseph speaks highly of the flexibility that he has gained as a solo practitioner. Unlike attorneys in larger firms, Joseph does not have to worry about "face time" in the office. He will often work at home in the morning, largely to capitalize on the quiet environment in order to draft documents.

For Joseph this time away is essential because administrative tasks, phone calls, and other distractions make it nearly impossible for him to write a brief while in the office. Speaking of the role the phone plays in his daily routine, Joseph says, "the phone is your friend, the phone is your enemy." Much of his time is spent on the phone, and he feels that he needs to be accessible by phone between mid-morning and 5:00 P.M. In a seemingly convenient arrangement, Joseph shares one receptionist with other solo practitioners on his floor, an arrangement he considers preferable and more client-friendly than using only an electronic answering system, as some solo practitioners do. Though he has employed researchers in the past and hires others to do his billing and accounting, he prefers not to have employees who are dependent on his ability to bring in business. At the same time, Joseph admits that his practice is probably not set up in the most "economical way" and believes that he should have an administrative assistant.

Although he does appreciate the hours that he is able to work from home, Joseph believes that having a separate office space is a necessity. Joseph explains that a litigator needs a conference room, access to a library, and, perhaps most important, the image that a commercial address generates, especially an address in a downtown location. Joseph notes, however, that there are many successful transaction and appellate attorneys who have built successful solo practices from their homes.

In addition to the demands that litigation places on Joseph, his personality also contributes to the decision to maintain an office in the heart of downtown Boston. Personable and energetic, Joseph enjoys interacting with others. For him, a solo practice does not mean hours spent alone behind a desk with little human contact. Instead, Joseph is regularly interacting with others, whether by meeting with a client in his office, arguing a motion in court, or squeezing in a conversation with a fellow attorney at the local law library.

Thus, for Joseph, the decision to "go solo" did not stem from a dislike of working with other people. Rather, the determination to strike out on his own was based on a more practical and entrepreneurial motivation—the desire to have his hard work generate money for himself, not for others. It's not that Joseph is in it only for the money. Instead, Joseph's manner suggests that he was drawn to the independence and self-reliance that a solo practice requires. Attempting to describe the personality of a typical solo practitioner, Joseph suggested, "if you see yourself as a cowboy, you are a solo practitioner." While hesitating before labeling himself a "cowboy," Joseph exhibits the adventurous spirit, self-motivation, and strong work ethic embodied in the cowboy persona. These traits, along with a deep interest in a client's story and the many skills developed during his prior experiences, have enabled him to build a successful and fulfilling solo practice. Cowboy or not, Joseph stands as an excellent example of what it takes to go it alone.

CARLTON W. REEVES

Small-Firm General Litigator

By G. Gregg Webb

The first thing that catches your eye when you arrive in front of the law offices of Pigott Reeves Johnson & Minor is the towering, rainbow-colored playground equipment at the elementary school across the street. Carlton Reeves would not have it any other way. His law firm is a vital sponsor to the school, buying books, attending job fairs, and, yes, purchasing those shining jungle gyms that soften the school's stone and brick façade. When asked about these contributions to his younger neighbors, Carlton characterizes them simply as "the right thing to do."

Carlton has crafted a legal career—and a life—out of doing the "right thing" for others. Carlton is black; he is unique, but mainly in his home state of Mississippi; he is well-educated; he is a veteran civil litigator; and he is one of four partners in a firm that he helped create. With his sought-after abilities, he could easily leave to others work on the smoldering social and racial issues that still plague his home state of Mississippi and could choose to focus on his own comfort instead. But Carlton rejects this approach. At every turn in his accomplished life, he has chosen to blend his own interests with those of his beloved Mississippi. As a college student, he labored furiously for political candidates who would change the racist policies of the state's political leadership. As a law student, he chose not to pursue lucrative opportunities at firms elsewhere in order to make his career at home. As a prestigious clerk, he learned from the first black justice on the Mississippi Supreme Court. As Chief of the Civil Division in the Mississippi U.S. Attorney's office, he wielded federal law as a tool for justice in the state. Today, as a founding partner in a firm with equal numbers of black and white lawyers, he has helped establish a new type of private law practice in Mississippi—one built on racial diversity and respect.

In many poor rural states, the best attorneys leave for rich jobs in large places. Carlton's story illustrates the priceless and boundless value of one man's decision to stay home. Carlton is the middle child in a family of seven brothers and sisters. His father was in the military, and the family moved often before Carlton was born. In 1968, the family moved back to their original home in Yazoo City, Mississippi, where Carlton's mother was virtually a single parent due to his father's continued career. Carlton attended public school there through high school. Growing up, he did not know any lawyers: his interests in law and politics emerged on their own. He remembers settling on a legal career early—in third grade to be exact—when he became aware of a lawsuit involving one of his favorite comedians, Red Foxx.

During his summers in high school, Carlton would go down to the courthouse in Yazoo City just to watch the trials and see lawyers in action. Likewise, he recalls watching the political conventions during the 1970s and early 1980s, particularly Nixon's impeachment hearings in 1974 and Barbara Jordan's speech to the Democratic Convention in 1976. As a teenager, Carlton worked on several campaigns for local candidates and helped mobilize voters. He developed a lifelong passion for political engagement. Carlton credits this early exposure to the political process, along with his own desire to join the fray, as fueling his desire to pursue a legal career.

After graduating from high school in 1982, Carlton attended Jackson State University in Jackson, Mississippi, as the first member of his immediate family to graduate from a four-year college. He immersed himself in social and political life at Jackson State while majoring in Political Science with a pre-law concentration. Carlton was successful in his pursuit to become president of his class before going on to run for president of the Student Government Association. Though he lost the election by only forty votes, the contest generated one of the highest turnouts ever among students.

Carlton also served as president of Jackson State's NAACP chapter, and campaigned for path-breaking political candidates, making speeches on behalf of Robert Clark's unsuccessful bid to become the first black Representative from Mississippi since Reconstruction. In describing the motivation behind his political activities, Carlton adopts a reverential tone as he invokes the "sacrifices that others have made . . ." in creating rights for Southern blacks to take a place in America's voting democracy.

Carlton had dreamed of becoming a lawyer even before attending college. Carlton's pre-law advisor at Jackson State, Charles Holmes, challenged him to "think big" in his law school plans and apply to the best schools possible. At that time the university was regularly placing its best students at top law schools in the country, including Harvard, Yale, and Georgetown. Carlton credits his Jackson State educators with giving him support, perspective, and confidence.

Carlton is not shy about attributing the opportunities he received to Jackson State's status as a historically black institution. In fact, Carlton believes that "every black student should go to a black college" because, he says, "it essentially prepares you for your life." Carlton maintains that historically black colleges give their minority students a wider range of opportunities than most would receive at conventional four-year colleges. He points to his own experience in gaining admission to an excellent law school as well as the chance he got to apply for a Truman Scholarship. Carlton also remembers the sting of visiting Vanderbilt University for the regional interviews and seeing how much better the facilities were at that nearly all-white institution. Carlton remains convinced that he would have missed out on these sorts of opportunities had he not been at a historically black college surrounded by mentors sensitive to his position as a young black student and devoted to promoting his future.

In 1986, Carlton continued his pioneering path by attending the University of Virginia School of Law as the first person in his family to go to a professional school of any kind. Though Carlton would not trade his time at UVA "for the world," UVA was not always a friendly place. In fact, Carlton was surprised to find upon arriving for his first year of law school that the institution was, in his opinion, even farther behind in responding to racial tensions on campus than the University of Mississippi. He cites as one small, but telling, example how the committee set up to deal with racial issues at the school, called the Task Force on Afro-American Affairs, was saddled from its inception with terminology that was dated even in those days.

Carlton not only faced the usual academic tribulations of a law student at UVA, but his years there also proved pivotal for race relations in the law school and within the larger University. Not surprisingly, Carlton was in the middle of the fight as a relentless advocate for minority students. One episode stands out for Carlton to this day. A fraternity had posted fliers across campus announcing a party and directing that "No Jews, No Wops, and No Nigga Babes" could attend. Carlton, along with Glenn Walters, a law school classmate, challenged the fraternity's actions through the school's judiciary committee. Exhibiting skills that would one day make him an effective litigator, Carlton and Walters found several black freshman female students from South Carolina who had been offended and intimidated by the racist announcement and prepared a legal assault against the posting on their behalf. The two law students presented the students' case to the judiciary committee—but lost. The committee found that the fraternity brothers had a First Amendment right to use such language in promoting their parties.

Though disheartened by the loss and the behavior it condoned, Carlton and his fellow students continued working to improve the racial climate at UVA. During the spring of 1987, a black student made Law Review for the first time, and at least two members of Carlton's class subsequently received this honor. Carlton served as president of the Black Law Students Association. Though this work had risks, Carlton considers the time to have been "well spent" and believes that he and his associates were able to effect real change during their law school careers.

Carlton counts the friends he made in law school as the most valuable product of his legal education, but he also enjoyed the classes he took. He had fun with his coursework because he selected courses he found intriguing instead of ones that would help on the bar exam. Carlton credits several experiences he had before law school for providing him with a foundation of knowledge so that he could choose courses he liked. His pre-law preparation also allowed him to devote more time to campus social issues during his first year, including working as a paralegal for a two-person firm in Jackson as a senior in college. He credits law-related courses he took at college and the CLEO (Council on Legal Education) Program for minority students as giving him an academic boost during his first year.

After graduating from law school, Carlton had the luxury of choosing where he wanted to live and what he wanted to do. He chose Mississippi. When he describes his decision, there is no hesitation or regret in his voice, "I wanted to come home because I saw home as a place that needed me, and I felt that there was a lot of work to be done at home." Carlton returned to Mississippi with his eyes wide open to the scarce opportunities available to young black lawyers in the state's largest and richest firms. Following his first year of law school, Carlton had hoped to work as a summer associate for a big firm in Mississippi. None offered him a position despite his attendance at one of the best law schools in the country and his being a native of Mississippi. Instead, he took a job in-state with the ACLU working on criminal cases.

By coming back to Mississippi, Carlton also declined a promising career in Charlotte, North Carolina, with the firm now named Ferguson Stein Chambers Gresham & Sumter, which legendary civil rights litigator Julius Chambers had founded in 1964. However, Chambers was the director of the NAACP Legal Defense and Education fund when Carlton was there. The firm has represented clients in many famous civil rights and employment discrimination cases.

Carlton had worked there as a summer associate following his second year of law school. He interviewed with them after graduation, but his plans to accept a job there were redrawn after his future wife was diagnosed with cancer in 1989. Ferguson Stein nonetheless served as an inspiration to Carlton with its fully integrated staff of white, black, Jewish, and female attorneys. Carlton's current attempt to show that an integrated and racially diverse firm can thrive in Mississippi is modeled in large part on North Carolina's Ferguson Stein.

Carlton also knew in law school that he wanted to pursue a clerkship. Carlton understood that most clerkships went to students with stellar grades and that his school was unlikely to be of much help in securing a clerkship because his grades were solid but unexceptional. He adopted a somewhat different approach to finding a clerkship. Instead of submitting his résumé to judges all over the country, Carlton focused on three judges in Mississippi with whom he felt a shared connection. One judge, U.S. District Judge Henry T. Wingate, who was then undergoing federal confirmation, had taught Carlton as an adjunct professor at Jackson State, giving Carlton a very rare "A" in his course. The second, U.S. District Court Judge William H. Barbour was from an old legal family in Carlton's hometown. Reuben Anderson, the third judge Carlton focused on, was the first black justice on the Mississippi Supreme Court. As Carlton describes it, "I had something in common with him. . . . I was black, and he was black."

Carlton interviewed with Judge Barbour and Justice Anderson, but there was no doubt in his mind that he wanted to clerk for Justice Anderson when they met at Christmas break during his third year. In Justice Anderson, Carlton found a "great friend" and professional "mentor." Carlton is effusive and sincere in describing Justice Anderson as "the best thing for my career" and a "father-type figure."

Carlton encourages all students to apply for judicial clerkships. He recommends that those interested in trial work and litigation do a trial court clerkship so that they can see first-hand the immediate evidentiary and procedural decisions that trial judges must make daily. Carlton advises students interested in honing their research and writing skills to seek appellate clerkships, where they will see legal advocacy laid out in written briefs and in oral arguments. According to Carlton, clerks receive insights into judicial decision making by discussing cases with their judges, which "will help you immensely" in practice. Even more important, a clerkship is an opportunity to connect with an older, accomplished lawyer—as Carlton did with Justice Anderson—who can serve as a trusted guide during the transition from law school into a legal career and beyond.

After clerking for a year, Carlton stayed on at the Mississippi Supreme Court as a staff attorney. Carlton's main duty was to prepare memoranda that helped the justices decide motions relating to the court's docket and to post-conviction relief for prisoners.

Carlton left the high court in February 1991 to begin a litigation practice in the Jackson office of the New Orleans-based firm, Phelps Dunbar. Carlton made important connections throughout the Mississippi legal community and gained valuable trial and appellate experience as a junior associate. He tried civil cases in both state and federal courts around Mississippi.

Carlton's big break came in 1995 when Brad Pigott, one of his current partners, was named U.S. Attorney for the Southern District of Mississippi by President Bill Clinton. Pigott and Carlton first met in 1991 at an alumni function for UVA Law School. At that time, Carlton was still clerking for Justice Anderson, but Pigott remembered Carlton four years later when he was looking for young, talented lawyers to shake up the U.S. Attorney's office in Mississippi. Pigott asked Carlton, at thirty-one, to join him as the Chief of the Civil Division. Carlton accepted.

He loved his tenure as an Assistant U.S. Attorney, though he concedes it was a job "that I really grew into because I was young." Carlton was immediately placed in charge of eight lawyers, all of whom were older than he was. Several of his employees had been practicing law for ten or even twenty years. In addition to this legal team, he supervised a support staff of seventeen. Instead of being intimidated by the challenge, Carlton spurred himself to make the most of the opportunity, applying the same tenacity and confidence that had served him well as a first-generation college and law student. He jumped into the federal government's litigation in his home state.

Carlton's primary role was to supervise the office's civil portfolio, making sure that the government was effectively represented in civil cases from the pre-trial stage all the way through the appellate process. This task involved the management of a vast array of actions ranging from defending the government against private lawsuits to collecting delinquent fines and student loans to pursuing fair housing claims against landlords. In addition to these managerial responsibilities, Carlton maintained a set of cases for which he served as the government's lead counsel, writing motions and arguing cases at both the trial and appellate levels. He adopted this burdensome practice in order to "live by example" before his employees and in order to sharpen his own skills as a litigator. As if these duties were not enough, Carlton also became active in Justice Department policy on the national level as a member of the Civil Chiefs Working Group.

Carlton conveys the essence of the Assistant U.S. Attorney's job in the sort of plainspoken and deceptively simple terms one expects from a native Southern litigator. In his words, "you have to go over there and do justice, whatever justice is. If justice is putting somebody behind bars on the criminal side or if justice is trying to enforce the Fair Housing Act. . . . Justice has to be the paramount consideration, and that may mean resolving a case short of trial because you know your agency has done wrong . . . or not resolving a case short of trial because you believe that there has been no wrong done. . . ." Whatever the situation, Carlton conducted himself with distinction in the U.S. Attorney's office and earned a Certificate of Commendation from the Civil Rights Division of the Department of Justice for his work on fair housing and education cases in Mississippi.

Carlton's tenure with the government was significant not only for the substance of his work and his exposure to diverse litigation, but also because the experience brought him in touch with the lawyers who would change his professional life. The job placed him in daily contact with U.S. Attorney Brad Pigott and one of Carlton's attorneys on the civil side, Cliff Johnson. The three men became close friends. Johnson had taken a course under Julius Chambers while at Columbia Law School, and he and Carlton began discussing their different experiences in Mississippi and their feelings about racial integration. As their relationship blossomed, they started comparing future plans and goals. In conjunction with Pigott, the three government lawyers realized that they shared a common dream for their state. They all believed that the time had come for Mississippi to have a truly integrated firm, with an equal number of black and white partners working side by side and in close collaboration with one another. The three experienced attorneys knew that no firm existed in Mississippi with fifty percent black lawyers and fifty percent white lawyers, though some firms had hired a few black partners in order to present a diverse façade, and many firms used black lawyers as litigators when they thought it might benefit their side before a particular judge or jury.

Pigott, Carlton, and Johnson had a loftier goal in mind. As Carlton puts it, "[t]here is no reason in the world why there should not be in Mississippi a place for black lawyers and white lawyers to work together on equal footing." From this idea a firm was born. The three men searched hard for another black lawyer and found him in the form of Mississippi native Douglas Minor, then an associate at Phelps Dunbar and a graduate of Harvard College and Georgetown Law. The four soon-to-be partners began plotting their strategy in earnest. Once again, Carlton sums up their exhaustive planning regime with a trial lawyer's way with words: "We met, and we met, and we met, and got to know each other." They recognized that private practice was a "different game" in which they would have finite resources to fulfill the same goal for which they previously had basically unlimited resources in the U.S. Attorney's office—namely, "to do justice."

In February 2001, the four lawyers opened their firm. They announced their presence mainly through word of mouth using their extensive network of legal contacts throughout the state. The partners also created brochures and bought advertisement space in newspapers. They included their pictures in this marketing material because they knew that the image of two black lawyers and two white lawyers in business together would be a "powerful statement" to many potential clients in Mississippi. Today, most of their clients come to them either as return clients or based on the reputation of the firm.

In his work for the federal government, Carlton had faced a staggering range of legal issues because of the government's involvement in many different areas of the law. Carlton handles nearly as diverse a portfolio of civil cases now. However, in private practice his varied workload is driven by the financial reality of supporting himself and his partners, not by the government's litigation agenda. Carlton counsels plaintiffs in commercial disputes, civil rights actions, and personal injury suits. He sues the government to recoup money for clients under the False Claims Act. He also maintains a healthy defense practice, representing corporations like 3M in lawsuits across Mississippi. Carlton notes that the type of case he takes "really doesn't matter" because he enjoys litigation itself. As he puts it, "I just like trials."

He has not allowed the financial risks of private practice to stop him from "doing justice" for poor clients in situations where fees are likely to be nominal at best. Carlton is animated in explaining why he takes such cases: "some things just scream out for justice so loudly that you . . . you feel obligated to do it." For example, he has brought claims on behalf of poor rural plaintiffs in wage and hour cases under the Fair Labor Standards Act. He also recently represented a group of black citizens as part of a congressional redistricting lawsuit that reached the U.S. Supreme Court.

Among Carlton's favorite cases is one involving a black woman named Johnnie Mae Johnson. Drew is a small town of 2,400 people in northwest Mississippi, roughly eighty percent of them black. Forty percent of its residents live below the poverty line. Despite its overwhelming black population, the city government was, until recently, dominated by whites. In 2001, Johnnie Mae Johnson challenged a white male incumbent who had been in office for years, to be alderman-at-large for Drew. She lost the election by a close vote. Rob McDuff, a well-known civil rights attorney, was enlisted to help Mrs. Johnson as her lead attorney. McDuff recruited Carlton to help build a case that would contest the result in court.

Mrs. Johnson alleged that the white poll workers had thrown out the votes of many blacks based on improper justifications. Part of the case for Mrs. Johnson required convincing black citizens whose votes had been rejected to testify in court that they had intended to vote and that they still wanted their votes to count. Many of the town's prominent white citizens filled the courtroom during this testimony and, in an effort to intimidate them, tried to stare down the black witnesses, many of whom were maids or nannies or otherwise employed by the whites. Carlton's eyes shine as he recalls how "these old ladies came up there and took the stand and told the judge that they wanted their vote to count. And that was very, very powerful." The trial judge reinstated some of the votes and threw out others such that the final tally was a tie, and the judge was forced to declare a new election. Johnnie Mae Johnson won the special election, giving blacks in the town a majority in local government for the first time. Her case and her victory spurred even more change in Drew, and the city elected its first black mayor in June 2005.

Carlton relishes cases like Mrs. Johnson's. He says, "[t]hose are the types of things that we want to do here," but the financial pressures of being in private practice force him to augment his social justice litigation with more lucrative casework. When asked about other drawbacks to private practice, he lists a common complaint among lawyers of all stripes: "[s]ometimes you feel like there's not enough hours in the day." He also notes that it can be "difficult" at times to make sure clients are satisfied. He explains that the best approach is to always keep them abreast of developments in their cases and that a good lawyer works hard to make sure his clients are satisfied "in the end."

Even with its frustrations, Carlton is satisfied with his decision to start his own firm. He points to "being your own boss and having a stakehold in something that you believe in" as among the advantages of his job. Because the partners have a financial stake in each other's cases, they work closely together, aiding in jury selection, editing one another's briefs, and collaborating on litigation strategy. Carlton sees his fellow partners daily and often goes to lunch with them, and their families all know and like each other.

Carlton says his lifestyle has not changed much since making the transition from government to the private sector. The firm has secured several "huge dividends" for its clients over the past few years, and though it might be tempting to take the money from these successes and use it for pleasure, Carlton and his partners invest the bulk of these large sums back into their firm for the next case or distribute it among their staff. Carlton notes the importance of rewarding the firm's eight employees and making "sure that they share in whatever you get."

When asked to list the qualities of an effective lawyer, Carlton focuses on adaptability. He mentions chestnuts like "precision," "preparation," and "thoroughness," but for Carlton, the ability to shift one's arguments to fit unexpected developments in the courtroom is the hallmark of a great lawyer. He notes that effective advocacy requires a strong constitution, since "[y]ou cannot allow yourself to be beaten down or intimidated for sure." Carlton flashes his own inflexible will by finishing his description with an exhortation to future attorneys to "[a]lways . . . remember that the bottom line is trying . . . to do justice, trying to get some justice for your client."

Carlton lives by example. When he was Chief of the Civil Division, he set the standard for his office, always maintaining a caseload in addition to his administrative responsibilities. As a law partner, Carlton helped create a firm that exemplifies the type of racially diverse and collaborative practice that is possible in the South in the twenty-first century. Thus, it is no surprise that Carlton himself serves as a paradigm for the advice he gives to those embarking on a legal career. He says "[g]et involved in your practice with some passion," and when you take a position on an issue, be sure to consider how it "might affect people other than your client." Carlton may practice law privately, but he serves as a very public example of the far-reaching impact that a gifted lawyer can generate by using his legal education to better his home state.

ADAM BERGER

Plaintiff's Toxic Exposure Lawyer

By Ariel R. Schwartz

As a city boy with a proclivity for parks, Adam Berger has made a career of halting environmental degradation and championing the rights of those who have been adversely affected by it. His career thus far has primarily involved working for nine years at Earthjustice in Seattle, which is a national nonprofit environmental litigation firm, and Schroeter, Goldmark & Bender, a plaintiffs' personal injury law firm.

Adam's childhood interest in urban land use grew into a broader interest in environmental issues, which in part led him to journey from the eastern to western seaboard. Seattle seems to agree with him. Despite the frequent beeping coming from his computer indicating that he has received new e-mail messages, Adam is relaxed — at least for a busy lawyer and a parent of two young children.

Adam developed his arsenal of legal tools while working at Earthjustice. His practice there primarily involved appellate litigation against federal governmental agencies such as the Environmental Protection Agency and the Department of Interior when these agencies failed to comply with their governing statutes. Working now at Schroeter, Goldmark & Bender, Adam is expanding his skills as an environmental and health advocate while litigating toxic exposure cases in which a person or property has been damaged and in suits on behalf of homeowners who unknowingly bought contaminated land.

His slightly cluttered office is sparsely decorated. One of the few items that adorns his walls is a certificate of admission to the U.S. Supreme Court, which hangs next to his college degree from Harvard and his law degree from Yale. Having graduated from these elitist institutions seems to have little effect on Adam's demeanor. He wears nondescript brown-tone clothing; he has shaggy, grey-streaked dark hair, an unruly beard, and a small stud earring in his left ear. Like his office, Adam's appearance is minimalist yet expressive.

Raised in Queens, New York, Adam is unsure of how he became an environmentalist or an aspiring lawyer, yet from an early age, he knew that he wanted to be both. He conjectures that perhaps as a child the excitement surrounding the first Earth Day in 1970 and celebrations in subsequent years piqued his interest in the environmental movement. Or perhaps, he speculates, his enthusiasm stems from his childhood adventures at a summer camp located on the New York-Pennsylvania border. This fledgling interest in the environment was reinforced by Adam's affinity for the sciences, an area in which his public high school had strong programs. Perhaps not coincidentally, he went to Benjamin N. Cardozo Public High School, named for the famous jurist who sat on both the New York Court of Appeals and the U.S. Supreme Court. The school's sports teams there were called the Judges, but, according to Adam, the name hardly intimidated the opponents.

Adam had no lawyers in either his immediate or extended family, yet he remembers always having had legal ambitions. When asked about why he knew he wanted to be a lawyer, Adam responds, "As a middle class Jewish kid growing up in New York, the cultural aspiration was to become a professional—either a lawyer or a doctor. I spent a lot of time in the Emergency Room—as a patient—and I knew I did not want to be a doctor. This sounds like a bad ethnic joke, but there was some truth to it."

The fact that his generation was the first in his family to attend college and to be politically and environmentally engaged did not faze him. Adam's father was the shipping manager at a plastic bag company. His mother worked at home transcribing tapes for attorneys (Adam never heard the tapes because his mother wore headsets). Adam's parents were not especially environmentally conscious, nor were they particularly interested in politics. Adam still does not know what his parents' political views were during his youth. Adam too is not particularly interested in partisan politics, yet his approach diverges from his parents' to the extent that a hallmark of Adam's career is his commitment to nonprofit policy advocacy.

One of Adam's few memories of discussing politics at home was when he was thirteen years old and was watching the televised Carter-Ford debates with a friend of his uncle. They became embroiled in a debate, and only in retrospect did Adam realize that his uncle's friend was the famous federal judge Jack Weinstein, who has sat on the bench in Brooklyn for over thirty-five years and is considered by many to be a great legal thinker and writer in the areas of evidence, complex litigation, legal ethics, and procedure. Yet this brush with the law — or, more accurately, with someone who helped define the meaning of the laws — went virtually unnoticed by young Adam.

Adam's experiences in both college and law school were characterized by a commitment to interdisciplinary education and problem-solving. While at Harvard, he considered majors such as biology, geology, folklore, and mythology. Ultimately, he settled on the interdisciplinary field of social studies. In part this decision was made by default, but in part he selected it because it enabled him to look holistically at urban problems by patching together various classes that related to urban studies, such as courses in urban economics, city planning and politics, and organizational theory.

One of his most memorable summer internships was working in the mid-1980s for the New York City government in the Mayor's Office of Midtown Enforcement. According to Adam, urban planning was very much in vogue, especially the mayor's project cleaning up Times Square. In anticipation of First Amendment challenges by peep-show owners if the City attempted to close them down, the interns were told to do research by visiting the establishments, but only for mundane chores such as counting the number of booths and seeing how much space was used for what purposes.

The experience of working in the New York City government was his first significant exposure to environmental impact statements, which are required by statute for proposed development projects. Responding to and critiquing such statements would become the bread and butter of his later work at Earthjustice. Yet the issues he confronted in City government were traffic flow and noise, whereas his concerns with environmental impact statements while he worked at Earthjustice were over issues such as rivers' water quality and sustainable wildlife populations.

Adam was admitted to Yale Law School during his senior year at Harvard but chose to defer enrollment for a year. Instead, he returned to New York City government, where his experience was colored by a huge municipal scandal in 1986 that broke out in the Parking Violations Bureau and brought the City government to a virtual halt. The problem was so extensive that even careerists were looking for new jobs. Although it was an unproductive year for Adam, the job gave him a sense of how bureaucracies work. Occasionally, particularly when he was working at Earthjustice, Adam found himself remembering the insights he had gained while working for the city, which often came to him when he would think about what litigation might accomplish in terms of influencing agencies' behavior.

Although he liked his classmates and professors at Yale Law School, Adam found law school less academically challenging than college. In particular, the ubiquity of baseless "bullshitting" by his classmates was irksome to him, especially when their comments were disconnected from the real world. Rapidly, Adam realized that he was tired of being in the classroom and really just wanted to practice law. Furthermore, he seemed to resent the stress emanating from his classmates over firm jobs and law review because Adam was interested in neither. Consequently, he sought refuge in clinical work.

After becoming involved with the landlord-tenant clinic during his second semester, he sought other opportunities to help economically marginalized people. His second year, Adam and some of his peers at Yale formed a clinic that sought to create transitional housing for homeless people who were trying to move from shelters to more permanent residences. This clinic involved collaborating with business and architectural students as well as a tax professor, who was eager to test applications of the recently enacted low-income housing tax credits. In part, this clinic was a response to Adam's frustrations with the law school, which "epitomized the disconnect between legal education and legal practice." The clinic was his way to bridge the gap.

Adam's plan to help pay for law school involved working at a well-paying law firm each summer. He never envisioned himself working at a big, defense-side firm for the long term but nonetheless found these work experiences to be beneficial because he learned basic legal writing skills, had exposure to a variety of practice areas, and was paid handsomely.

Working as a judicial clerk for the year following law school also provided Adam with invaluable exposure to the litigation process. He chose to clerk for Mark L. Wolf, a federal district court judge in Boston, because he knew that he wanted to be a litigator and thought that a district court clerkship would be the best opportunity to learn firsthand about the litigation process. During Adam's clerkship, from September 1989 to September 1990, there were only two civil trials in Judge Wolf's court, but there were numerous criminal trials, partly because, according to Adam, Judge Wolf was an early proponent of pushing parties to settle by employing a variety of mediation and alternative dispute resolution techniques. At the time, Adam felt that the "role of the judge should be to preside over cases, not to beat up on parties to settle." However, Adam has come to accept, along with much of the legal community, that "most cases do settle and probably should settle and they need some nudging along." In retrospect, Adam has come to appreciate Judge Wolf's proclivities and the experience Adam had while clerking.

Adam's trip to interview with a Seattle firm during his second year of law school turned out to be particularly fortuitous because he was able to squeeze in a visit to the Earthjustice office. Earthjustice, formerly the

Sierra Club Legal Defense Fund, is a public interest litigation firm that primarily represents environmental nonprofits in natural resources and environmental litigation, especially in public lands management and endangered species protection cases. After that trip, Adam accepted an externship with Earthjustice for the fall semester of his third year.

Since the Seattle office of Earthjustice had only three attorneys, two interns, and a full docket, from the beginning Adam was drafting briefs and overseeing cases. After the externship, Adam knew that he wanted to work at Earthjustice upon completing his clerkship with Judge Wolf. However, it was not until after Adam had sent out cover letters and résumés to a host of environmental organizations did he realize that Earthjustice's attorneys wanted him to join their team.

Initially, Adam's primary frustration with Seattle was his inability to get a date. He "wasn't having any good luck with dating," so he swore that he would leave Seattle if he could not get a date within two years. Adam eventually succeeded: with the woman who would later become his wife. At the time, Harriet was a graduate student; now she is a postdoctorate fellow in anthropology at the University of Washington. His marriage and later his two children were integral to Adam's decision to put down roots in Seattle.

Adam found Earthjustice to be a great starting place for an inexperienced attorney. Because the organization was perpetually short-staffed, he felt that there was no wasted effort and no busy work. From the first day he had cases that were primarily his responsibility. If anything, Adam remembers, "I suffered from lack of sufficient supervision and guidance because I had to actively seek out the more senior attorneys to ask questions, or I just heard about the case from them when I messed up." In part, Adam attributes this sink-or-swim office culture to the fact that it was a small, personality-driven office, which was characterized by more freedom and responsibility than some of the other Earthjustice offices. Once Adam became a more experienced senior attorney, he tried to work with the junior attorneys so they would not feel as if they were floundering.

After working several years at Earthjustice, Adam felt he was overextended: he was litigating a host of cases that ranged from advocating for sea lions in Alaska to halting geothermal development, to protecting old-growth forests in the Northwest. He also argued several notable Endangered Species Act cases. Consequently, when he was promoted from Associate Attorney to Project Attorney, he asked that his new position allow him to focus on cases relating to salmon preservation. Reflecting back on this request, Adam notes, "Be careful what you ask for. I asked for more focus because I was being stretched thin, but the downside was that once I specialized I was not learning a new area of science or the law each week. I got quicker at these type[s] of cases, but the intellectual challenge had faded." Haunted by the motto, "Your wins are only temporary, but your losses are forever," Adam started feeling frustrated that the same battles were being fought over and over again. He began to dread the thought of bringing another salmon case.

At one point while at Earthjustice, Adam toyed with the idea of taking a clinical professorship teaching environmental law at Stanford Law School. However, due to the high housing prices near Stanford, the fact that they were expecting their first child, and his wife's need to be near the University of Washington to finish her doctorate, Adam chose not to take the position at Stanford. Nonetheless, personal factors were still driving Adam to look for a new position. His wife was close to finishing her doctorate in anthropology, and because she was going to be in the academic job market, Adam wanted to prepare to be geographically mobile. He felt that the skill set he had developed at Earthjustice would not be sufficiently transferable, especially if they ended up moving to a smaller legal market. After talking to a former colleague who was working at the plaintiff-side firm of Schroeter, Goldmark & Bender, Adam realized that working there would enable him to develop some of the legal skills that he hoped to acquire. After nine years at Earthjustice, during which he argued countless cases in the district courts, six cases before the Ninth Circuit Court of Appeals, and twice opposed petitions for certiorari in the Supreme Court, Adam decided to move on.

Many aspects of Adam's work at Schroeter differ from his previous professional experiences, especially insofar as his practice now is much more trial-oriented, yet his docket continues to focus on challenging systematic environmental degradation and risks to human health. Litigating toxic exposure claims, consumer fraud class actions, nursing home liability cases, medical negligence cases, and homeowners' contamination suits, Adam is once again learning science on the fly.

Adam's work at Earthjustice taught him how to analyze complex scientific causalities in order to determine whether the government was meeting its statutory obligations. Now, as a plaintiffs' lawyer, Adam is using that same set of skills to determine whether the defendants were negligent and thereby caused needless injuries to his clients. Particularly in toxic exposure cases and homeowners' contamination suits, Adam, like most plaintiffs' lawyers, has the challenging role of trying to prove that the defendants had a duty to his clients that they breached, and the breach had caused the clients' injuries. The fact that Adam has stayed involved in legal work that is intertwined with scientific determinations does not surprise him: he feels that being exposed to science and scientists is a big part of what keeps him interested in legal work. Also, he believes that the work he does as a plaintiffs' lawyer is consistent with his work at Earthjustice because in each job he was able to hold accountable those who engage in behaviors that have adverse environmental and health impacts.

One of the greatest differences between Adam's work at Earthjustice and the work he has done over the last seven years at Schroeter is the dramatic change in his clientele. At Earthjustice, his clients were typically institutions that were often litigation-savvy and engaged him in the strategic aspects of the lawsuits. Now Adam characterizes his clients as not particularly sophisticated about the legal system and having much more personally at stake with their claims, which can often make the process more emotionally challenging for the clients. Although Adam sometimes misses litigating public law cases that have policy ramifications, he believes that advocating for people who have suffered as a result of someone else's failings is important. Furthermore, he values the opportunity to acquire new professional skills, including trial work experience.

When asked about his feeling toward the contingency fee system and, more specifically, working on a contingency fee basis, Adam responds that he thinks that the contingency fee system is important because without it many people would not get representation. Yet Adam finds himself thinking more about money than he did while at Earthjustice. In part, Adam hypothesizes that this change might be a result of his increased financial obligations now that he has children. Yet he acknowledges that there are several other issues at play: while at Earthjustice, Adam had few worries about money because he was salaried and there was a development office that carried out fundraising activities. Adam would sometimes have to meet with donors or submit information for grants, but for the most part the finances of the organization were at the periphery of his professional responsibilities.

As a shareholder at Schroeter, despite the fact that the firm is financially successful, Adam worries about the profitability of his cases and how he is going to support his share of the overhead. On each case, the firm is laying out money, sometimes as much as several hundred thousand dollars. Consequently, as Adam explains, "If a case doesn't pan out, then you are out that money. I need to be concerned about picking too many 'bad cases,' not ones that aren't meritorious, but ones that won't be profitable."

Sometimes this involves telling clients with meritorious claims, "[T]here won't be enough money at the end of the day to make it worthwhile for the firm or the client." Although it always bothers Adam to have to turn down a meritorious case for financial reasons, he often does. "One of the things I had to get over is the belief that I can somehow make financially precarious or evidentiary weak cases work."

Despite his worrying, Adam finds his quality of life at Schroeter to be "pretty good," especially relative to other lawyers in the community. Adam notes, "There is no pressure to jack up billable hours, and no need to be in the office just to show that you are a hard-ass litigator." In part, Adam attributes the reasonable quality of life to the fact that the majority of partners are women, many of whom have families and value spending time with them. Like many of these partners, Adam spends his time outside of work with his family, including attending his children's sports activities and hiking with them on the weekends. Occasionally he sneaks some time for himself to play a game of pick-up frisbee or soccer. As is the case with many legal careers, the work can be unpredictable and time-intensive, sometimes requiring Adam to bring work home on nights and weekends. Even when he is not actively working, he finds himself "almost always thinking about the job — planning, strategizing for the next day." Sometimes having law constantly on the brain causes him to think that he should have had a different career, but overall he feels fortunate about the opportunities he has had as a lawyer in terms of the people he has worked with and the places he has worked.

While practicing at Schroeter, Adam continues to be involved in the nonprofit environmental law scene by serving on the board of directors of the Washington Environmental Council. Also, since leaving Earthjustice, he has twice taught an environmental law seminar as an adjunct professor at the University of Washington Law School. Now that he is a trial lawyer, Adam is a member of both the American and Washington Trial Lawyers Associations.

Seattle has changed in the fifteen years since Adam arrived. He finds that it has become busier, bigger, and more expensive. When asked whether he continues to see himself living in Seattle and working at Schroeter, Adam is unsure. He speculates that he will continue to engage in this type of personal injury work for another ten years, but he is not sure what he sees himself doing afterwards. Adam continues to feel like he is still learning how to do the job. He believes that law students do not realize how long it takes to learn the skills necessary to be good at the jobs they will ultimately pursue. As a law student he probably could not have envisioned himself feeling like a relative newcomer after so many years at a job.

Occasionally, especially when he was at Earthjustice, Adam received calls in which the caller explains that she wants to go into environmental law and asks which law school she should attend. Adam usually responds, "Don't go to law school as a means of obtaining an ideological end if you don't like the law and the way that lawyers think." Although Adam admits it is hard to figure out "the way lawyers think" before attending law school, he finds that prospective law students are often woefully naïve about the fact that "law is a very structured way of approaching the world and approaching problems and therefore one needs to work within the rules and to be very detail-orientated to be effective as a lawyer." Adam emphasizes that the "big picture" is important, but unless one can deal in details, one should find a way other than a legal career to achieve one's ideological ends.

However, Adam believes that if a prospective law student discovers that she does in fact have the temperament to be a lawyer, then the most important parts of finding a public interest legal career are getting to know people who work in the organizations in which she would ultimately want to work, striving for good grades, trying out a variety of legal jobs and experiences, and, most important, not becoming "locked into a life-style that keeps you from going to the job you love." Adam emphasizes that it is not, as some people will suggest, impossible to have a public interest legal career. Yet, according to Adam, one has to be proactive about seeking out alternatives to the big-firm career because public interest opportunities will not come by default.

STUART OLLANIK

Plaintiff's Product Defects Lawyer

By Rhett O. Millsaps II

The salesman at the Chrysler dealership had convinced Susie B. to indulge herself, so she chose the upgraded version of the van she'd been eyeing. "Nicer seats" were among the premium features touted in closing the deal; "ejector seats" would have been a more accurate description. The seats had not been properly manufactured, installed, or crash-tested, but that reality wouldn't begin to come to light until another vehicle crashed into the van occupied by Susie and her brother John. Both their seatbelts snapped, and their seats' pedestals bent far forward, which sent Susie into the dashboard and John into the steering column.

Susie, then an Emmy-winning Fox sports graphics producer, was left with such severe and chronic back pain that she had to trade her rising-star Los Angeles television career for a less demanding job as a producer at a local-access channel in Pennsylvania. John, a musician, was paralyzed and severely brain-damaged, and never able to travel again with his music. Both were in their twenties, with bright futures snuffed out by the careless actions of someone, somewhere in a corporate web with no clear center of responsibility—but with a phalanx of lawyers and virtually limitless resources to marshal in the defense of the corporation. Fortunately for Susie and John, there was a David to match this auto industry Goliath: Stuart Ollanik's small, specialized firm.

When Stuart comes bounding into the conference room of his small plaintiff's firm in Arvada, Colorado, the air seems to crackle with life. He's jovial and ebullient, with a firm handshake and a Cheshire Cat's smile. He's a stocky guy, solid, the kind who's happiest leading his son hiking up the side of a mountain (the bigger the better, one suspects). He projects a force of will, fueled by his passion, that makes Stuart an easy interview subject but a daunting figure to imagine on the other side of a courtroom. He roots for the underdog—whom he has made a career of championing with great success—and says he became a lawyer because he "love[s] being part of a system where regular people can challenge larger institutions."

It's no surprise that Stuart is a Dick Gephardt fan or that he was raised in the middle-class Midwest. Stuart grew up in St. Louis, Missouri, the second of three sons in a family that, he says, "approached life from a moral perspective." His mother was a secretary, his father a pharmacist and the first in his family to attend college. His was the kind of family that kept up with the news and discussed important issues of the day at the dinner table, always striving to be mindful of their place in the community and the larger world. Stuart's favorite subject in school was social studies, and he has a hard time pinpointing the exact age when he became "very involved in politics."

Stuart's experiences in high school undoubtedly put him on the path to where he is today. He is adamant that one person really can make a big difference in the world. Ralph Nader had just come onto the national scene, and Stuart points to him as an early hero and role model. Stuart became active in community causes and formed a citywide student coalition to address local environmental issues. In 1976 he and fellow student coalition leaders met with presidential candidate Jimmy Carter to discuss their concerns, focusing on the harmful effects of proposed dam projects in their area and around the country. He recalls with pride one of President Carter's first actions in office: calling for a moratorium on dam building. This experience was particularly empowering for Stuart, who decided early on that he would head to Washington, DC, to study political science, already aware that law school likely lay in his future.

While attending George Washington University, Stuart worked part-time on Capitol Hill for Missouri's Senator Thomas Eagleton, a "Democrat who understood the populist message," as Stuart put it. Like most freshman Hill interns, he started out opening mail and gradually took on more responsibility over time. He also wrote for and was an editor of the school newspaper, which sparked thoughts of graduate school in journalism, though his heart ultimately remained true to his more direct interest in law and policy. This interest was fueled by college courses like the one most salient in Stuart's memory, which was taught by a professor affiliated with the Center for Science & Public Policy. The class focused on the space program and aimed to teach students how to apply scientific knowledge to public policy—an intellectual pursuit that would prove fundamental to Stuart's legal career to come.

After college Stuart deferred law school for a year to work for Senator Eagleton's reelection campaign. He cashed in on his years of toil as a lowly Hill intern and returned to Missouri as the campaign's press coordinator for the eastern half of the state. When voters returned Eagleton to Washington that November for a third term, Stuart followed him to Washington, but not to Capitol Hill. He spent a couple months as a telephone fundraiser for a children's research hospital before becoming a media and legislative affairs assistant at the National Transportation Safety Board. It was there that Stuart first became intimately acquainted with the brutal reality of America's car culture. He was disturbed by highway safety statistics showing that automobile accidents claimed more than 40,000 lives each year, and the numbers were rising. What's more, those statistics were punctuated by personal tragedy: Stuart's first cousin was killed that year in a car crash and another first cousin was killed in a 1987 car wreck. While these experiences made strong impressions on Stuart, however, they would not come to bear on his career until several years after law school.

Stuart the outdoorsman lost to Stuart the policy wonk when it came time to pick a law school—he returned to Capitol Hill by way of Georgetown University Law Center. Stuart says that he enjoyed law school throughout, though he admits that he did his share of complaining over the heavy workload at the time. He entered law school with no clear direction in mind; instead he hoped to find his way by sampling the myriad opportunities before him. He was surprised to find how much he liked his courses in Contracts and Corporations, but he never saw himself at a corporate firm, even after spending a second-year summer at a respected firm in St. Louis. Stuart wanted something more personally interesting, and criminal law seemed to fit the bill after he became enthralled by Prof. Michael Seidman's Criminal Procedure course.

In his second and third years of law school, Stuart spent much of his time taking advantage of Georgetown's renowned clinical programs. He worked in the Center for Applied Legal Studies during his second year, taking on Social Security appeals and consumer protection cases for local DC residents. In his third year, Stuart says he spent most of his time "representing kids charged with crimes in a rotten system" through the juvenile justice clinic. The opportunity allowed him to delve into the nitty-gritty practice of criminal law, which he loved, working with kids accused of crimes ranging from truancy to murder. He was appalled by the terrible condition of the juvenile system facilities and learned that many of the counselors were crooked: they dealt drugs to the juveniles with whose care they were charged. Stuart, never one to shy from challenging an institution gone awry, got word to a Washington Post reporter about what he had learned. Nothing came of it immediately, but Stuart would return to DC after law school to find a story in the Post exposing corruption in the city's juvenile detention system.

When the real world came knocking during Stuart's third year of law school, he interviewed with the big corporate firms along with most of his classmates. The corporate path didn't seem to go in the right direction, but it was easy, and Stuart felt it was a solid backup if nothing more exciting came along. Then one day, as he pondered his future as a legal lemming, Stuart noticed a flyer on one of the many bulletin boards. An Alaska Supreme Court Justice was coming to campus to interview potential clerks. Seeing an opportunity for adventure, Stuart signed up for an interview.

Over the course of his chat with the justice, Stuart revealed his love for criminal law. His interest in the area came across so intensely that the justice recommended him to an Alaska appeals court that handled only criminal cases, and Stuart soon found himself Anchorage bound. He spent the summer driving from DC to Alaska, backpacking along the way. He loved the appeals court judge and the clerkship, describing it as one of the most rewarding experiences of his life. He also fell in love with, and later married, one of the clerks for the Chief Justice of the Alaska Supreme Court.

Stuart and his wife took their first post-clerkship jobs in Alaska. Stuart went to work with Jim Gilmore and Jeff Feldman, two of the top criminal and civil litigators in the state at the time. Because they operated a four-attorney shop, Stuart worked very closely with the two litigators and took on much more responsibility than a large firm would have offered. He racked up substantial time in court, which was unusual for a new associate, and learned the art of deposition, a skill crucial to his current work as a plaintiff's lawyer. Stuart and his wife were far from their families, though, so their days in Alaska were numbered.

Stuart recalls stopping in Boulder, Colorado, on his way to Anchorage and suggested to his wife that they might settle there. They were drawn to the opportunities for outdoor recreation, so Stuart decided to interview for jobs in the area. Stuart landed an excellent position in Denver: he was hired as second chair to Michael Bender—who would go on to become a Colorado Supreme Court Justice—in a high-profile criminal defense case. Stuart, who is Jewish, represented a member of the Aryan Nation accused of killing Alan Berg, a controversial, Jewish talk radio host. Stuart's client was convicted, which marked a turning point for Stuart. While Stuart had thrived representing low-level offenders, especially juveniles he saw as deserving of second chances, he found high-level criminal defense work to be less personally rewarding. When he saw an ad for an opening in the Colorado Attorney General's office, he took the opportunity to apply for the job.

Stuart was hired as an Assistant Attorney General handling hazardous waste litigation for the state of Colorado. He'd always been interested in environmental law, and his intense trial experience was a huge selling point for the Attorney General's office. Stuart further honed his court-room skills in bringing polluters to justice, but that stint was relatively short-lived, too. When Gale Norton, future Secretary of the Interior under President George W. Bush, became Colorado's Attorney General, Stuart felt the office was moving in a direction he couldn't support. After almost three years in the job, he decided to leave.

Stuart's next move grew out of a connection he had made between leaving Bender's office and joining the Colorado Attorney General's office. Stuart had spent a month traveling in Asia, but had a month free upon his return. He had run across an ad posted at a local law school by a lawyer named Jim Gilbert, who was looking for someone to help write an article on medical malpractice suits. Gilbert's practice focused almost exclusively on automobile manufacturing defect cases, such as SUV rollovers and the infamous exploding Pintos. Gilbert also revolution-ized product liability litigation by helping found the Attorneys Information Exchange Group, which shares among member lawyers information, such as depositions and other factual research, from product liability suits all over the country. Gilbert and Stuart had worked well together collaborating on the medical malpractice article, so Gilbert asked Stuart to join his firm.

Since 1991, Stuart has worked with Gilbert at what would become Gilbert, Frank, Ollanik & Komyatte, P.C. The firm consists of the four named partners, a senior lawyer, an associate who recently graduated from law school, an engineer, and a handful of paralegals and other support staffers. Stuart and his team are highly specialized. They focus almost exclusively on automobile manufacturing defect cases. They juggle between ten and twenty cases at any given time, with Stuart and Komyatte each managing half the load. The work is very collaborative among the lawyers, however, and Gilbert lends his three decades of technical experience to every case.

It's clear when Stuart describes the details of his work that one can never have too much experience in the product liability business. The cases are extremely technical: to win an automobile design defect lawsuit, one needs to have a virtual encyclopedia of information regarding gov-ernment regulations and industry standards to prove that harm was caused by defective design and not by the fault of the driver or some other culprit. This means that the cases go through many stages before they finally reach trial, so there isn't really a "typical day" in the life of a plaintiff's lawyer like Stuart.

First come the pre-litigation fact-finding and technical research phases, when a mountain of work must be done to ascertain whether a suit against a manufacturer is even viable. In the fact-finding stage, Stuart is on the road, taking sworn statements from those with first-hand knowledge of the calamity in question. After the events surrounding the injury are reconstructed, Stuart dives into the technical research stage to determine whether the harm might be attributable to a design defect. The work at this point is voluminous: it requires Stuart to develop a precise understanding of the mechanical devices at issue by talking with experts and reading technical documents and depositions.

If a design defect is suspected and a suit is filed, the litigation phase that Stuart finds most tedious begins: written discovery. At this stage, Stuart spends enormous amounts of time drafting extremely detailed technical questions to be answered by the defendants. The defendants, of course, usually are multinational automobile manufacturers, whose lawyers and engineers are extraordinarily adept at quashing litigation by revealing as little as legally possible. The onus thus lies with Stuart to draft questions that can't be answered without divulging the critical details necessary to build the plaintiff's case. Because the defendants' lawyers also will use every legal maneuver available to avoid answering such questions, Stuart spends a lot of time using legal motions to compel the defendants to comply with his written discovery requests.

Once written discovery is complete, Stuart begins preparation for engineer depositions. Deposing the engineers involved is one of his most intense tasks because the engineers are usually loyal to their employer, the defendant. Stuart is sensitive to their plight as he understands the dilemma created by conflicting responsibilities to give detailed technical answers while remaining loyal to one's employer. Nonetheless, thorough engineer depositions are critical for the upcoming battle of the experts.

In the expert phase, Stuart prepares the plaintiff's expert witnesses for their depositions and testimony at trial. He also works with the experts to prepare cross-examinations of the defendants' experts when they are deposed, hoping to undermine their testimony so that the plaintiff's experts come out on top. Winning or losing this battle of experts can be crucial to winning or losing the whole case.

After all the experts have been deposed, Stuart must prepare for trial. This entails a lot of organizational work such as making exhibits and drafting outlines of witnesses' testimonies. Stuart also must figure out how to present his mountain of technical evidence to the jury, which will be composed of twelve "regular folks" drawn from the community. To do this, Stuart will convene many randomly selected focus groups and present and re-present all of the issues he'll bring at trial until he feels comfortable communicating them to a jury.

Many cases never reach trial because the defendants settle before that point. Others have mixed resolutions, with some defendants settling but others holding out to the bitter end. That's how Susie and John B.'s case, Stuart's sweetest victory, played out.

Susie and John B. hired Ed Steinbrecher, a local Los Angeles lawyer, who brought in Jim Gilbert, Stuart's partner, and Stuart to sue Chrysler, the company with ultimate responsibility for the quality of products sold under its brand; the auto dealership, for misleading Susie about the upgrade; the conversion company, for doing a shoddy job of upgrading the van; the seat manufacturer, for selling car seats with sharp edges under the upholstery that could and did sever the seatbelts; and the pedestal manufacturer, Coachmen Industries, for selling defective seat pedestals. In a bold move for a major automobile manufacturer, Chrysler actually paid to settle the case and then joined forces with Stuart and his co-counsel to go after the other parties. All other defendants settled except for Coachmen. At trial, the jury found against Coachmen and awarded thirty-five million dollars to John and Susie. Some fault was attributed to other entities, so the judgment amount would have been reduced to about seventeen million, but Coachmen settled the case for essentially that amount in the weeks following the verdict.

Stuart believes justice was served and hopes the case will deter companies from similar dealings in the future. If not, he'll be all the more prepared for the next fight, when he'll venture out once again from Arvada to begin the long road to trial. The beauty of working in a national market, Stuart points out, is that he doesn't have to live like many high-powered lawyers in a major financial center. He can live and do much of his work in his chosen home of Colorado, where he can enjoy the outdoors with his family whenever he has time. Having such an environment as his backyard is all the more important as a litigator, because his time commitments fluctuate depending on the litigation. In 2005, Stuart worked seven days a week for the first five months of the year but then afterwards had plenty of time to take trips with his family. It doesn't help that he sits on the boards of several nonprofits, including the Two Rivers Institute and Trial Lawyers for Public Justice, but Stuart wouldn't have it any other way. He feels a responsibility to give back to his community and his world, an impulse rooted in those nightly discussions at the family dinner table back in St. Louis, where he learned that one guy with modest beginnings can be a force for change in the world.

Stuart has earnest advice for young or budding lawyers: "use the law as a tool for what matters to you." Stuart recognized a turning point when he saw the notice on the wall about interviews for a job in Alaska. He could have taken the easy path with a corporate firm position that was practically handed to him, but he knows it would have stifled his spirit. Instead, he resolved, "my law degree is going to be a tool for me, not a straightjacket," and he used the opportunities before him to blaze his own trail. "Find a niche where you can do good and do well," he says, and you will be happy.

EMMA LEHENY

Labor Union Lawyer (Private Firm)

By Molly Pietsch

Emma Leheny was brought into this world with an innate desire for social justice. By the time she could read, Emma could not help but comment on the "Men Working" sign as she drove to school with her mother. She remembers saying that the sign was unfair, only to realize that only men were working at the construction site. She revised her statement by saying, "no, it's the job; it's the job that's unfair."

It is not surprising that Emma has dedicated her career to public interest work. After a variety of legal internships, a federal clerkship, and a Skadden Fellowship, Emma now works as a partner at a small union-side labor law firm in Pasadena, California.

Emma's upbringing in Amherst, Massachusetts, surrounded by an activist culture, a father who was an English professor, and a mother who was a high school English teacher, helped foster Emma's commitment to social justice. Her parents' friends gave her t-shirts with Che Guevara quotations printed on them, and there is a kindergarten picture of her wearing a women's symbol with a fist in it without really knowing what it meant. She fondly remembers eavesdropping on a lot of interesting conversations among her parents' activist friends.

Emma not only observed the activist culture, she was an agitator herself. In high school she often (voluntarily) found herself in the headmaster's office, debating about whether it was sexist to call ninth graders "freshmen." After discovering that there were twice as many boys' basketball teams as girls' teams, Emma calculated how many girls had tried out versus those who were turned down and learned that there were enough girls to start another team. She brought it to the attention of the athletic director, who claimed that there was not enough interest. After Emma wrote an editorial for her school newspaper, the school formed a third girls' basketball team. Despite her activism, Emma always approached situations in a respectful and diplomatic way, which was part of what eventually attracted her to a career in law.

Emma was fortunate to receive a full scholarship to a college preparatory academy where her mother was a teacher, but she never adjusted to the environment of social privilege. After realizing at the beginning of high school that she had surpassed most of the world in educational access, she decided she needed to spend her life giving back. She is not able to pinpoint exactly when she viewed her future career as a mandate to be involved in public service and social justice, but obviously the need germinated early. Emma always remembers thinking about her potential career as always being part of her logic: she wanted to seek out and change what was not fair about the world.

All the while, she felt pressure from her family and peers to continue to pursue the best education she could. Her parents were the first in their families to go to college and thus considered education as a "sort of holy land." Emma applied early to Brown University and enrolled in the fall of 1987. The school provided a nice balance: the academic prestige her parents valued and a reputation for supporting outspoken students and liberal platforms.

Soon after Emma settled into her new academic home, she was again writing letters to the school newspaper. She remembers one she wrote during her first semester about Brown's decision not to sell its investments in South Africa. The school paper had written a supporting article entitled, "Balancing Money and Morals." Emma's response was titled, "Money Over Morals."

One issue that touched Emma on a personal level was when strong anti-gay and anti-African-American hate speech erupted on campus. During informal support groups set up around campus, Emma "outed" herself, smiling as she recounts the story, "I'm obviously not black."

Even as an agitator, Emma always acted within the institution, using argumentation and persuasion to get her views across. It is an approach Emma continues to use in her practice: she makes a point not to elevate her rhetoric unless she has to, with opposing counsel or anyone else. She always tries to see how far she can go with diplomacy.

College was also a time when Emma came to terms with her majority status, as a white, prep-school educated, middle-class female. After enduring the anti-gay and African-American hate speech, Emma dedicated herself to gaining a better understanding of the minority groups around her. She took an African-American Studies course and did her final project on the black communities at Brown. For her senior thesis, she chose to write about novels by James Baldwin, who, as a gay, African-American writer in the 1960s, was rejected by both groups when gay themes entered his novels.

Despite her enriching academic experience at Brown, no professor stands out as a mentor during her college years. Rather, Emma credits much of her inspiration and eventual career as a lawyer to a woman named Diane Sprague, who is a social worker in Providence, Rhode Island. Through Brown's public service center, Emma received a fellowship the summer before her senior year of college working with Diane doing intakes of at-risk teenage mothers. As Emma puts it, Diane was "doing an unglamorous job in a really compassionate way." Diane took an interest in Emma, and at the end of the summer asked her: "Well Emma, what are you going to do with your life?" At that point Emma knew she wanted to be an advocate but was not sure if she wanted to be a social worker or a lawyer. Diane wanted her to focus and nudged Emma into choosing: "I want to see you decide which one."

Although none of Emma's family or close friends were lawyers, Emma wanted "to take being an English student and social justice and make it into a career." With her "bookish upbringing," she decided to choose the one that required the most books—the law—and that was basically the extent of her really complicated decision-making process.

She applied to law school her senior year. Knowing that she would be paying for it herself, Emma knew she was going to have to really invest in and like her chosen law school. She also knew law review competitions, summer associate positions, and big firms were not for her. Looking exclusively for public interest programs, Emma decided on Northeastern.

As the fall after graduation approached, Emma realized that she was not ready for law school. Her colleagues now joke that she ended up in labor law because she had had the widest variety of wage-earning jobs. Having spent her teenage years and all through college at odd jobs—babysitting, cleaning dorms at her prep school, maple-sugaring, working in Brown's cafeteria—Emma also spent the two years prior to law school in other jobs. She worked in a restaurant for six months, taught nursery school for six months, and spent her next year as a supervisor at a group home for teenage girls.

After two years, Emma reconsidered law school. Her parents' voices played in her head. "Education is the way to do meaningful work. Once you have the education you can do the work that you love." Although Emma eventually followed her parents' advice and decided to go to North-eastern Law School, she greatly appreciates the time she took off. Feeling uncomfortable with her privileges, Emma had to learn for herself that the law was the best career for her.

Like most law students, she remembers law school as a "tough road." Although Northeastern has its notable differences from other law schools, such as no grades, no law review, and a unique clinical opportunity that requires completing four internships before graduation, still "it was a law school," with the usual academic and financial stresses.

Emma's first clinical internship led her to her career as a labor lawyer. Leaving the East Coast behind, she went to the Legal Aid Society— Employment Law Center in San Francisco. That experience crystallized in her wish to pursue a career involving workers' rights in California. While at the Center she had the opportunity to work on impact litigation matters and spent most of her time working on an Americans with Disabilities Act case. Knowing she wanted to stay in labor law, she asked her colleagues there where she should work next.

They guided her to the law firm of Rudy, Exelrod, Zieff & True, a boutique, plaintiff-side discrimination firm with a fancy office and big jury verdicts. Although she enjoyed her time there, she spent most of it working on sexual harassment matters and found the work emotionally very difficult. For her own comfort level, Emma sought something that allowed her to be "close enough to the fight but far enough away so that I could sleep at night."

She then had the opportunity to intern with Judge Thelton E. Henderson, the chief judge for the Northern District of California. If Emma had to pick one hero, it would be Judge Henderson. She greatly respected how Judge Henderson, someone with strong convictions about social justice, was able to mediate them within the institution of a judge-ship. His attitude toward his work is something that still guides Emma. His approach would be: "These are my convictions; this is the law; how much can we accomplish within these parameters?"

Emma also spent time at another law firm, Altshuler, Berzon, Nussbaum, Berzon & Rubin, which is similar to the firm where she works now. That office also did mostly traditional union-side labor law. Through her internship Emma gained exposure to the basics of labor law and was certain that she wanted to stay in California and continue to practice labor law.

However, before she embarked on her career as a labor lawyer, Emma secured a clerkship with Circuit Judge Warren J. Ferguson, who sits on the Ninth Circuit. Coming from Northeastern with no grades or law review, her career services office told her to not even bother applying for a clerkship. Looking at the majority of judges' information sheets that stated they were seeking students in the top ten percent with all the usual credentials, Judge Ferguson's information sheet stood out. His sheet had only one line, which said "commitment to social justice." By no small coincidence he hired Emma. During her interview, Judge Ferguson asked Emma what the most important case she was going to handle in her career was going to be. She started thinking — class-action, employment discrimination, Supreme Court — but before she could answer, Emma recalls him saying:

> Let me tell you. It's 5:30. [Y]ou have deadlines the next day, you are absorbed in all of your cases, you hear a knock on your door and it's a woman and she can't pay you, and you want to go home, and you have all of these important matters, but she needs help with the custody of her son, a very unglamorous case that no one is going to read about, and she needs it right now.

Judge Ferguson was always concerned with who in the case is the "little guy," a concern Emma greatly respects.

Emma then decided to apply for a fellowship before starting her labor career and received a Skadden Fellowship to work at the Western Center on Law and Poverty. Although the Center did not focus on labor matters, she appreciated the exposure to another area of public interest law: impact litigation concerning government benefits. One of her cases that stands out was a class action that challenged a federal food stamp policy. There was a disconnect between the food stamp program and disability benefits. Under the disability law, there was a waiver that still allowed someone to be eligible for benefits if he or she owned a car, but under the food stamp program, if someone owned a car of a certain value, he or she did not qualify for food stamps. The named plaintiff in the class action was a single mother with several children, one of whom was severely disabled. The mother was provided with a van with a lift that was probably worth about $25,000. If she kept the van, she would not qualify for food stamps. The mother was forced to decide between food for her children or a car to take her daughter to the emergency room. The government settled the case and changed the rules in the mother's favor.

Although Emma enjoyed her time at the Western Center, the experience helped her to realize that she was not as interested in impact litigation as she was in direct client representation. She found that kind of litigation to be attorney-directed and found herself more comfortable with the role of deferring to her client.

With that in mind, Emma set out to find a job. Another factor that entered into Emma's decision process was finances. She realized that she could not realistically pay her loans working for a legal-aid type office and live in Los Angeles. At that point, her loans were higher than her rent, which in a place like Los Angeles is hard to believe. Unfortunately, Northeastern at the time did not have a strong loan repayment program. Being a realist, and having worked at two law firms, Emma decided a small union law firm was her best option. She knew she would be paid less than her peers at corporate firms, but more than at a nonprofit firm.

Emma also decided to look just in California. While at Northeastern she had thought that she could do her best work located near where she had come from, but her work at the Employment Law Center during law school showed her that California was an extremely interesting place to work on labor issues. She also found the public interest community to be more diverse. Emma concentrated on Los Angeles, knowing that she had to stay in a more urban or industrial setting to work with unions. The size of the city and breadth of work that Los Angeles offered allowed her to specialize and not risk there being a lack of work.

Emma looked only at small public interest plaintiff-side firms working on employment matters. She picked Rothner, Segall & Greenstone because she liked the people who worked there, and she has been there ever since. Their beautiful craftsman style 1920s home converted to office space probably didn't hurt either.

With all of her previous experience, Emma began at Rothner, Segall & Greenstone as a fourth-year associate. She considers herself a technician, doing only what her clients can't do. Being in the deferring role, Emma finds that some of the work is difficult, especially when she would love to second-guess some of the choices her clients make. It also means that some of the cases she does are very hard to win. For example, Emma takes on many discharge cases, which she arbitrates under collective bargaining agreements. A union may decide to take the case for many reasons: to show support for the grievant or to make a point to management. But these do not always result in getting the employee's job back or winning.

Nonetheless, Emma prefers doing direct client work. She enjoys the contact and that the cases are client-driven, not attorney-driven. Although technically the unions are usually her clients, she has the opportunity to work directly with union members whom she represents at the request of the union. Also, as a labor-side union lawyer, she enjoys learning the nitty-gritty details of people's jobs and figuring out what the relationships are like at the workplace.

Emma has the opportunity to work with a variety of unions. A few of them are internationals, others are district councils of large unions, which are intermediate organizational bodies that oversee local unions, and some are locals. The unions are also diverse, such as the writers' guild (which represents all of the screen and television writers west of the Mississippi), teachers, painters, and cleaners.

Emma also enjoys her day-to-day work. She even gets a "kick out of what is considered mundane." How much she enjoys her job took her somewhat by surprise. When she started out, she thought that if she stayed for two years that would be a success. She has now been at Rothner, Segall & Greenstone for five years and has never paused or thought about leaving. She credits that to feeling like she is still constantly learning. That's not to say that everyday is blissful; some days are tough. As a recently made partner, she now finds herself even more accountable to her clients. In addition, her firm is small, sort of like the "Wizard of Oz." They try to have a big presence, but if you look behind the curtain, there are only a few staff members.

As a private practitioner, her responsibilities have changed over time. When she first arrived, she did more research and writing, which then evolved into her being introduced to clients, handling more aspects of cases, then a whole case, then establishing the client relationships where she is taking a second person to her hearings. She remembers being given a lot of responsibility as a young attorney. As a partner, she now often passes on to a young associate an entire disciplinary proceeding, which is a full evidentiary hearing—like a trial without a jury.

Now she may field a half a dozen phone calls a day from clients, some on the picket line wanting to know if they can block a delivery truck, another to call about a worker whom the union thinks is going to be fired who is about to be called into the meeting. Emma spends time developing unglamorous fact-intensive cases that never get into the newspapers. She gets e-mails from teacher's union staffers inquiring about whether legal staff time should be allotted, or from a union rep on-site inquiring about whether the union is obliged to represent an employee in a sexual-harassment case. She also has ongoing court litigation, with probably half a dozen cases open at any given time.

At Rothner, Segall & Greenstone, a lot of nontraditional labor law is done to advance the interests of unions and workers. A couple of years ago the firm filed suit under a state law to prohibit employers from referring their employees to public health programs like Medi-Cal. Employers who wanted to cut back on their insurance premiums were essentially saying to their employees, "since I pay you so little you are a low-wage worker, why don't you apply to Medi-Cal?" The employees felt as though they were being asked by their employers to apply for welfare. A partner in Emma's office found an obscure provision of the Califormia Insurance Code that had never been enforced. It prohibited such action, and Emma took the case to trial, albeit without success.

Last year the office filed two class actions seeking overtime pay on behalf of reality television producers, who are actually writers that script portions of reality TV. As a new and unregulated sector of television that does not involve typical actors, writers, and directors, there is no union that represents them. Numerous networks and production companies are being sued in the proposed class actions. Emma calls it "traditional wage and hour with a twist."

Emma feels like she leads a balanced life. Rothner, Segall & Greenstone does not have a billable minimum; the firm asks only that the attorneys are productively responding to their clients' needs. She estimates that most labor law firms in town like hers expect attorneys to bill between 1,700 and 1,900 hours a year. In the evenings, if she is in the office until seven, she is the last person to leave. Like most lawyers, there is an occasional weekend that she finds herself working. She says that if you come in on a Saturday, about half the office staff will be there. People also work at home. By observation, she finds the work environment also accommodating for parents. Three of the partners in the office have children, and they all manage their schedules to complement their demands at home. Some come in from nine to five, but every Saturday, others come in early and leave early.

Regarding Emma's personal life, being gay at times has affected her legal practice. Her coworkers know she's gay, but she rarely raises the subject except to exchange personal stories. She does not come out to the judges, opposing counsel, and union clients because she feels that in some cases it might complicate the relationship. In that way, she feels she is a bit different from her heterosexual colleagues, who often refer to their spouses, even in professional settings. There have been only a few situations involving "ugly, overt homophobia" in the course of Emma's career, one dealing with a coworker who condemned homosexuality and another where an individual in the legal community had made offensive comments. Although she does not reveal her sexual orientation to clients, when Emma has worked with some individual employees who are gay or lesbian, many of whom are closeted in the workplace, she believes the fact that she is gay has helped her earn their trust. At times she is able to only offer empathy, as the individual may have no legal claim.

Emma also dedicates a considerable amount of time outside of work to organizations in the legal community. She is a contributor to the California Labor and Employment Law Review and to the Developing Labor Law, Cumulative Supplement. She has lectured at the California State Bar Association Labor and Employment Conference, and is a member of the Los Angeles County Bar Association Labor and Employment Executive Board.

Overall, Emma loves what she does. She finds that even if there is alleged wrongdoing on the part of an employee, she still believes in the right to due process for each individual and the need to make employers accountable to stabilize the workplace. On a personal level, she feels very fortunate to be a labor lawyer because she has come full circle. Her grandparents were wage-earning people, and her great-grandfather was a union agitator in a cotton mill in the north of England. Her grandfather's dream was that his kids could go to college, a dream that Emma's parents passed on to her. Now she comes back to help people not so different from her own grandparents.

NED BURKE

Labor Union Lawyer (In House)

By Emily Rae Woods

"You gotta believe in the movement." And Ned Burke does. He believes workers deserve safe working conditions, equitable compensation, and fair labor practices. Those goals have led him to spend the last six years of his life practicing labor law and fighting for the rights of workers everywhere.

Ned is best described as the "social justice variety" of union labor lawyers. He's not the stereotyped movie version of a thug whose tool is his threatening disposition and whose workplace is plagued by corruption. Instead, Ned comes across as a gentle person—one who genuinely cares about people, as signaled by his warm nature and disarming laugh. Joking about the stereotypes that suggest labor lawyers who work for unions come in two flavors, "Communists and gangsters," Ned embraces the idea of himself as a Communist labor lawyer—one whose chief objective is to empower workers rather than to gain power for himself.

Ned took his time before focusing on labor law. After finding that he was unable to join the military because of his hearing loss and not being particularly interested in law or politics, Ned chose to study history in college. He had an eventful couple of years before the school asked him to leave for "having too much fun," as he puts it. He went on to complete his bachelor's degree at a different college and eventually ended up going to law school, his "fallback plan." As it happened, Ned spent most of his time at Chicago-Kent Law School reading about history instead of the law—and he eventually went on to get a master's degree in history and to pursue a doctorate in the subject from the University of Chicago, one of the top schools in the nation. His law practice didn't really take off until it was apparent to him that his dissertation was not going to be completed before he was forty. And so, after being a stay-at-home parent for several years, Ned remembers deciding that it was finally time to "focus more intently on my career."

After working for several years as a solo practitioner, Ned became an associate at Katz, Friedman, Eisenstein & Johnson, a premiere labor law firm in Chicago. During his three years there, he practiced federal litigation. The time spent working at Katz Friedman helped Ned build the connections that are so important in labor law. Ned didn't have any attorneys in his family — most of his family members were doctors, nurses, or mathematicians — but his family was heavily involved in politics and had a deep respect for unions. His grandmother, Anne Zimmerman, was a significant source of inspiration for Ned's career. Deserted by her husband and forced to forge a living for herself and her three-year-old daughter (Ned's mother) in the backwoods of Montana, Zimmerman turned to nursing. Years later, she was elected the president of the Illinois Nurses Association, and Ned credits his grandmother with helping to invent the idea of collective bargaining for nurses. Ned was "extremely close" to his grandmother, who knew the "seamy side" of labor law and did her best to deter her grandson from following in her footsteps. But, as she was soon to learn, Ned believed in the cause. And there was no stopping him.

Much of Ned's work at Katz Friedman involved representing union members in arbitration proceedings. An arbitration decision, Ned explains, cannot be appealed, and the arbitrator is not bound by previous decisions. So, "oftentimes, common sense can win the case." Ned fondly remembers one relatively minor case where he managed "to pull a rabbit out of a hat." The case centered on whether a furniture company employer had the right to fire an employee who had falsely called in sick to work and who had been caught lifting heavy stuff outside of work after claiming to be suffering from a wrist injury. The evidence mounted against Ned's client was "fairly compromising" (there was video footage). "Flying by the seat of my pants," as Ned characterizes it, he began questioning the human resources witness. "Has it ever happened that people call in sick who aren't really sick?" he asked. The witness had to admit the only case that had been documented was his client's. "Have you ever noticed there are certain days when the number of sick calls spike?" "No," she combatively replied. "So, it has never been your experience that on the first day of deer hunting season, sick calls spike? What about muskey season?" Ned persisted. They were in Wisconsin, where the start of hunting season was thought by many to be deserving of a national holiday. "That's on a Sunday," the arbitrator interrupted the questioning, "but I get where you're going with this." Ned knew then that he had found a commonsensical way to demonstrate to the arbitrator something that management officials often forget: "It is *human* relations and humans make mistakes and screw up sometimes . . . but this woman deserved to keep her job." And she did keep her job, thanks to Ned.

Ned continued to litigate similar cases at Katz Friedman until he was approached by the Illinois Nurses Association and asked to run the operation for their union of roughly 4,500 nurses. The union was well known for being "a revolving door" in the sense that its staff were generally driven out quickly—something very unusual for most unions. Despite this, the significant salary cut, and his grandmother's warning that he would "bitterly regret" the decision, Ned decided to accept the position.

The shift from a law firm position to a union position is a relatively common career move for someone in Ned's line of work, particularly today, as more unions are finding it beneficial to have in-house counsel at their beck and call to handle the emergency legal matters that frequently arise. It helped Ned that Katz Friedman had a reputation as a feeder for such union jobs, that Ned came from a family of nurses and healthcare professionals and that his grandmother had served as the association's president for years.

His work at the Illinois Nurses Association involved directing the field staff, arbitrating grievances, serving as counsel before the state labor boards, and acting as the chief negotiator for all major contract negotiations. While at the association, he built a track record that he was "pretty pleased with," he says modestly. In fact, Ned built a strong reputation for himself in the profession as a top-notch negotiator who was willing to fight hard for his member nurses.

The contract negotiation with the University of Chicago hospital was one instance when Ned really proved himself. The campaign itself lasted eighteen months. It began, as most do, long before the current contract was set to expire and ended, as almost all do, after the expiration date. As chief negotiator for the contract, Ned "bargained hard" with management until they said the phrase labor lawyers know all too well: "This is our last, best, and final offer." So Ned knew that they weren't going to budge any further, and he would have to present their proposed contract to the nurses and let them vote on whether they would accept its terms.

Membership votes are usually kept confidential, but Ned decided to generate some public heat around the vote on what he considered was a "substandard" contract. So he got creative. It just so happened that the University of Chicago hospital is situated just off the Midway—a well-known street in Chicago. The widest street west of Paris, this expansive boulevard hosted the 1892 World's Fair. It was at this historic location where Ned decided to hold the vote.

Throughout the beautiful summer day, the nurses made their way outside to place their votes under a giant tent while enjoying lots of free food and socializing — and the press (invited, of course, by Ned) was there to broadcast the fanfare on the evening news. At the end of the day, Ned had some young nursing students publicly perform a count of the ballots. When the count was finished, he walked into the late-night meeting with the hospital management and reported that the vote was more than nine to one against their contract — a "resounding defeat" for them, announced Ned and, as a smile crept across his face, "it was fun to see their faces." For the first time, they were dealing with a union that was fighting hard for their members, and management was "knocked back on their heels."

In the end, Ned won the battle and secured a solid thirteen percent raise over the next three years for the nurses. Thinking back on the success, Ned says he was "pleased and happy" both with the contract terms and with the way the attorneys and negotiators interacted. "We had a very high regard for each other. I'm still not *friends* — you can never be friends with a management lawyer — but I'm *friendly* with those guys. It was a well-fought battle and we got what we wanted from them."

But eventually the "toxic" politics of the volatile association proved too much for Ned, and his grandmother's premonition came true. As the union faced the very real threat of being raided by another nurses' union, Ned found himself unable to gain approval for funding necessary to fight against the raid. Finding it difficult to unite the elected leadership in his vision, Ned chose to leave. The massive turnover notorious at the Association continued and, shortly after Ned left, the elected leadership fired almost everyone else holding an executive position. Generally, union staffs tend to have a great deal of longevity. "This one did not," says Ned.

Ned now works for Teamsters Local 705 in Chicago, a union of over 20,000 members, mostly truck drivers and parcel deliverers, where he has been since 2005. The Teamsters union is run by twenty-three staff members and eleven elected officials — all of whom work full-time in paid positions. Ned's hours are unpredictable but the work is very interesting. In addition to more traditional legal work, Ned still remains involved in the things he's really good at: coordinating contracts and strikes and organizing campaigns. He works about fifty to sixty hours a week — which frees up his evenings and weekends so he can spend time with his thirteen-year-old and eight-year-old daughters, something he values and enjoys. He also finds enough time to sail (which he once did competitively) and cycle thirteen miles to work each morning — "an addiction" he discovered he loved while a law student.

The Teamsters office is located on what is commonly referred to as "union land." The surrounding area has been union turf for years, as evidenced by the concentration of union headquarters on the nearby blocks and the lack of foreign cars traveling the streets. Ned's office, on the seventh floor of an ominous black building, is a buzz of activity — to the point where it is sometimes necessary to work from home to avoid the constant interruptions and commotion in the office.

Ned enjoys being in the thick of things. "A few weeks ago," he whispered, "I snuck into a railroad yard and just wandered around. It really is amazing. Those cranes are enormous; the trucks are unbelievable." Stolen glimpses into his members' workplaces give Ned a keener sense of the enormity and importance of their work. "At a Nabisco plant, an employee left his work station for a couple minutes and ten thousand Waverly crackers hit the floor. That's how fast and hard these places are," he adds with a hint of admiration in his voice. One can tell from talking to Ned that he has tremendous respect for the hard work and determination of working-class people — something that is absolutely essential for his line of work.

Strikes carry with them immense power, particularly for the Teamsters. With transportation, Ned explains, if you coordinate a successful strike, you can "cripple the employer almost instantly." A recent strike coordinated by his union lasted a mere hour and a half before management "gave us *everything* we wanted," Ned reports. The strike was a strategic one, accomplished during a shift change so that the trucks, unable to cross the picket line, caused traffic to back up considerably. Ned chuckled to himself as he remembered how the boss immediately came to them and offered to back down. Ned recounted the legendary Caterpillar strike — awed himself by the hugeness of the players — "a *giant* union with a $2 billion strike fund up against a *giant* corporation." Over 400 unfair labor practices claims were filed — more than in any other case in history. It is those "unbelievable" strikes, the truly big fights, that inspire labor lawyers everywhere.

But, as the Caterpillar strike taught us, strikes can be devastating. People in Ned's position need to know what they're doing because "a poorly planned strike can destroy a union just as easily as it can help a union," he warns. "I'm no brilliant labor tactician," he assures me, "but I'd say a strike that lasts more than a few days has the potential to kill the union." In general, the longer the strike, the more it tends to militate against the union. The Teamsters were nearly bankrupted by a freight company strike that lasted nearly two years. Such strikes put a considerable strain on the union's finances because it must provide the workers with enough back-up compensation so they don't have to cross the picket line to work out of necessity.

To avoid strikes, the Teamsters depend on strong negotiation tactics. When asked what sorts of skill set makes for a good negotiator, Ned replied, "theoretically, a monkey could negotiate a contract. The economics are what they are. The members are what they are." Even so, there are some qualities that can improve one's chances of success in the heated negotiation room. You have to be "thick-skinned" and let insults bounce off you because, as Ned knows, "you get insulted *a lot*." You also have to be able to show your members that you are willing to fight for them. You have to scream and shout. "But," cautions Ned, "you have to be a good actor so you can bang the table without actually being emotionally overwrought." Keeping your wits about you in the room is critical because you must be able to pick up on subtle cues. Ned, in particular, is well suited for this work. Born with significant hearing loss, he began interpreting nonverbal cues early on in life. Even today, he gets about a third of what is being said from lip-reading and facial expressions. For Ned, this extraordinary perceptiveness gives him an edge over the competition.

As to whether women are out of place in this rowdy world of loud voices and intimidating table-banging, Ned is quickly reassuring: "women are uniquely suited" for this work because they don't come from a place of privilege. As such, they are often better able to grasp the give-and-take of negotiations and to understand that compromise is inevitable. People of color can be very successful in this line of work for the same reason, according to Ned.

A monochromatic movement from its start, the labor movement hasn't always been receptive to women or minorities — and things are slow to change. Ned admitted that for the most part the established leadership still runs the show in labor law firms: "They own the place and they ain't leaving and they ain't going to make you partner." Yet, in spite of a few stubborn founders, more females and minorities are finding their place in the movement and "it is much better for it," says Ned, who actually prefers his female colleagues to the males. He jokes about regret-ting his shift from "a very high estrogen to a very high testosterone environment," but does sincerely regret the low numbers of women in the ranks.

It's important to remember that labor law involves much more than fighting with management. A large part of the work of Ned and his col-leagues focuses on bringing the union members together in a united front. As in other areas of litigation, sometimes it is better for the client to accept a settlement offer rather than take the matter further in the courts — and Ned is charged with the responsibility of advising his clients when that is the case, which isn't always easy. Convincing management to agree to contract terms seems simple when compared with the seemingly insurmountable task of convincing the membership, whose numbers range in the thousands, to agree as well. And Ned's job involves making even the most discordant group appear cohesive so that he has more bargaining power.

According to Ned, the most frustrating part of his type of work is that "you lose *a lot*," particularly in arbitration proceedings. "Frankly, some of these guys deserve to be fired," he says with regret. In representing them, the union lawyers put on the best case they can under the circumstances. But substandard employees do exist, and the majority of the time the arbitrator upholds the management's decision—which can be discouraging.

Another difficult aspect of his work is the shifting political trend, which currently cuts against unions. The federal government "is not on our side," declares Ned. This means that the scope of his union's ability to function is limited by the National Labor Relations Board, which has been very pro-management under the Bush Administration. Ned is constantly looking for ways to avoid the oppressive NLRB and comments that "this is an exciting time because we have to find new creative ways to do what we do, or we're going to be out of business."

Why did Ned choose Chicago as his home? It turns out he has lived in Chicago, which he lovingly refers to as "the best city in the world," his whole life. He enjoys the city's waterfront, its unique communities, and its famous live theater venues. When his oldest daughter reached middle school age, however, he decided it best to move to one of the Chicago suburbs so she could attend a better school, but he still looks forward to moving back to the heart of the city "the minute my kids are older."

As it turned out for Ned, Chicago is an excellent place for him to find work doing what he loves. There are some parts of the country that are better for union work than others. A regional divide exists. Ned advises, "Don't go South and think you're going to be a union lawyer." Many of the Southern states have right-to-work laws that allow non-union employees to take jobs in unionized industries, thereby undercutting the trade's collective bargaining abilities. Ned points to California as a union-friendly place to pursue a labor law career or Las Vegas, Nevada—the most unionized city in the country. Positions in labor law tend to be more competitive in the big cities, whereas in less populated areas, such as Springfield, Illinois, union lawyers are "as busy as it gets."

When asked what advice he would give to someone interested in labor law, Ned stressed the importance of forming union ties and political connections early. Labor lawyers generally get their jobs through personal networking, so it helps to be in a union, to do a clerkship at a labor law firm, or to volunteer for an externship. It's really "a matter of pounding the pavement to get this type of work," says Ned. You must be persistent.

In this area of the law, hands-on experience matters far more than grades or where you went to school. Ned advocates casting a wide net. A nationwide job hunt is easier with labor law because it's not necessary to pass the state bar to do the type of arbitration and negotiation work it involves. Never work for management. According to Ned and others on the union side of labor law, it is the death knell for any union aspirations you may have had. But, most important, Ned says again, "You gotta believe in the movement. You really do gotta believe in the movement."

LISA KRIM

University Counsel

By Elizabeth Pederson

It is clear that Lisa Krim loves her job. The work as an Associate Counsel at Georgetown University is challenging and diverse; the hours have some degree of flexibility; and she likes her colleagues. When asked about any downsides, nothing immediately comes to her mind. She finally notes that the need for prompt advice doesn't allow her to "anticipate issues proactively" and then spend significant time thinking and writing about them as she could when working for a law firm.

Lisa's story is that of a woman who has the world at her feet professionally but loves her family. A slight, dark-haired woman with a warm smile and direct eyes, she is a woman who made conscious choices to achieve balance between her personal life and her career. Those decisions led her away from a lucrative job with a big law firm and instead to seek her current part-time status at Georgetown. Lisa chose a non-firm job: she chose to be a lawyer but also to be a wife and a mother.

A seated statue of John Carroll, Georgetown's founder, guards the entrance to Healy Hall, the building that houses the offices of Georgetown's General Counsel. Lisa's office is behind two slightly scuffed wooden doors that mark the entrance. Her office is tidy without being sterile—family photos smile in a row near the desk, and framed finger paintings liven up one wall. Bursting file folders manage to contain the chaos on a shelf, beyond which a large window looks out onto the well-manicured grass and stately buildings of the oldest Catholic university in the United States. The hushed silence in the humid heat of a Washington DC summer evokes the calm of a place of worship.

Lisa's job centers almost exclusively on counseling and advising. "Most of the days, we're reacting to and triaging issues that come in. A lot of what we do is getting the right people to figure out a particular issue." The job is focused on prevention, and she does not litigate. Put simply, her role is to prevent the university "from making bad decisions that would make people want to litigate" against the school.

Lisa particularly enjoys the diversity of her work. On employment issues, she fields questions on a wide range of topics from applying and interpreting existing University policies to figuring out whether new policies are needed. For example, if a supervisor is not pleased with an employee and wants to let the person go, Lisa will guide the supervisor through the proper procedures and help him or her understand any legal risks involved in the decision. Or, when new regulations governing overtime pay were issued, Lisa worked closely with a team from human resources to educate the University community on the changes and on the logistics of implementation. She also helps draft policies that satisfy her desire to serve as an agent of positive change, such as the paid-leave option now given to certain faculty who are new parents or who serve as primary caregivers. In another instance, she worked to bring training on the issues of harassment and discrimination to over 5,000 university employees.

Lisa also advises student, faculty, and staff committees who review student conduct, academic integrity, and other matters. She fields issues such as complaints by parents about their child's grades, to complications that arise from privacy laws that protect student records, to disputes about the University's responsibility to protect students from harm in situations like accidental death or potential suicide.

It can be very difficult to break into work at a university General Counsel's office. The reason, Lisa says, is simple: "People love this work and they don't leave!" To obtain such a position, Lisa recommends that one "get trained somewhere else." There are a few opportunities in the field for people just out of law school, but the need for previous training and experience generally makes it difficult to get this kind of job right out of law school. "You have to make judgment calls," Lisa says of the job. "There are often things that aren't black and white, and there isn't a partner who will make the decision for you. You have to be able to evaluate the legal risk and make decisions. You've got to be able to deliver answers, and you need legal background for that. It takes time to learn, and you have to have confidence to be able to do this job."

Lisa herself has been with Georgetown since 1998, when she took what was supposed to have been a temporary position as Staff Counsel. The advertisement in the *Legal Times* sought "a true generalist" with two to three years of experience, and the position was conceived as a two-year job to assist the lawyers in the General Counsel's office in their different practice areas. Lisa took the job, and her husband also took a job in the area. After an Associate Counsel left the office, Lisa's position became permanent.

Lisa didn't grow up wanting to be a lawyer. Raised in Westchester County, New York, her father was Vice President for Financial Control at Citigroup, and her mother was a high school English teacher. Lisa's exposure and interest in the law didn't manifest itself until her undergraduate days as a public policy major at Stanford. During a meeting with her advisor, Lisa complained about all the ways she thought the law should be changed, particularly with regard to women's rights issues. Her advisor told her, "You better know what you're talking about. If you want to change the law, you need to be a lawyer." This conversation stayed with Lisa. "My goals included being a change agent, and I wanted to be a credible one."

From the beginning, Lisa knew her priorities. After graduating from Stanford in 1991, she moved to Los Angeles with her boyfriend, who is now her husband. She had a job with a big law firm through the Stanford Intern Program, which she describes as a "glorified name for a paralegal job." She did not enjoy her work as a paralegal and applied to law school because she "had seen that the lawyers could do so much more than the paralegals could do. There was this almost impenetrable barrier in the legal field between those who have law degrees and those who don't." Lisa made the choice to apply to law school in the Los Angeles area for personal reasons and was admitted to UCLA.

Lisa's time as a paralegal was not entirely intellectually satisfying, but it did have positive ramifications in her law school experience. In part as a result of the paralegal work she had done for a partner, she was offered a summer associate position in the firm's New York office during her first-year summer. Lisa also credits her paralegal job with providing her valuable exposure to the legal profession and to lawyers who prepared her for the law school experience. "I was lucky to be around lawyers who gave me really good advice. They said, 'Trust your instincts; you know how you need to learn.'"

Her instincts served her well. By any measure, Lisa excelled in law school. Graduating third in her class in 1995, she was Editor of the UCLA Law Review and earned American Jurisprudence Awards in Torts, Contracts, and Legal Research and Writing. She liked law school but admits, "I think I liked it because it came easily to me. . . . It's like the lightbulb went off—it clicked." She acknowledges that law school does not come easily for everyone. "It was really lucky that I happened to pick a path that matched my skill set." The classes Lisa took that have been most helpful to her current career were those that honed her logical thinking and precise writing skills. "I use the writing skills every day, and find myself revising documents of all sorts that were initially drafted by very intelligent, highly credentialed individuals. Because of my training as a lawyer, I can almost always make the writing more logical and more effective at achieving its purpose."

Although her paralegal experience left Lisa thinking that she hated big firms and would never again work in one, she ended up spending her first summer as a lawyer at a New York branch office of a large firm. She got her "first taste of big firm life from the other side" and her first exposure to labor and employment work. She enjoyed both. One of the best aspects of working for a firm is that "they take the time to train you." In Lisa's opinion, the writing and the feedback provided wonderful opportunities that helped her grow as a lawyer in ways that she deeply appreciated.

Although she enjoyed the work, Lisa did not love working in New York City. Consequently, she spent the summer after her second year with a different firm in Los Angeles, primarily doing basic litigation work. Again, she received great training and enjoyed the people with whom she worked. Unlike many summer associates, Lisa was never fooled by her summers of firm work. "Life is great as a summer associate, but . . . I had no illusions about what life was really like for lawyers at a law firm because of my year as a paralegal."

During the first semester of her second year at law school, Lisa's Constitutional Law professor recommended her for an extern opportunity in the White House Counsel's office. Lisa consequently spent the second semester of her second year working in the Clinton White House, primarily on ethics issues. She also helped to vet potential nominees for the open Supreme Court seat that eventually went to Justice Stephen Breyer. Lisa gained valuable knowledge about the "quiet work" that goes on in the White House Counsel's office, which taught her that "the best work can be the work that nobody ever knows about." In her current job at Georgetown, Lisa does similar "quiet work," preventing legal problems through training, the careful wording of university policies, and sound legal advice.

After law school, Lisa became a district court clerk. She knew that she wanted to stay in Los Angeles and applied only to Central District courts in California. She wanted to work in a district court in order to learn the "nuts and bolts of what went on" in court proceedings. She felt that she already "knew how to read cases and put them together and write bench memos," which discouraged her from pursuing an appellate clerkship. Still, her choice was not without controversy. "I was getting a lot of encouragement from the law school to apply to appellate court judges, to [Supreme Court] feeder judges. I think again for personal reasons, for lifestyle, I opted for the district court."

Lisa credits her clerkship with the Honorable J. Spencer Letts of the Central District of California with teaching her a lot about the limitations of the law. "So many people come to the law looking for redress that the law really isn't designed to give." Lisa observed that people were inclined to use employment law when their feelings were hurt, not realizing that "there are a limited number of things that constitute illegal harassment or discrimination." Judge Letts was very pragmatic, and if he thought something was wrong, he would do what he thought was right. Lisa describes him as "a little bit of a maverick." He was also committed to imparting his knowledge to his clerks and spent time engaging them in legal dialogue. Even though his politics were not an exact match for Lisa, she found him to be "a fabulous teacher," who provided her with a different way of thinking about the law. The clerkship also taught her that she didn't want to do criminal law. "I wasn't sure that I loved being in the courtroom and it would have been very difficult for me to deal with the harsh reality of crimes day in and day out." Later, she also ruled out litigating. Lisa was lucky that she chose a clerkship with, for her, the right judge. "So much depends on the judge, and my judge just had so much to offer."

During her clerkship year, Lisa re-interviewed at firms. She did not expect to like the environment, but she nonetheless took a job at O'Melveney & Myers LLP, a large Los Angeles-based firm, in order to pay off her student loans and get the training that the firm could offer. She chose labor and employment law because she found the work intellectually stimulating and enjoyable. As it turns out, "labor and employment is a terrific training ground," she says, partially because she often worked in a team including just herself and a senior partner. Consequently, she was very involved in the cases and built many different skill sets very quickly. She was also fortunate to be in a small department with close colleagues who invested in helping her to develop as a lawyer. When her firm began expanding its employment practice in Washington, DC, a year after she started her job in Los Angeles, Lisa was part of the move. Midway through her first year at the firm, she had married her long-time boyfriend, who had completed his Ph.D. and had an offer for a postdoctorate position at the University of Maryland. The timing of the move worked out well for her personally. For Lisa, the move felt like "coming home." She enjoys the intellectually stimulating environment of DC and the fact that "you run into interesting people everywhere you go."

After two years at the firm, Lisa felt that she came away with an impressive set of legal skills. Of course, if practice makes perfect, then there was a reason that Lisa was building skill sets so rapidly: she was working sixty hours a week or more and traveling often. "What's hard about law firms is that you only really keep track of how many hours you bill. To bill forty hours, you're there at least fifty or sixty hours." Stops at the bathroom, lunch breaks, and brief conversations with coworkers all consume minutes—and eventually hours—of time that can't be billed. Lisa describes the workweek as "grueling," though she concedes that "in two years, I got an extraordinary level of skills and breadth of experiences."

Despite her appreciation of the work and her colleagues, Lisa eventually decided to leave law firm life because she couldn't see a way to balance it with everything else. She knew she wanted to have children and couldn't see that happening with the demands of the firm. "It became clear to me that the firm was moving in a direction that was not consistent with what I wanted for my life." Part of the problem lies in the very nature of firm work: the lawyer's time is the commodity for sale. "If I was going to be the commodity for sale, then it wasn't going to work," Lisa says. "The goals and values of the firm were not consistent with my goals and values."

Before she decided to apply only for district court clerkships, Lisa had a talk with one of her female law professors that she has never forgotten. "She strongly encouraged me not to take myself out of the running for the more competitive clerkships. She made what I found to be a very compelling argument that we don't have enough women clerking for the Supreme Court because women like me take themselves out of the pipeline, and it's something I've carried around and that has recurred thematically for me." Some women don't advance to the upper echelons of their professions because they never have the opportunity. Other women, like Lisa, have the opportunity but are unable to embrace it in a way that is consistent with the other priorities in their lives. Lisa stands firmly behind her decisions. "For me the right choice was to choose the district court clerkship. It wasn't without guilt and a feeling like I was letting down women lawyers and giving up the possibility of more."

As she made the decision to leave her law firm job, Lisa struggled with the same issues. Ultimately, Lisa realized that she couldn't function as a change agent within the firm hierarchy. "If I'd wanted it, I had the skills to be partner, but even if I became partner, I wasn't going to be able to change the direction and value system of the firm." Even with this realization, Lisa still wondered, "Am I part of the pipeline problem because I'm taking myself out of the running for a big firm partnership?" It would be one thing if she could justify her decision with the hope that by *not* accepting hours and a work environment that were inhospitable to family life, she might inspire change from within the firm. She was without such illusions, however. "There are always others who are willing to make the sacrifices," Lisa notes, even though "there are probably too many women who have my credentials at that time [in their careers] who take themselves out of the running." In her current position at Georgetown, Lisa is aware of lifestyle concerns and their effects on firm associates. Now, as the client, she can somewhat influence the issue by looking for firms that offer more support to their employees and therefore attract teams of litigators that are diverse and include women.

Lisa herself has been able to work part-time. As she points out, "There's the idea of part-time and the reality of part-time." Luckily, Lisa's supervisor supports the reality of it, and she ". . . is supportive of it in a real way." Even part-time, Lisa is still working between thirty and thirty-five hours per week. But if Lisa gets a call to pick up her sick child, she can do that and then get on her home computer at night to finish working, though she prefers to keep work separate and "be focused at home when [she's] home." Lisa also feels the need to be present for her clients. "In the regular course of things, it's important that I be here and that people see me and that I interact with people."

Lisa credits her hard work for her balancing success. "My plan," Lisa confides, "was to try to be so good that by the time I wanted to make choices to be part-time or take time off, I would be so valued by wherever I was working that my employer would be receptive to making nontraditional arrangements with me." Lisa believes that many women have employed this strategy with great success. "It's all a business," she explains, "and whether you're dealing with a law firm or some other kind of institution, they aren't going to accommodate your request for special schedules or time away just because you want it; they're going to give it to you because you're good and they recognize your value to the institution. The better you are—it's all supply and demand—the more career flexibility you are likely to have when it comes time to make a balance between family and work."

In regard to achieving balance, Lisa is hopeful. "It can be done." She has been fortunate to have a number of women mentors throughout her career who have shown her different ways to achieve balance. Lisa's current supervisor, Georgetown's Vice President and General Counsel, provides both support and daily inspiration to Lisa, as she balances great responsibility and tremendous career accomplishment with her own children and family. Lisa herself has modeled her career around the knowledge that "work has always been a piece of what's important, but not everything. . . . I've always had different pieces of my life that are important to my happiness, and I think I've made a lot of choices to try to achieve balance." Lisa takes her ambition in stride, recognizing that women can work for more than forty years, and there will be a time when her family needs her less, and she can focus more of her attention on her professional life. She feels that it should be okay for women to get on and off the career track. "I guess my view of it is: be in it, stay engaged, keep growing, keep learning. There is time to scale back in your career while your family needs you and there's time to be totally devoted to it when the kids grow up." For now, Lisa appreciates the opportunity to work part-time. "This is where the myth of the superwoman has gone," Lisa says, "you can't do it all at the same time, but there *will* be time to eventually have done it all."

Section3

Criminal Law

DAVID O'KEEFE

Assistant District Attorney

By Carly J. Kaufman

David O'Keefe started practicing law after an established accounting career following a period of volunteering that opened his eyes to new possibilities. With an understanding of the tremendous impact those who argue and decide law can make in individual lives, David decided to find a way to protect civil liberties, especially liberties often compromised due to sexual orientation.

David was born in 1963 in the small town of Greenlawn, New York, as the fourth of five children and attended public school. His father's accounting job supported a comfortable existence. David, a tennis player and a runner, spent a summer in Ecuador and eighteen months working at a Burger King before attending the University of Virginia. At UVA, David majored in business with a focus on accounting; he also studied computer programming. He spent two summers working at an importing company and one as a computer programmer for Mobil Oil. At college during the school year David worked at a crisis intervention phone center as a training director and in his fourth year served as president of the gay and lesbian student organization.

After graduating from UVA, he followed his father's example and spent the next six and a half years as an accountant for Coopers & Lybrand in New York, with a six-month rotation in Tokyo. David enjoyed his auditing and mergers and acquisition work (the latter being an especially busy and fun area in which to work in the 1980s). While at Coopers & Lybrand, he also volunteered with an organization called the Gay Men's Health Crisis (GMHC). He was involved mostly in outreach and training and became involved in fundraising after leaving Coopers & Lybrand to go to law school. During that time he also attended various marches and protests concerning gay rights. As David became disenchanted with the structure of Coopers & Lybrand and his clients (his main client was Drexel Burnham), he decided to act on his desire to become involved in civil rights law. David gave up his $60,000 salary and enrolled in New York University Law School.

David graduated from law school in 1995 with a new tool to help him make an impact. When asked about his classes, he says he only "survived" law school. Although David had graduated from college seven years before, he lived in the dorms, rooming with a classmate who was straight out of college. He was not at the top of his class because he was more interested in actually working than he was in his classes, which he felt reflected more a professor's subjective belief than consistent objective analysis. In order to have something to do besides briefing cases and to help pay for school, he spent up to thirty hours a week during part of his first year working as an accountant. David took out loans in addition to liquidating his 401(k) plan, pension plan, and every one of his savings accounts to pay for law school. Despite his financial situation, he never seriously considered taking a job with a large law firm.

Throughout law school David stayed active in the gay rights movement and even spent his first date with his now-partner in 1992 at an anti-violence march organized by the Gay and Lesbian Anti-Violence Project in New York City. The march and its aftermath also helped David decide what he wanted to do professionally. After the march, David and his date were riding the subway when a thief snatched a chain from his date's neck. Dealing with police and prosecutors gave David a look at the system from the inside. The experience served as an example of how unsafe the City, especially its subways, were at that time. David often felt unsafe in New York City and hoped to better the city through his professional life.

The summer after his first year of law school he worked (in exchange for a $3,000 stipend from NYU's public interest program) at the Gay & Lesbian Anti-Violence Project. David loved the experience, particularly because he worked for Matt Foreman. He describes Foreman as "one of the best street organizers." That summer and into his second year, David was an advocate for clients in trying to decrease the violence and the stigma in society attached to being gay. As an advocate he would do things such as lobby a policeman to respond to kinds of situations that the police had previously ignored. Working with Foreman taught him that he would prefer to be involved with law and crime on the street level, where David believed he could see the most direct effects of his work. Although gay rights remain important to David, he decided that professionally he preferred to make the streets safer for all, not just one group. His experience at the Gay & Lesbian Anti-Violence Project highlighted for him that he felt most inspired when directly working with victims within the justice system.

David spent his second summer at the U.S. Attorney's Office for the Southern District of New York. This experience had less of an impact on David than had his job the previous summer. David spent most of his time researching and drafting memos, but he craved direct contact with those in need. He also realized that although he liked government work, he was not on the path often required to get into the U.S. Attorney's office – he did not want to clerk and then spend a few years at a white-shoe law firm before being qualified to work there. He thought that working for the District Attorney would be a better fit. The Manhattan D.A.'s office hires about fifty lawyers directly out of law school each year, and being at the top of one's class at a top law school is not necessarily required. According to David, the D.A.'s office hires a much more diverse staff in terms of work experience than the U.S. Attorney's office does. He also noticed that at the federal level, as opposed to at the state level, one spends a lot more time writing and researching and less time developing investigative skills, which interested him more.

David sought out an opportunity to work at the Manhattan D.A.'s office before graduating from law school and found that NYU's prosecution clinic was his favorite law school experience. It solidified for him that he wanted to be a prosecutor. He was given about ten cases at a time from the D.A.'s office in his first opportunity to represent "the People of the State of New York." In the prosecution clinic, he dedicated about fifteen hours a week during his third year prosecuting domestic violence and assault cases. This experience enabled him to work with the justice system at the street level and to see the impact of his work. David also found that the D.A.'s office allowed him to "do what's right" in a case.

Although he has over the years developed a great respect for public defenders, David believes that their focus is often on keeping their clients out of jail. He prefers the prosecution side because it allows him to try to achieve whatever he believes the correct solution should be; for example, he can ask that a judge remedy a situation by ordering drug rehabilitation for his client rather than jail time if that is what is best for society. David's work in the prosecution clinic led to a full-time position in the trial division of the Manhattan D.A.'s office, where he has worked for the past eleven years.

David commutes in from his co-op, where he lives with his partner. He wears a suit jacket and a tie every day. When he started in 1995, he made

$34,000[1] a year—a large drop from the $60,000 salary he was making as an accountant. David works with a few hundred lawyers (women hold a little less than half of the legal positions) working as Assistant District Attorneys (ADAs) under Manhattan District Attorney Robert Morgenthau. The ADAs are responsible for investigating (with the help of the police) and prosecuting crimes in the borough of Manhattan. Because Morgenthau has been in office since 1975, the office is quite apolitical, so there is little talk of political affiliations. Although Morgenthau is in his eighties, David does not foresee him stepping down soon. David enjoys a stable environment full of well-connected people, for which he gives credit to his boss. Although he is paid by the city of New York, he considers himself as working for Morgenthau.

David's office at One Hogan Place is clustered with other government buildings in downtown Manhattan in an area with little charm. Though the building appears stately, it is inadequate: it has only two conference rooms for about 300 lawyers and their various witnesses, police officers, and victims. People from various walks of life line up in the marble lobby waiting to pass through a metal detector. The building houses many courtrooms and the offices of most of Morgenthau's staff. The ADAs are noticeable because of their formal business attire in contrast to the many uniformed police and casually dressed people from many backgrounds.

There are six trial bureaus in the Trial Division. David and the fifty other lawyers in his trial bureau all focus on street crime. Other divisions focus on areas such as organized crime, while specialty groups outside the six trial bureaus focus more specifically on areas such as sex crimes.

In 1995, when David started, he shared an office with several other ADAs and spent almost two full years prosecuting misdemeanors. At that time he practiced triage, constantly trying to evaluate which of his 200 cases was the most important while juggling various institutional assignments. Thereafter, his caseload evolved into about twenty-five or thirty felonies at a time (usually the cases were drug crimes or theft). Now that David has been there for about eleven years he has fewer but more difficult cases, and he has his own office, which houses a basic desk and table with four chairs; there is little room to walk because boxes connected to current cases are stacked up to the ceiling. Remnants of construction and odd pieces of furniture dot the hallway. The office has a moldy feel because the natural light is filtered by dirty windows.

---

1. Starting lawyers at the Manhattan D.A.'s office now begin making around $48,000 per year with modest raises almost every year based in part on merit and in part on years worked.

One whole wall of the office is lined with boxes labeled "Girven." Captain Girven, a policeman in the New York Police Department, was shot in August 2003 after interrupting three men on their way to rob a gambling spot on 154th Street. David presented the case to the grand jury and was in charge of prosecuting the four suspects on counts including attempted murder, attempted robbery, and criminal possession of a weapon. All four defendants were convicted and are serving state prison sentences.

The best known case David has been involved in is known as the "Carnegie Deli" case. David assisted another ADA named Steven Nuzzi in successfully prosecuting the case in the New York Supreme Court. On May 10, 2001, Sean Salley, 30 (a former roadie with funk musician George Clinton) and Andre Smith, 21, entered an apartment above the Carnegie Deli. The apartment was used by Jennifer Stahl, 39, an actress in the movie "Dirty Dancing," and other people in the music industry and show business worlds as a high-grade marijuana boutique and a recording studio. The defendants used duct tape to bind the five people in the apartment: Jennifer, her hairdresser, two friends visiting from out of town, and her assistant in charge of opening the door. The defendants robbed Stahl of about 1.5 pounds of marijuana and $800 in cash and then shot all five victims in the head.

David and Steven worked with the police to track down the killers with the help of the apartment building surveillance camera film and a tip from a viewer of the television show "America's Most Wanted." The viewer told the authorities that one of the defendants was living in a Miami homeless shelter. One valuable clue came from a paper found on an uncooperative friend of the defendants on which was written a few phone numbers and names; on this paper, a "Dre" was listed with a phone number that was eventually connected with Andre Smith. Once authorities tracked down the defendants, Steven and David spent months readying for the six-week trial. Their preparation consisted primarily of interviewing witnesses and working with the police to track down clues. For example, one of the defendant's claims was that the gun went off by accident, killing Ms. Stahl. By looking at the gunpowder evidence, they were able to prove that the gun went off while it was held up to the head of Ms. Stahl. In July of 2002, the two defendants were sentenced to 120 years to life in prison for murder and robbery.

The Carnegie Deli Killers case was atypical in a few respects: there were two ADAs working on it, and unless a case is very large, an ADA usually works alone. Also, due to the high-profile nature of the crime, the New York Police Department provided anything that the D.A.'s office requested. In many cases, it can be a bit of a struggle to convince police to give their time to accompany ADAs to pursue witnesses or follow up on other clues from a crime scene.

In other respects the Carnegie Deli Killers case was typical. First, despite the high-profile nature of the case, Steven and David were nonetheless forbidden from speaking to the press—a policy in all cases. Second, Steven and David were almost entirely on their own. Although there are other ADAs who may answer questions, once an ADA takes on a case (either through a contact in the police department or through an intake procedure known as ECAB) he or she has almost total control. Even in high-profile cases the ADA(s) in charge of prosecution need not gain approval of their strategies before going to court. David enjoys this autonomy, but with it comes great responsibility.

This responsibility can cause much stress. David usually works from 8:45 A.M. until 7 P.M. five days a week. He is paid no overtime, and the work is driven by his caseload. He sometimes works seven days a week, often from 7 A.M. until midnight, when he is trying a case; he once worked seven days a week for over three months. David would like more resources, especially when it comes to technology to use in investigations, and more office space in which to work with witnesses.

David feels his biggest frustration when he meets people who do not care about the system's effect on society. For example, he recently dealt with a gunshot victim who wanted nothing to do with the prosecution of the man who shot him. David ended up putting the victim in jail overnight to ensure that he would be in court to testify against the accused. David believes his move was necessary because the system is bigger than one victim who is reluctant to testify: if this shooter gets off because the witness has refused to testify, then others will attempt to intimidate witnesses in the future. David cites money as the main reason people leave the ADA's office; it is difficult to support a family on an ADA's salary.

Despite the low compensation and the stress, most ADAs really enjoy their work. ADAs do not need to keep track of or bill their time, and there is very little bureaucracy in the office. The job allows ample opportunity to get out of the office and follow up with a witness or investigate a crime scene. Given their autonomy and their direct role in keeping New York City streets safe, they constantly see the effects of their work.

The Manhattan D.A.'s office has lawyers from many different types of law schools. The diverse backgrounds make the office able to respond to the diverse types of crimes. David believes there is no one way to be a successful prosecutor. However, he says the best ADAs are not working there as an intellectual exercise; it is important to be grounded and aware of the real-world effect of every decision.

David mentioned when his next trial will start: "Well, it is supposed to start August 1st, but the case is a real mess. Basically, two groups of rappers shot at one another and my witnesses are mainly drug dealers."

David's advice to a lawyer just starting out is to "take risks early in your career and do what sounds most interesting." David took a risk early in his career, and after eleven years in Morgenthau's office, he is not yet ready to leave. He still loves seeing the direct effects of his work. He still loves working to solve crimes at the street level.

DONALD CABELL

Federal Prosecutor

By Julia Lipez

Security guards prevent people from entering the federal courthouse in Boston without permission, especially if they are carrying electronic tape recorders. Although Donald Cabell himself approved the tape recorder, the Boston U.S. Attorney's office is located in the courthouse, and nothing comes into that courthouse unless the marshals okay it.

After a trip to the marshal's office with Donald's secretary, the tape recorder was allowed. On the other side of a common area full of boxes and case files, Donald finished a meeting with an FBI agent. He came out shortly thereafter, going into a small conference room, also full of case files, where he apologized for the delay, noting that he had just "had a flare-up in a case." He then asked for just another minute, explaining that whenever someone gets arrested, he has to "call at least eight people." The offense was traveling across state lines to engage in illicit sex, and Donald had to call the duty attorney who would handle the defendant's initial appearance to tell him not to move for detention. After a few other phone calls, Donald finally settled into his chair, explaining that he had a two o'clock hearing, and that his parents were in town, and he was trying to get things settled so that he could leave at a reasonable hour to visit with them.

This hectic scene, Donald commented, was just another "typical Monday morning," and Donald, it seems, thrives on the action. He entered the Major Crimes Division at the U.S. Attorney's Office (USAO), expecting to stay between three and five years, and ten years later, has not left. Like his unexpected tenure in the office, his path getting there was anything but direct.

Donald had lived in four different states by the age of six. His father was in the Air Force, and the family moved around before finally settling on Cape Cod, Massachusetts, where Donald grew up. He knew by the age of eight that he wanted be a lawyer. His inspiration was not a family member or adult friend but, rather, Perry Mason, whom Donald enjoyed watching on TV as he won "his courtroom battles." Donald confirmed his desire to be a litigator when he participated actively in debate and mock trial in high school and college, which, he said, "excited the hell out of me." At that point, Donald only wanted to be a trial lawyer, in part because he thought, like many young people, that lawyers only worked in the courtroom.

Donald went to college at the University of Massachusetts at Amherst, where he majored in Political Science and completed an informal concentration in French. Even though he already knew he wanted to be a lawyer, he decided that he would take time off before going to law school. He worked in the UMass admissions office for a year and then took his first airplane ride ever, flying to Paris, where he studied humanities and French at the Sorbonne. Because he loved UMass-Amherst and the opportunity the admissions work gave him to visit high schools, Donald went back to the admissions office after his year at the Sorbonne. He worked there for another year, and then, repeating his pattern, went back to the Sorbonne for another year.

At this point, Donald had been out of college for four years and decided that he needed a change of pace. In 1986 he moved to Boston, where he worked for the mayor in the Office of Fair Housing, investigating discrimination complaints. That experience reinforced Donald's desire to go to law school. He said that he performed the functions of a judge, jury, and a lawyer; he investigated complaints, he made findings, and then he negotiated with discriminatory landlords on behalf of tenants. He also worked with lawyers in the office, some of whom had attended Northeastern Law School in Boston. Donald decided that he wanted to be a civil rights lawyer, perhaps focusing on housing and poverty law, and chose Northeastern because of its "public interest-oriented spirit."

Northeastern has a "co-op" program that allows law students to engage in actual legal work. Donald attended regular classes for the first year and then over the next two years participated in four co-ops, each lasting three months. He loved the co-op program because it allowed him "to figure out what he didn't want to do."

Because he went to law school with the idea of being a civil rights attorney, Donald completed his first co-op at a legal services clinic on Boston's North Shore, where he assisted clients with issues such as eviction for nonpayment of rent, domestic abuse, and applications for Social Security benefits. Despite his desire to work in poverty law, Donald "hated" his experience at the clinic. His goal had been to empower people, yet he found himself dealing with repeat clients and generally just helping them from one crisis to the next rather than improving their lives.

As he was forced to reexamine his career goals, Donald spent his next co-op working at an insurance defense firm of approximately 100 attorneys. He credits the firm with giving him excellent research, writing, and litigation experience. Still, he found the work unsatisfying because he had no opportunity for client contact; the clients, he said, were companies, not human beings.

Still unsure about what he wanted to do, Donald found himself at his next co-op in a situation he always swore to his friends he would avoid: a large law firm. He worked as a traditional summer associate at the former Hale & Dorr and found the experience to be more enjoyable than he had expected. He said he initially took the job because he thought it would look good on his résumé, but he also found that the firm gave him good contacts and afforded him the opportunity to work with talented attorneys. Hence, after graduation Donald accepted a job with Hale & Dorr, where he focused on securities and commercial litigation. Although he had a "great" experience at the firm, he "chafed at the bit" to get opportunities to take depositions and appear in court. He left after two years to join the small, "irreverent" law firm in the North End where he had completed his fourth co-op while at Northeastern.

Donald worked as a litigator at the firm, concentrating on employment law and large commercial litigation. While he found more opportunities to appear in court, he still did not see the courtroom as much as he thought a litigator should. Around that time, President Clinton selected Don Stern, a senior partner at Hale & Dorr with whom Donald had previously shared a secretary, to be the U.S. Attorney for the District of Massachusetts. Donald had once offhandedly mentioned to Stern that he thought it would be fun to work as an Assistant U.S. Attorney (AUSA).

In 1995, without giving much thought to working at the U.S. Attorney's Office, he decided to interview for an opening in the Major Crimes Division. Stern hired him, and after soliciting advice from two partners at the small firm who told him, "run, don't walk" to the USAO, Donald accepted the job. He also took the advice of a friend who told him that this would be a real chance to overcome the feeling of butterflies that he felt every time he entered the courtroom.

Donald has stayed at the USAO longer than he had planned in large part because, he says, "he has never been as stimulated" as he is as an AUSA. He describes the Major Crimes Division as a "catch all" for any offense that does not involve drugs, organized crime, or white collar crime. Firearms offenses are his "bread and butter," but he also prosecutes bank robberies, immigration offenses, arson, theft of government property, pornography, and computer-related offenses. He credits the variety of work in the Division with being one of the reasons he has stayed so long. He likes the fact that he gets to work with different government agencies and that every case presents a "new legal issue." Despite his love of the job, Donald's adjustment to the USAO was not easy.

He described his first days on the job as "daunting." He explained that as a young associate, he had no autonomy at the law firms and no sense of how the work he did fit into the case as a whole. At the USAO, in contrast, once an attorney gets a case, it belongs to him or her from beginning to end. Donald said that from his first day on the job he had almost complete autonomy to determine the case strategy, what charges to bring, how to present the case in court, and what evidence to use. It was difficult at first, Donald says, because, "it's all on you." He spent the first two years adjusting to that change and found it especially difficult when, he said, "you had something going to trial and you realized you didn't know how to do a trial."

Donald is no doubt an expert at trying cases now; he appears in court at least once a day, whether at an initial appearance, an arraignment, a probable cause hearing, an evidentiary hearing, a detention hearing, or a trial. Donald also has the opportunity on occasion to argue appeals in front of the First Circuit Court of Appeals. When asked to describe the difference between trials and oral arguments, Donald said that appellate arguments are more nerve-wracking because the attorneys have to anticipate and respond to questions from three judges, whereas trial strategy can be mapped out ahead of time. He described a recent day when he argued in front of the First Circuit in the morning and then went right from the argument to the last day of a trial, where he had to cross-examine the defendant in a "nasty" case, and then deliver a closing argument. He said he spent the evening trying to figure out which activity took more out of him, the trial or the oral argument — and he is still not sure. Nonetheless, he described the experience as exhilarating: "there's always anxiety, [but] you're really pleased with yourself when you're done. Whatever goals you set for yourself, this is the type of job where you're always going to be confronted with more than what you might have otherwise envisioned yourself doing."

When asked to describe the office environment, Donald explained that the office is best understood in the context of the people who work there: everybody is there because they want to be there. USAOs generally do not hire people straight out of law school; most new hires have been out of school between three and five years and thus have consciously made a choice to leave behind another working environment. Donald described the office as collegial. He said that while he and other attorneys do not actually collaborate on cases, they always discuss their cases with one another and solicit advice from each other on the legal issues those cases raise. The caliber of the attorneys working at his office is "extraordinarily high," according to Donald, and he stated that he is in awe of most of the people with whom he works.

More and more people are staying at the USAO for many years, which is no doubt due in part to the pleasant working environment. Donald said that when he first started in the office, the usual plan was to stay for between three and five years and then to return to a large law firm. Since then, however, people are staying longer and longer, and, according to Donald, there are attorneys who have been in the office for up to twenty years. It is a "lifestyle choice," explained Donald. He said that while the attorneys at the USAO do not make as much money as those at law firms, they can "make it to their kids' softball games." He does not work much less than attorneys at large firms: he averages between fifty and sixty hours a week. Nonetheless, he says that he has more ability to manage his time than he would at a firm. Donald and his wife both work, and they have school-age children. He says that he comes into work at 5:30 in the morning three days a week so that he can leave in the afternoon and be home when his kids get off the school bus.

Donald takes a practical attitude towards his work. When asked whether it is ever difficult to prosecute someone, he acknowledged that there are times when he might have sympathy for the defendant but stated that it does not usually affect his decision to prosecute. Rather, any sympathy he felt for the defendant would influence the length of sentence he chose to seek. He also said that often he feels good about getting defendants off the street, particularly when the case involves a violent bank robbery or an assault.

Donald occasionally deals with recidivist defendants, which is frustrating if he thought that the defendant got the message the first time around. Sometimes, however, he knows he will see a defendant again in court, particularly when substance abuse is involved. He sees varying levels of substance abuse among defendants. He said that it depends on the type of crime, noting, for instance, that there is a high correlation between bank robberies and heroin abuse. In addition, he said that most defendants in violent crimes come from broken households, where there was either alcohol abuse or domestic abuse or both present when the defendant was a child.

He also said that most defendants he sees do not have particularly severe juvenile records but that he does see escalation in defendants' records; often he will see a defendant who had petty larceny convictions as a juvenile, and had gone from there to breaking and entering to armed robbery. It is the escalation in violence that Donald finds worrisome, which is why he attempts to help young defendants who have made mistakes before they commit worse crimes. He gave the example of a case he had in which a group of young people from Alabama drove illegal guns to Boston and sold them to an undercover agent. Donald met with the defendants multiple times throughout the course of the prosecution, and he said that while what they did was "stupid, criminal, and completely worthy of prosecution," he also tried to help them at sentencing by requesting a variety of rehabilitation programs. Since then, Donald has received thank you letters and updates from the defendants and their parents. One of the defendants is about to graduate from college and told Donald that he sees the prosecution as the event that turned his life around. Donald explained, "sometimes it's not the biggest case that impacts you." Rather, he likes to focus on the cases where good people made bad decisions. In those cases, the prosecution process for Donald is about putting the defendants in positions where they will not make poor decisions again. According to Donald, the work of AUSAs is "not just locking people up and throwing away the key."

For Donald there is value in all facets of his work. Just as he enjoys helping young defendants who made a mistake, he also values making the streets safer for the public. He said, "It sounds so corny, but the more and more I'm in the job, I think what we do is so valuable. You recognize how much crime is out there and how many people are trying to do harm in so many ways. Honestly, we're talking about civic responsibility and serving the greater good. I honestly feel that what we do, in keeping the community safe, is one of the most important things you can do."

Although Donald himself hardly could have planned the route that eventually brought him to the USAO, he did have advice for law students interested in a career as a federal prosecutor. He said that "being able to hit the ground running is a really sought-after quality." Thus, young attorneys should "try to get into the courtroom as early and as much as possible." When asked how attorneys should get that experience if they are working in a large firm, he responded that "the trick is to be assertive." He recalled a Hale & Dorr program that enabled him to appear in state court one day a month as appointed defense counsel. Any experience that allows a young attorney to have full responsibility for a case is helpful for applying to U.S. Attorney's offices. Donald also advised law students to take courses that teach them to read and write well. Ultimately, Donald said, "I could not have anticipated the path I took to get here, and therefore, I'm a firm believer that if it's gonna happen, it's gonna happen."

One thing is clear: Donald enjoys his job. Just as he could not have predicted how he would end up there, he says that he cannot anticipate where the next ten or twenty years will take him. He does know one thing: "I've been here five years longer that I ever imagined, and I still enjoy every day here."

ED SWANSON

Private Criminal Defense Lawyer

By Mike Kass

Ed Swanson loves his job. Seven years ago, he and a colleague, Mary McNamara, left the federal public defenders office in San Francisco to open their own law firm, Swanson & McNamara. Business is good. The work, a mix of criminal and civil cases, is meaningful and fun. It's also newsworthy. Recently, Ed and Mary McNamara received front-page press for their defense of Victor Conte, the lead defendant in the BALCO case, who was charged with conspiring to provide steroids to professional athletes. On top of all this, Ed is the proud, openly gay father of two young children, remains an active volunteer in the Bay Area legal community, and teaches trial advocacy to law students and practicing attorneys.

Since graduating from law school fourteen years ago, he has worked as a policy advisor on land allocation and health issues in South Africa; as a judicial clerk in a federal district court; as a federal public defender; and now as an attorney in private practice. These jobs were not part of any long-term plan on Ed's part: rather, in weighing the opportunities available at each stage of his career, he has been careful to choose only those that he would enjoy — he never once settled for a position that would serve merely as a stepping stone to bigger and better opportunities. "Everything I did I liked, and then I liked the next thing more," he says. "I just want to be sure that what I'm doing continues to be the thing I most want to do. That's sort of been my guiding principle as I've moved from one job to another."

Ed grew up in the Midwest as the oldest of four children. He first came to the San Francisco Bay Area to attend Stanford, where he studied international relations. Ed thought he wanted to work on international development issues. After graduating from college in 1985, he spent a year researching foreign policy issues for Congressman Jim Bates in Washington, DC. Ed then transferred to the House Select Committee on Hunger, where his duties involved organizing committee hearings and drafting aid-related legislation to present to committee members.

By the end of his second year with the Committee on Hunger, Ed had decided to attend law school. His decision was motivated in part by his belief that a legal education would provide good preparation for a career in politics. He became interested in politics in high school, when his parents had been active campaign volunteers. Ed's time in Washington focused on this interest. "As a staffer working on committee hearings," he explains, "I would write the opening statements and the questions that were going to be asked. I would sit in the back row and hand these up to the various committee members. I felt like I wanted to be asking some of those questions, and I wanted to follow up on my own without having to get someone else to do that."

Not many politicians walk right out of law school into an open congressional seat, and there was the consideration of what to do while awaiting his chance at public office. The practice of law seemed appealing: "It seemed to be a profession where you could be judged more on merit than just on your ability to schmooze, which is a lot—it seemed to me in my early twenties—of what Washington was about. I was really drawn to the idea of going somewhere where using skills that you developed and applying them in a courtroom and making arguments [that] could actually make a difference." He also liked the idea of working closely with people: "When you're doing international development work in Washington and you get ten million dollars for Mozambique, you're not going to see, most likely, any of the Mozambiquans who are actually going to benefit from that. That was frustrating to me. I wanted to be in an environment where I was actually looking at the people I was trying to help."

Ed enrolled in Stanford Law School thinking initially that he wanted to be a prosecutor. He remembers, "I was really clear that in the criminal justice world, that's the person who has the power, so if I wanted to do the most good I could with my law degree in the world of criminal law, it would be as a prosecutor." Criminal defense, at that point, was not an interest of his. "There was one former county-level public defender I met in Washington who was working for Senator Leahy, and he didn't make the job sound very appealing," Ed explains. "It sounded to me like you were going to be representing a lot of guilty people with hopeless cases, trying to gin up some sympathy for these not very sympathetic characters."

In law school, Ed took every criminal course available and received a lot of career-related guidance from two of his criminal law professors, Barbara Babcock and Bob Weisberg. He spent both of his summers during law school working in the field of criminal prosecution.

During the first summer, Ed worked at the California Attorney General's office, where he assisted on appellate briefs regarding trial errors or suppression motion challenges. "It was not a good job for me," he says. "It had none of the people contact that I was looking for."

The next summer, Ed worked for the Alameda County District Attorney's office. "It's a great office," he says. "But it was really clear early on that this was not a good fit. It didn't feel right to me. My perspective on the issues . . . and the perspective of the attorneys in that office were so different that they would turn to me and say, 'Ed, can you tell us what the Stanford/ACLU perspective on this is?' And there's a lot to be said for someone having the Stanford/ACLU perspective and working in a prosecutor's office. Someone like that can be a really good prosecutor, but the work did not bring me any real satisfaction." During his summer in the DA's office, Ed prosecuted a DUI case before a jury. He won but, in his own words, "didn't get any positive feeling out of winning." It was difficult watching the defendant's family, seeing them react to the verdict and the sentence. "This was not [the defendant's] first DUI, so there were going to be real consequences."

On another occasion, Ed was asked to research whether the office could prosecute women who used crack during pregnancy for the harm caused to their unborn children. "As you might imagine," he says, "my perspective on that issue didn't synchronize with that of some of my employers. My argument was that it doesn't matter if you can or if you can't [prosecute]: this is not going to result in those women coming in and getting treatment and healthcare; it's going to result in driving them out of the treatment system, further jeopardizing their health and the health of their children."

Deciding that prosecution wasn't the right path for him, Ed took on a part-time externship at the Santa Clara County Public Defender's office during his final year of law school. "I loved it. It felt like coming home," he says. "It was just so clear to me from the day I walked in that I was in the right place with people who shared my perspective on [criminal justice] issues. And I got to work with clients." Ed spent most of his externship working on motions to suppress—usually for drugs or guns. He remembers winning his first motion. "It was a drug case. A bunch of drugs had been found out in the yard behind someone's house, but it was a yard shared by a number of people, and there really was no way that you could prove [my client] had exclusive control over it." The judge granted the motion to suppress the drugs, ending the case. "I lost plenty of suppression motions that fall as well, but I certainly remember that experience being really satisfying and being able to deliver something like that to the client, who was expecting so little. I mean, for crying out loud, he has a law student working on his case in a public defender's office, so you're already down two strikes in his mind."

Ed never worked at a large law firm, but he briefly considered it. "I think it is very hard to go through law school and not end up at a big firm. I think the gravitational pull of the big law firms is almost overwhelming because they're on campus to interview—unlike the rest of these employers. You have to hardly lift a finger to interview with them. They're willing to pay you as a law student, and they're willing to pay you a lot of money as a lawyer. No one's ever going to say, 'Why did you become a partner at this big law firm?' It's such a clear measure of success in our profession. It's not like becoming a public defender, where people are going to say, 'You could have done anything; you ended up as a public defender?' I had no intention of ever going to a big firm, and before I knew it I was interviewing at a big firm. I remember one of the people interviewing me said, 'You've done such interesting things. Why would you want to work here?' For me, it was one of those moments of just, 'Oh yeah, okay; thank you for reminding me.'"

Ed had a similar experience while applying for appellate clerkships during his second year of law school. He had the opportunity to interview with several DC Circuit Court judges for some of the most selective and prestigious clerkships available. "It was just sort of the track," he explains. "It was definitely the thing you do next if you can, so that's why I was attracted to it." During the interview, one of the judges' current law clerks said, "I see that you worked on Capitol Hill, and I know that's a really exciting, fast-paced job. You should know that as a circuit court clerk you can go entire days without talking to anyone else. All you'll be doing is looking at the computer, writing, and researching." Ed describes it as another epiphany moment. "I'd been thinking about possibly going to South Africa after graduation to work over there instead of doing a clerkship. After hearing him say that, I realized then I could spend a year working in South Africa or sitting here in front of a computer. It was a no-brainer. So I canceled the rest of my interviews and pulled out of the whole process of applying for clerkships."

He spent the year after law school at the Centre for Applied Legal Studies in South Africa. "It was a great year," he says. "Nelson Mandela had been released from prison, and they were beginning the talks about how they were going to transfer power" to the black community. Ed worked on two big projects that year. One involved helping to design a land claims court to adjudicate claims between blacks who had been kicked off of agricultural land and the white farmers who had acquired that land. Another project involved health policy — helping to create an umbrella group for local AIDS-related organizations and helping to draft a charter of rights for victims of AIDS. AIDS was just then entering the national consciousness in South Africa. "It was such an incredible time to be there. Everything was possible. Everything was hope. There was just so much optimism. You had yet to run into the reality of what it was actually going to be like to get shelter and water and electricity and jobs for a population that hadn't had [anything] for years and years."

At the end of his term, Ed returned to the Bay Area for a clerkship — this time at the district court level, with Judge Thelton Henderson, then chief judge of the Federal District Court for the Northern District of California. He explains, "I thought [clerking at the district court level] might be more to my liking, with a little quicker pace [than a circuit court clerkship] and getting to actually see things happen at the trial level. That was a great year." At the district court level, Ed got the chance to see cases from the judge's side of the bench, to see "how judges perceive attorneys and their arguments, and what works and what doesn't; who is respected and who isn't and why." "It's an amazing lesson in that," he says. "You don't get another chance like that as a lawyer."

At the end of his clerkship, Ed joined the federal public defender's office in San Francisco as an assistant federal public defender. He spent the next five years there.

"At the federal defender's office in San Francisco," Ed says, "you hit the ground running. You are given some 'duty days' in which whatever cases come in on that day, they're your cases. Some of the heaviest cases I ever got I got in my first month on that job," including two career offender bank robbery cases. "In the beginning, for your first few months, you have another, more experienced attorney who shadows you and second chairs [your trials]." After that, "it's not that you're totally alone — there's a lot of sharing information and support and all that — but you're handling your own cases; you're making your own decisions. It's between you and your client if the case is going to go to trial or if you're going to cut a deal. It's a lot of responsibility." But, Ed says, he quickly came to enjoy the independence.

In his first trial, Ed defended a postal worker who was charged with having stolen a check from the mail. The man's thumbprint was on the check, so "it was going to be tricky to say he hadn't been the one to take it out," he says. Nevertheless, Ed managed to obtain an acquittal. "Your first trial is an overwhelming thing, and you don't know where you're supposed to stand or how to deal with the court," he reflects. In that first case, there was a piece of evidence that the jury was not supposed to see, but the prosecutor took it out and was about to approach a witness with it. "Rather than, as I should have done, asked to go to sidebar to make sure this was handled properly, I jumped up and said, 'Your Honor, that's been partially redacted.' The judge thought I was grandstanding. I just didn't know any better."

Ed remembers the anxiety he felt at his first trial. "It's such an enormous responsibility to be a defense attorney at trial, where it's so very clear that the only thing standing between your client and prison is you." But he soon found that he loved the trial work. "It is unlike anything else that I know professionally in that you're so incredibly focused. You've got to make a thousand decisions a day; you've got to be reading people on the stand [and] sensing the jury peripherally, trying to figure out where your opponent's going. It's such an engaging and exhausting experience, but there's nothing better about [being a lawyer] than . . . being in trial."

Looking back on it, Ed remembers having a good win-loss ratio his first year. "I would have been wise to hang up my spurs after my first year," he says. "I certainly picked up a number of losses after that." He describes what it feels like to lose a case. "By the time you're in trial, you've so come to believe the rightness of your position — if not in the innocence of your client, at least in the [prosecution's inability to] prove this case beyond a reasonable doubt — that when you lose a case, it's extremely hard. . . . It feels like you've been rejected by the jury. . . . And then to know what that actually means for your client is . . . awful." But there's little time for reflection: "When you're in trial, you have to put so much on the shelf to focus your attention on that case, the minute trial is over you've got pots boiling over everywhere. So you just have to turn around, and get right back to it."

Ed worked hard in the public defender's office. "I worked nights. I worked most weekends. I'm sure I didn't work 'big firm' hours, but I worked a lot." When in trial, "you barely go home." But trials were infrequent: "Some cases I'd get dismissed altogether," he recalls, but the majority of the work is plea bargaining. In general, "sentencing guidelines and the ability of government to charge mandatory minimum sentences" often make it too risky for defendants to take a case to trial. "I probably did an average of two or three per year, which, compared to a county public defender, is nothing. They can do that in a month."

Trial work aside, Ed is glad that he joined the federal public defender's office rather than that of the county public defender. Ed explains, "Typically, your case load is light enough that if you're willing to work pretty hard, you can do everything that you think needs to be a done on a case. That makes the job really satisfying." By contrast, in a county public defender's office, "you really have to do triage and try to decide which cases . . . have some fight in them and are going to need your attention, and which don't." The cases that are brought in federal court "are often much tighter for the prosecution" than those brought in state court. In the Northern District of California, Ed explains, "the U.S. Attorney's office is careful to bring cases that they feel are very strong." That tendency "makes your job as a defense attorney that much harder."

One of the challenges of being a public defender is earning the client's trust. While Ed found that the case load in his office enabled federal defenders to provide the sort of high-quality representation that clients could expect from good private attorneys, many clients seemed to feel "that as a general principle, you get what you pay for." While a lot of clients proved to be very grateful for the work of the federal defender's office, in many cases "you would have a lot to overcome in order to build a relationship of trust with them." This, Ed explains, "is not the case in private practice. In private practice, they have selected you, they're paying you, they want to believe that they have got the best [representation] that there is."

Ed greatly enjoyed his time in the federal public defender's office. In part this was due to the culture of the office in the Northern District of California: "It's a pretty small office. It's a cohesive office. It's not competitive." He describes his former boss, Barry Portman, the appointed federal defender for the Northern District of California, as "an incredible person to work for." Ed explains that being a public defender can often be an emotionally grueling job. "It is common that after several years of being a public defender and representing folks who often have pretty desperate cases—and often desperate lives—you get worn down. . . . You lose some of that enthusiasm that you initially bring to the job. Barry—you would think he'd been hired last week. . . . What I miss most now that I'm in private practice [is] being around someone who can consistently find the joy in this work because you can lose sight of that pretty easily."

The federal defender's office in Northern California has a rule that public defenders have to move on after five years. This enforced turnover helps to keep defenders from getting stale in their work, and it opens up vacancies so that young attorneys can acquire federal criminal defense experience. Ed did not originally plan to open his own law firm after working as a public defender. The idea came from his current law partner, Mary McNamara, who joined the public defender's office at roughly the same time Ed did. Neither he nor McNamara was enthusiastic about the prospect of trading in the independence that they had enjoyed as assistant public defenders for the hierarchy of a large law firm, but they faced difficult challenges in starting out on their own. "We didn't have any sense of how we were going to find work or if we were going to find work." It's hard to open a firm coming from the public defender's office, Ed explains, because public defenders don't have a paying client roster that they can take with them. In addition, Ed's and McNamara's years in public service left them without a lot of savings that they could draw on. "We decided we were not going to do family law—period. But we were pretty open to most anything else if it would keep the doors open."

Starting out, Ed was nervous about their ability to cover expenses: "I remember thinking of ourselves as Apollo 13; that if we would be able to get back alive—that would be a success. But pretty early on, we had enough work to keep us afloat, and since then it's continued to grow." From the very beginning, their work came largely from referrals—passed on by local attorneys they knew. When these attorneys were unable to take on a case due to a conflict of some sort, they would direct the client to Swanson & McNamara. Ed and Mary McNamara watched expenses carefully—moving from one office to another in the first couple of years when the rent rose too high. But they were fortunate. They had enough business to hire an associate after their first six months and gradually brought on other staff: an office manager, a paralegal, and, eventually, another associate. In that first year, Ed earned around $110,000.

Today, about seventy percent of Ed's time is spent on criminal defense cases, the remainder on complex civil cases. A small percentage of the criminal defense work comes from the Northern District of California Federal Indigent Defense Panel—a body that appoints lawyers to defend individuals who are unable to use a lawyer from the public defender's office because of a conflict of interest. Ed also does some *pro bono* work—usually for former clients of his from the public defender's office. He charges an hourly fee for the rest of the work, and most of it still comes in the form of referrals from other local attorneys.

To expand their network, Ed and McNamara write legal articles and stay engaged in the local legal community. Ed sits on the board of California Attorneys for Criminal Justice and has been active in Bay Area Lawyers for Individual Freedom (BALIF), an association of local lesbian, gay, bisexual, and transgender attorneys. When asked what advice he would give to a young lawyer interested in starting a firm, Ed suggested that you should first "build[] a community, a strong network of people who know you as a lawyer" and who can refer cases to you. "Until you've established a reputation among your community, it's just going to be very hard, at least to do the kind of work that we do. We don't do insurance work, so we don't have anybody who can steadily send us work. We've got to get referrals all the time."

While the majority of his cases are criminal defense in nature, Ed has found that he greatly enjoys the civil cases, which range from trade secret cases and other commercial disputes to employment litigation. He explains that the procedural and substantive legal issues in civil cases can be "so much more intellectually challenging than what you see in the criminal world." In part, it's also nice, from time to time, to litigate on an even playing field: "The playing field in the criminal [justice system] isn't level . . . despite the presumption of innocence and the government's burden of proof. When you're representing someone in the courtroom who's shackled and wearing an orange jumpsuit, they're not in the same shoes as government. They're not treated the same way by the jury, and, depending what court you're in front of, . . . by the court as well."

But criminal law remains his passion. "The kind of case that appeals to me the most is the criminal case where there's really something you can do [besides working out a good plea bargain], be it a good suppression motion or a triable case. It doesn't really matter to me if it's a securities fraud or insider trading case or a felon in possession of a weapon case."

He has found that it is harder to take cases to trial as a private attorney, and he misses that aspect of his work as a public defender. On average, he'll try one case a year. "You do a lot of work pre-indictment to avoid your client being charged at all," he explains. "The presumption in most cases is you're going to stay away from trial, and a lot of our clients want to keep it as quiet as can be." And then there is the economic side of going to court. "Taking a case to trial in federal court costs an incredible amount of money. Someone who has got a case that is triable and has the funds to do it doesn't come along all that often."

As for his work-life balance, Ed says, "I still work a lot, but since I've had kids, I now don't work on my weekends until Sunday night. I get home for dinner most every night, although I then work at home a lot."

By the time he became a federal public defender, Ed had decided against pursuing a career in politics. It was "something I was less interested in, and it seemed less practical," he explains. As for practicality, while there are some who start as public defenders and enjoy successful political careers, such as former San Francisco Supervisor Matt Gonzalez, Ed observes that the public defender's office is "certainly a harder place to start than being a former prosecutor." Looking back, Ed says, "I'm glad I didn't go into politics. . . . and being able to structure life to be home at night and not out at some fundraising event is a big deal."

Now, fourteen years out of law school, Ed continues to hold out for work that he enjoys. "I only really will take a case if I feel that it's something I can bring some value to. If I feel that there's not a whole lot that can be done in a case and someone else can do the same job and do it more cheaply, then that's something I'll pass on to someone else."

While it was not his original intention to open his own firm, Ed is grateful that his career led him in this direction. "I've got a much more interesting variety of cases now than in the federal defender's office," he says. "I'm still working on things I've never done before, learning new things as I go"—both in terms of substantive areas of the law and in peripheral aspects of case management, such as dealing with the press frenzy surrounding the BALCO case. He has also enjoyed the process of building a business. "It's a great thing to create a place to work that you like and that people who work with you enjoy. That's a really satisfying experience."

Looking forward, Ed says, "I don't have a sense of what I want this firm to be like or what sort of job I want to have other than this. I could imagine there could come a time when this is no longer particularly engaging." Right now, he's doing the thing he most wants to do. When that changes, if history is any indication, Ed will find something else—something that he will enjoy even more.

JANICE BERGMANN

Habeas Corpus Specialist

By June Shih

Janice Bergmann's office on the eleventh floor of a glass-windowed high rise in downtown Fort Lauderdale is equipped with many of the trappings of a typical litigator. A large computer screen and desk dominate the room. Treatise binders line the walls, and case files are piled on every available surface. But there are a few signs that Janice is not your average lawyer in private practice. A stack of letters written on lined notebook paper sits on a shelf near the door — letters from federal prisoners begging for help with their cases. And two colorful child's paintings hang prominently on the wall — "Mama #1 Supreme Court" reads one inscription.

Janice is a habeas corpus specialist. She is an expert on all the deliberately complex and constantly changing intricacies of the law that grants prisoners the right to challenge their convictions and detentions on constitutional grounds. As an assistant federal public defender for the Southern District of Florida, Janice regularly represents prisoners in their habeas corpus appeals before judges of the Eleventh Circuit in Atlanta. And in 2005 she made her inaugural appearance before the U.S. Supreme Court in Washington.

But representing prisoners and arguing the finer points of habeas corpus before federal judges is just one part of Janice's life. So are changing diapers and reading bedtime stories to her preschool-aged sons. Nearly two decades after graduating from law school, Janice, who is married to Bernardo Lopez, a fellow federal public defender, is the only one of her three best women friends to still be working full-time in the legal profession. She attributes that feat to being lucky enough to find jobs that have allowed her to remain true to both her professional and her personal ambitions.

Growing up in the conservative middle-class suburb of Bronxville, New York, Janice had little inkling that she was destined for a career that would take her from bail hearings in Alaska to death row appeals in California to oral argument before the U.S. Supreme Court. Though her friends and family had often joked that she should become a lawyer because she was so "argumentative," Janice's childhood dream was to teach chemistry. She followed that dream to Colgate University, where she double-majored in chemistry and math. After she graduated she took a job in the research and development division of a pharmaceutical company.

She lasted eight months before realizing that she was not suited for a career in chemistry. She quit her job, traveled around Europe for a while and then decided to try living in Boston. Eventually, she found a new job canvassing for Mass PIRG—the Massachusetts arm of Public Interest Research Group, a grassroots student-run advocacy organization. Knocking on strangers' doors and asking for donations was good training for a future as a public defender. "You get used to having doors slammed in your face," Janice recalls. "I learned how to deliver a message really quickly and to appreciate each day's small victories."

Janice was soon promoted to a position assisting Mass PIRG's senior lobbyist. At the group's headquarters in Boston, Janice saw lawyers in action for the first time in her life. The chance to see firsthand how a handful of public interest attorneys, working for very little pay, could strategize, lobby, and succeed in passing so many new and progressive consumer and environmental reforms, including the state's first bottle bill, inspired her to pursue a law degree. "I didn't realize what lawyers did until I got to Mass PIRG," she says. "They became my role models. They talked me into going to law school."

Janice chose Northeastern Law School because of its "nontraditional" image and emphasis on public interest careers. Northeastern lacked the cutthroat competition that characterized other schools, she said, because at the time the school had no grades or law review. "People went there because they wanted to be public interest lawyers."

Janice enrolled, thinking that she would specialize in environmental law—following in the footsteps of her mentors at Mass PIRG. But during her first year, she found her interests leading her down another path.

"I fell in love with the Constitution," she says.

"I discovered that environmental law was all regulation—it was worse than the tax code," she says. "Constitutional law just interested me more . . . it had the most impact on people's lives." But she quickly learned that very few jobs in the legal profession actually allowed lawyers to "do constitutional law" on a daily basis.

Northeastern requires its students to spend four quarters serving internships in real-life legal settings. Janice used that time to find ways to practice constitutional law. She spent three months with a small but prominent private civil rights firm in Charlotte, North Carolina. The firm's lawyers had brought and won many landmark school desegregation and voting rights suits. She was impressed by the firm's record of public service, but seeing lawyers who were able to have both a satisfying work life and a satisfying family life made an even more lasting impression. "The lawyers there were smart, worked hard, but their jobs were not the focus — their families and churches were," she recalls. "I liked the balance."

After her internship in North Carolina, Janice headed to San Francisco and an internship with the staff attorney for the Ninth Circuit Court of Appeals. It was in that office that she first became interested in habeas corpus law. The staff attorney's office vetted all *pro se* appeals — those filed by citizens without attorneys — and determined which appeals should be more carefully considered by the judges. The vast majority of *pro se* cases were habeas corpus and section 1983 civil rights appeals written by prisoners. And since habeas appeals dealt exclusively with constitutional issues, Janice naturally gravitated toward those cases.

After three months as a staff attorney in San Francisco, Janice headed to another internship in the Alaska Public Defenders' office, where she worked as a "bail slave," accompanying newly arrested defendants to their bail hearings. Meeting criminal defendants for the first time gave her a more nuanced understanding of why people commit crime — and the sometimes practical reasons that lead people to break the law — such as the homeless who committed petty crimes that would allow them to spend the Alaska winter in a warm jail cell. "It was shocking to learn how mundane and profound the criminal system could be."

Though she had a job offer from the Ninth Circuit's staff attorney's office in hand, Janice also tried life in a major commercial law firm in Boston before making a final decision. Despite the $1,000 a week salary — more money than she had ever made in her life — she hated it. The associates seemed "very unhappy," and the cases the firm took — defending tire manufacturers who had been accused of placing defective products on the market or suing potato farmers in Maine on behalf of a large potato chip maker — did not appeal to her. And of course there were very · few opportunities to practice constitutional law. "I didn't want to wake up in the morning and go there," she says. "It was not important to me to make fancy dollars."

Janice decided to take the job in the Ninth Circuit staff attorney's office. Like other law students, she says she was concerned about paying back her student loans, but not enough to put off or give up a career as a public interest lawyer. "You just do it," she says, "I knew I needed to live a moderate lifestyle . . . but ten years [of paying off debt] go by faster than you think."

She stayed three years with the Ninth Circuit, rising to become the acting director of the thirty-five attorney office. She discovered that she very much enjoyed reviewing cases and researching and writing legal memoranda for the circuit judges. Her interest in habeas corpus and in section 1983 civil rights cases continued to grow and deepen. "I kept doing habeas and I kept liking it," she says. She also began to rule out another field of law: criminal appeals. "Direct criminal appeals just didn't involve issues that were interesting to me," she says.

Her passion was habeas, but she wasn't sure how she was going to be able to make a living "doing habeas." Most litigants were *pro se* prisoners. And only a very few public interest organizations, such as the ACLU or prisoners' rights groups, were actually willing to pay people to work on habeas appeals. But Janice was undaunted. As she was preparing to leave the staff attorney's office, she had lunch with a friend who worked at the California Appellate Project (CAP), an organization that assisted attorneys with their death penalty appeals. "You don't want to do death penalty work," he told her. "That only made me want to do it more," she recalls.

Timing was on Janice's side. In the early 1990s, California's death penalty cases were just beginning to make their way into the federal court system. While CAP had plenty of experts on the state appeals process, it lacked experts on habeas in the federal courts. Janice was one of several lawyers hired to fill that need.

One of the first major cases to cross her desk involved Robert Alton Harris, the first man sentenced to die in California's gas chamber since the state restored its death penalty in 1978. In a last-ditch effort to save his life, Janice and CAP helped Harris's attorneys pull together a case that challenged the constitutionality of the gas chamber. The lawyers argued that the gas chamber violated the Eighth Amendment ban against cruel and unusual punishment. The Circuit Court granted Harris a stay of execution, which was later overturned by the Supreme Court with an unprecedented order that no more stays be granted in Harris's case. Janice says she didn't sleep in the five days preceding "Robert's" execution—a date she still remembers: April 21, 1992. She takes some comfort in knowing that their lawsuit, which continued after Harris's death, ultimately resulted in California doing away with the gas chamber.

Janice's opposition to the death penalty grew as she got to know more death row inmates. "It's shocking how normal they are," says Janice, who remembers her clients by their first names. "They're real people." She began to understand the arbitrariness, the "lightening strike aspect" of the death penalty and the circumstances of a defendant's prosecution and representation. "Your punishment depends on how rabid the prosecution is and whether you are lucky enough to get a competent trial attorney," she says.

While at CAP, Janice also had a chance to play a small but important part in history. In 1992 Thomas Miller-El, a death row inmate in Texas, was in the midst of challenging his conviction on the grounds that the prosecution had deliberately and unconstitutionally excluded African Americans from his jury. He had just lost his direct appeal to the Texas Court of Criminal Appeals, and a call went out to the death penalty defense community for a lawyer to help write a cert petition to the U.S. Supreme Court. Miller-El had just one week before the petition was due — and just one banker's box of materials and research. Janice volunteered to write the petition, her first-ever Supreme Court petition. The petition was denied, but it bought Miller-El the time he needed to find new lawyers who could file a habeas corpus suit on his behalf in the federal courts. Afterward, Miller-El wrote Janice "one of the nicest letters I have ever received from a client." The case continued for another thirteen years, until June 2005, when the Supreme Court agreed with Miller-El that African-American jurors had indeed been unconstitutionally excluded from his jury. His sentence and conviction were overturned.

In 1996 Congress zeroed out funding for Janice's position at CAP: no more federal funds would go to assist CAP in advising federal habeas capital cases. At the same time, Janice's husband had accepted a clerkship with a Ninth Circuit judge in Pasadena. Luckily, demand for someone with Janice's expertise remained high, and she found a job writing a manual on capital habeas cases in the Ninth Circuit for the federal public defenders' office in Los Angeles. Janice continued to develop and share her expertise after she and her husband decided to move closer to family in south Florida. She spent two years as a post-conviction specialist, training and advising federal defenders on habeas corpus issues. Finally, in 2000 she returned to litigation by joining her husband as an appellate attorney for the federal defender in Fort Lauderdale.

In 2004 she was assigned a case involving the question of when the one-year statute of limitations for filing habeas corpus cases began to run. In November the U.S. Supreme Court granted certiorari, and Janice was scheduled for oral argument in March 2005. For four months, Janice had "no life." She was "thinking, reading, and writing obsessively" about the issues of the case. Some days, she even talked to herself. "A Supreme Court case has a life of its own and the life it has is yours," she says. Her husband was supportive and became the primary caretaker of the children during those months. When the March oral argument date arrived,

Janice was prepared—fielding tough questions from nearly all the Justices. "I don't think the argument could have gone much better," she says. But she lost the case 5 to 4.

Today, although she remains on a variety of capital habeas lists and is still a consultant on the issue for the ABA, Janice no longer takes capital cases; she focuses exclusively on noncapital habeas appeals for both state and federal prisoners. Capital habeas attorneys need to "give up their lives" to their careers. After having given birth to two sons in her early forties, Janice's priorities shifted. She's seeking more of the balance in her life that she first saw with the civil rights attorneys she interned for many years ago in North Carolina. She prefers keeping more regular hours and being able to spend more time with her family.

But twenty years after first falling in love, Janice's affair with the Constitution is still going strong. Working in habeas appeals, defense lawyers get to do "amazing stuff . . . stuff that is so interesting and affects people at the same time," she says. "My husband and I marvel often about what nice lives we have—we have great jobs, are able to live comfortably and work with smart people. I even got to argue at the Supreme Court."

She is satisfied with her career choice. "Criminal defense attorneys are incredibly patriotic," she says. "They believe in the Constitution, in justice. They believe everybody deserves a chance at those protections. . . . If justice doesn't work for the most despised people in our society, then it doesn't work for anybody."

Section4

Other Government Lawyers

RAYMOND CHEUNG

EEOC Employment Litigator

By Lauren E. Brady

When Raymond Cheung was growing up, he was the one always interested in intellectual interaction, in parsing an argument, in the merits of issues and political debates. That same passion for an intellectual challenge is what led him to decide to major in anthropology in college. Professor Vincent Sarich taught Raymond's class at the University of California at Berkeley in a modified Socratic style by encouraging his students to challenge each other intellectually and forcing them to think on their feet. True to his own critical approach, Raymond had many disagreements with Professor Sarich, but his love of the rhetorical aspects of the class led him to choose anthropology as an early career path.

At Berkeley, Raymond was exposed to a variety of political viewpoints. It was, in his words, an eye-opening experience. It was a time during which Raymond began fine-tuning his political sensibilities. As he describes it, while he'd always had a gut sense of what was right and wrong, during college he began to refine the way in which he viewed the world, gaining a more nuanced view of rights and social responsibilities. He spent his semesters engaged in rigorous academic exploration and his summers hard at work to pay his tuition. Work was a constant throughout Raymond's life, even from his earliest years.

The son of immigrants, Raymond was born in Hong Kong and grew up in Oakland. His parents worked long hours in a restaurant, and he was a self-described latchkey kid throughout primary school. He helped out at the restaurant as early as he can remember and even as a young child developed a very intimate understanding of what happens in a workplace. He saw his parents constantly working to support the family and was attuned to the great inequalities in treatment they faced at the restaurant. As immigrants, they were picked on by patrons and coworkers because of their inability to speak English. People mimicked their accents and teased them behind their backs. Raymond describes his reaction to this type of discriminatory treatment as very visceral — the type of feeling that people cannot understand without living through it and being personally affected by it. Without that personal connection to discriminatory treatment, Raymond says, people can only think about experiencing prejudice abstractly. Despite these experiences, Raymond wasn't immediately drawn to law or to civil rights. In high school he was involved in debating, and he began to refine his political consciousness during his time at Berkeley. But his path to law school was instead marked by a very interesting and completely nonlegal post-college career.

Just after his graduation from Berkeley in 1988, to supplement his degree in physical anthropology, Raymond spent a year excavating and analyzing human skeletons in Cairo. This type of overseas fieldwork was a logical extension of his undergraduate major, but for Raymond, classifying mummies was just a stop on the road toward a legal career. He also tried graduate school in New York but left after two years, because he was troubled by the detachment from daily life he felt he and his peers were experiencing. "They were disconnected from the issues, and the problems that people have," he says. He left New York looking for a more fulfilling career, where he could delve into work that had an impact on people's daily lives.

Back in the Bay Area, Raymond briefly worked in a number of jobs and finally decided on law school. He knew from the beginning, when he entered the University of San Francisco as a first-year law student, that he would be drawn to public interest work. But, he says, "I tried to go in with open eyes about what I wanted to do. I wanted to try to be embracing of other things, but I soon realized that I couldn't." He quickly became involved with the public interest community at USF and in the Bay Area. He was co-president of USF's Public Interest Law Foundation and was involved with the law school's clinical programs. During his first summer, Raymond worked at the nonprofit Benchmark Institute in San Francisco, an organization that provides training for legal services attorneys. He remains involved with Benchmark today as a member of its board of directors. It was an ideal first-summer legal job, says Raymond, because it provided him with the opportunity to interact with many different public interest organizations. Armed with that sampling of what was available for new lawyers who wanted to work in public interest, he returned to school in the fall with a renewed commitment to public interest law.

During his second year of law school Raymond took an externship with the San Francisco Neighborhood Legal Assistance Foundation, where he was responsible for assisting clients with public benefits matters, including Social Security and MediCal claims and appeals. During school Raymond found himself drawn to his Civil Procedure course, a class that many students consider dry: "I thought that 'civpro' was the coolest class ever," he says; "I suppose that makes me a dork." There was something about knowing the back story of a case—the type of information an attorney learns through the strategic decisions involved in civil procedure—that intrigued Raymond. Knowing the way a case developed and understanding the legal problem from the perspective of the people who experienced it can be a powerful tool in litigation, Raymond says. It also explains his concern for remaining connected with everyday issues and real-life problems as his legal education continued.

During the summer after his second year, the same troubling fear of becoming disconnected from issues, coupled with his passion for public interest work, drew Raymond to the Employment Law Center at the Legal Aid Society of San Francisco, a place where he could be involved with cases that would have immediate impact on the lives of hardworking families. As someone who grew up with an intimate sense of that life, Raymond's internship with the ELC was a natural fit. It was, in his words, "a pivotal summer, and one that forever directed my career."

During that summer of 1993, Raymond assisted attorneys litigating a wide variety of employment cases involving English language-only rules, sexual orientation discrimination, and national origin and accent discrimination. His experiences as a child seeing the discrimination his parents faced resonated in the work Raymond did that summer. Raymond assisted Christopher Ho, a lawyer at the ELC whom he considers a brilliant attorney, in litigating the Ninth Circuit English-only rule case, *Garcia v. Spun Steak Company*. The case was a fascinating intellectual exercise for Raymond and provided him the opportunity to learn from a seasoned professional doing cutting-edge legal work on behalf of minorities. From that time forward, Raymond would identify employment discrimination work as his passion. "It's what I loved to do," he says.

When asked if he enjoyed his time at law school, Raymond hesitates. There were classes that he loved, he says, but other aspects that he didn't like. He was frustrated with what he considered the conservative bent of his legal education and his fellow students. He was also unhappy with the excess of rote memorization: "This is what you do; this is how you practice law." On the other hand, he found his legal theory classes and constitutional law seminars "a lot more interesting—something to sink your teeth into, as opposed to the nuts and bolts of what certain laws might be on a certain issue."

Raymond graduated from the USF School of Law in 1994. He found his first job in San Jose, California, at the Asian Law Alliance (ALA), a nonprofit legal services organization. It seemed to be the perfect fit for a new attorney interested in direct legal services public interest work. As a staff attorney, Raymond was primarily responsible for litigating housing cases, including fair housing issues, unlawful detainer actions, and contract disputes. In addition to the usual aspects of trial practice, Raymond was able to interact directly with clients and provide counseling on housing, employment, public benefits, and immigration issues. As a housing attorney with a background in employment discrimination, Raymond saw the crossover issues that most clients with housing problems faced. "When you do intake for housing cases, you find that most people face a whole suit of problems," he said. With this in mind, Raymond lobbied to add an employment component to the ALA's practice areas and provide a more holistic representation to clients.

After successfully acquiring funding to support his idea, Raymond created "Justice at Work," an effort aimed at educating recent immigrants about their employment and labor rights. As program director, Raymond represented clients at employment-related administrative hearings, wrote informational materials on employment rights, and gave presentations at adult-education and English-language classes for new immigrants. Raymond also became acutely aware of another issue prevalent in public interest law practice: financial strain. Although he was doing work that he considered important and fulfilling, Raymond wasn't making enough money to pay back his student loans. Fortunately, USF had a loan repayment assistance program (LRAP) that made working at the ALA financially viable, but he admits that the financial burdens of law school made it difficult for him to decide what he wanted to do with his legal education. Even a government salary doesn't go far, especially in the Bay Area, Raymond notes. The financial aspect of working somewhere other than in a traditional law firm is something that every law student poised to take on a public interest career must consider, he says, but with LRAP programs available, that decision should be much easier.

Raymond remained at the ALA until 1999, when he took a position with the U.S. Equal Employment Opportunity Commission (EEOC). He has remained with the EEOC in San Francisco since that time and is now a senior trial attorney. San Francisco Regional Attorney William Tamayo, the attorney who hired Raymond there, speaks glowingly of Raymond: "Ray was committed to making the law work for people that have been historically neglected or underserved. He believes in civil rights and will work the long hours and put in much energy to help out victims of discrimination. He is a thorough litigator, writes well, knows his arguments, and can think at the macro and micro levels. He also understands the stakes involved in terms of the lives of the charging parties, the precedents that can be set, and the importance of the government protecting individual rights."

Raymond considers working at the EEOC as a career goal, as a place where he can focus solely on employment discrimination. It has been his only position with a government office, but Raymond is quick to point out that he considers himself a civil rights attorney who just happens to work for the government. Working for the government was not the draw that brought Raymond to the EEOC—instead, it was the practice area and the kinds of cases he would have the opportunity to work on that led Raymond to take a government position. Also important was the fact that he would continue to work in intensive litigation. The competitiveness of high-impact cases attracted him. "You have to love that part," he says, "If you don't, you'll burn out. It's the rush that you get in competitive litigation that I love."

Despite being a government office, the EEOC is a relatively small agency. The district office is located on the fifth floor of a tower on the Embarcadero, which overlooks San Francisco Bay. The attorneys' offices are relatively small, with hallways filled with filing cabinets and boxes. It's a place, Raymond says, where people really care about their work. "You can get a better-paying job at the Department of Justice," he says, "But this work is less partisan—and more important." However, the EEOC is the type of agency that both Democrats and Republicans can find reasons not to like, so the office doesn't always get the level of resources it needs to effectively fight civil rights violations. That said, Raymond notes, they are definitely able to rely on a level of funding far above most nonprofits doing similar work.

There is one thing Raymond misses working at the EEOC—the constant contact with clients. At the Asian Law Alliance, Raymond was able to see the faces of the people he was helping. "These were people who came in to our office with a gut sense that something was wrong," Raymond says. He saw his job as translating that sense into a legal claim. As an attorney at the EEOC, he doesn't get the chance to have that first contact with individual clients. The office is charged with investigative and enforcement functions, and, although the agency does workplace outreach programs, he has fewer opportunities to educate workers on their rights than he had at ALA. In larger class action cases, Raymond often never meets any of his clients. This distancing is troubling to

Raymond at times, and he considers it one negative aspect of working in his current position. However, the position does offer him the flexibility not only to litigate class actions with major impacts, but to bring other cases in which he can interact with individuals in a very personal way. "To many of the people that we see, by the time they get here they've had to deal with very difficult situations for a very long time."

Raymond considers one class action to be the most important litigation he's been involved with in his career. *Arnett & EEOC v. Public Employees Retirement System* is an employment discrimination case in which the Commission secured a $250 million settlement for a class of 1,700 retired and disabled public safety officers and invalidated a California statute that discriminated against older public safety officers. The lawsuit grew out of a violation of the Age Discrimination in Employment Act of 1967 (ADEA). The class of officers suffered discrimination through a policy that reduced their industrial disability retirement benefits in proportion to an officer's age at the time he or she was hired. Raymond deems *Arnett* the most intellectually challenging case he has litigated. "We made new law, and changed a discriminatory statute," he says, but points to an even more fulfilling part of the case: the sheer number of individuals who were helped significantly by the settlement.

Most of the cases at the EEOC are staffed by one lead attorney, but some have large teams of lawyers working from multiple district offices. Raymond considers the hours and the workload reasonable. "It depends on the level of commitment you put into it," he says. He's heard the criticism that nonprofit and government attorneys don't work as hard as firm lawyers, but believes that the real difference is the kind of work public interest attorneys engage in during their workdays. "I've modeled my career on the practice habits of other attorneys who work very hard," he says. That ability to find role models in the public interest arena is an important aspect of the practice area, Raymond notes, especially for new attorneys. The public interest community in any given city, but especially in San Francisco, is a very small community. "You get to know a lot of people, and you maintain those contacts and develop those networks." Through those networks, Raymond met a number of people doing public interest work he now considers role models, including his current boss at the EEOC, William Tamayo. "Bill is a standard-bearer for his dedication to public interest," Raymond says. "I made fun of him when he first went to the Commission—he paid me back when he hired me." Raymond also admires Bay Area civil rights attorney Eva Patterson, for her ability to forward a topic and to be a spokesperson for an issue.

While he may point to others as role models in the field, Raymond Cheung very clearly has forged a path of dedication to upholding civil rights and fighting for those who lack a voice—the kind of dedication that many new public interest lawyers will no doubt look to when searching for their own inspiration.

ALISA KLEIN

Federal Civil Appellate Litigator

By Jason Peckenpaugh

This should be an easy case for us, thought Alisa Klein. But on June 3, 1996, the day Alisa made her first appellate argument, her side was in trouble. She was representing the Office of the Comptroller of the Currency, a federal agency that was appearing as an amicus in support of a national bank that was sued for allegedly violating a financial privacy law.

"You realize that the law and equities are entirely with the other side," a judge with the Fifth Circuit Court of Appeals told the bank's lawyer. Alisa, who has a quick wit, initially thought the judge was joking. But the silence in the courtroom told her the judge was serious. "I thought, they're giving our side an incredibly hard time," she remembers. "This type of realization tends to get the adrenalin flowing."

When Alisa's turn came to speak, she launched into her argument with characteristic zeal. It is perfectly legal for a bank to share a customer's financial data with the government, she explained, when the customer is laundering money. The following week, the Fifth Circuit ruled for Alisa's side without issuing an opinion — a sign the judges did, in fact, view it as an easy case.

Nine years later, oral argument can still make Alisa's heart race. But this rush, along with the intellectual heavy lifting required by a caseload that ranges from medical marijuana to Medicare is what makes litigating for the federal government exhilarating for her. It's why, at thirty-eight, she can't imagine doing anything else. "I'm not leaving my dream job," she says.

Alisa's dream job is representing the federal government in the high-stakes world of appellate litigation, which she does as an attorney with the appellate staff of the Justice Department's Civil Division in

Washington, which includes the Office of the Comptroller of the Currency. From her spartan office, which overlooks an interior courtyard at Justice headquarters, Alisa has worked on the biggest federalism cases heard by the Rehnquist Court, including *United States v. Raich*, where the Supreme Court upheld Congress's ability to regulate the use of marijuana for medical purposes.

Alisa has litigated cases involving politically sensitive issues, including anthrax contamination at postal facilities and federal management of Native-American lands. She has handled highly technical cases, including an "unbelievably complicated" case on the overlap of the Medicare and Medicaid statutes. She's even represented the Justice Department against a class of Justice attorneys seeking compensation for unpaid overtime.

And these days, Alisa does it working a forty-hour week. Leaving at around 5:00, she heads home to Chevy Chase, Maryland, a leafy suburb of Washington, DC, where she picks up her two children, ages six and a half and four, from the babysitter. Her husband, a partner at the Washington law firm Wilmer Cutler Pickering Hale and Dorr, arrives home soon thereafter. With two young children and full-time legal careers, free time is scarce for both lawyers. A book club—it has "been going strong for almost eleven years"—remains a guilty pleasure.

Alisa is petite and animated. In conversation she speaks at a breakneck clip, her words unspooling in rapid-fire but grammatically perfect sentences. With her easy laugh and dark, darting eyes, she exudes a fascination with her cases and a reverence for a certain way of practicing law—intellectually rigorous, yet courteous—that she learned in clerkships and applies every day at work. You sense she has found her calling, and in the Civil Division she has discovered a small cadre of like-minded coworkers who share this calling.

"This office tends to draw people with an academic bent but not an academic temperament," says Alisa. Every other year, Alisa and her supervisor, Mark Stern, co-teach a seminar on federalism at Georgetown University Law Center. Other colleagues also teach on the side but share her preference for full-time work at the Justice Department, where they have a hand in resolving real-world legal disputes.

Many were drawn to the Civil Division's appellate staff by the chance to make appellate arguments as an entry-level attorney—an opportunity that simply doesn't exist for most associates at a large law firm. "It would be very unusual at a traditional law firm for . . . the most junior person to be the one who goes off and does the argument," notes Alisa. "Here, there is a tremendous focus on cultivating young attorneys, on making sure they have the chance to do arguments."

New attorneys aren't just thrown into court. When a case comes up on appeal, a supervisor will share advice before the attorney starts work—and then take a red pen to the resulting brief. "To write something and then have someone show you how to make it better is the best legal writing training," says Alisa. "Next time, ideally, you make it better yourself."

Veteran attorneys face revisions as well. In big cases, Alisa says attorneys "will do thirteen or fourteen iterations of briefs, even before we circulate it to the client (agency) or other Justice divisions." It may take a village to write a brief in the Justice Department, but rewriting ensures a top-notch final product.

Of course, working for Uncle Sam isn't all roses. It can be hard to get a foot in the door at the Justice Department; presidential administrations sometimes impose freezes on new hires, and permanent personnel ceilings mean support staff are in short supply. "My secretary, who helped six or seven attorneys, left months ago, and we don't have authorization to fill her slot," says Alisa. And the government will never pay lawyers or support staff as much as law firms do.

However, an experienced Justice Department attorney still can expect a six-figure salary. "My view is that federal government salaries are very generous," says Alisa. With its fascinating caseload and high standards for legal work, the Civil Division has many lawyers willing to devote a career to working for the government. Robert E. Kopp, the director of the appellate section, has been there since 1966.

Alisa was born in 1967. Growing up in the 1970s in Lafayette Hill, a suburb of Philadelphia, she was a shy, bookish child. As the daughter of two psychologists, Alisa was not drawn to the law as an inevitable career path. But after studying the social sciences at Princeton's Woodrow Wilson School of Public & International Affairs, a feeder for top law and policy graduate schools, Alisa decided to try law.

First, though, she wanted to see what life at a law firm was really like. After being accepted at Harvard Law School, Alisa deferred for a year to work as a paralegal with a New York firm, Davis, Polk & Wardwell. The experience taught her that issues of business and finance—the cornerstone of New York legal practice—didn't pique her interest. But what did?

Alisa wasn't sure. But she arrived at Harvard with a plan: "I very self-consciously tried to do many different types of legal jobs when I was in law school, just to get a sense for what they were like." While in school, Alisa worked for the U.S. Attorney's office in Boston, watching seasoned attorneys conduct criminal trials. She interned at a legal services center, helping low-income residents secure disability benefits. Summers were spent in Washington, where she worked at Public Citizen, the Ralph Nader-founded watchdog group, and Shea & Gardner, a small DC law firm.

Law school wasn't all about outside jobs: during her first year she won the prestigious Sears Prize, which is given to the top two students in the first-year class. She also made Law Review and participated in clinics. All this left little time for mock trial, although Alisa remembers enjoying Harvard's moot court competition for first-year students. Thinking back on her law school experience, she counts Federal Courts as her most useful course for what she does today.

Through hands-on work experience outside school, Alisa found what interested her. "I'm much more interested in government and social policy, which tends to be a DC practice." But Alisa owes her career path to an unusual series of events that transpired after she applied for clerkships — and crossed paths with a particular federal judge.

In the summer of 1993, Alisa was a newly minted Harvard Law School graduate. She was spending her days at Shea & Gardner while studying for the bar exam at night. One day she received a phone call from her mother. "Did you hear? Your boss has been nominated!"

Alisa's boss was Ruth Bader Ginsburg, who had just been named to the Supreme Court by President Clinton. Ginsburg, then a judge on the DC Circuit Court of Appeals, had offered Alisa a clerkship months earlier. But because Supreme Court Justices rarely take clerks fresh out of law school — they prefer law graduates who have clerked for a year — it seemed doubtful that Alisa would follow Ginsburg to the High Court.

Alisa was, understandably, a tad shy about broaching the topic with Ginsburg. "I didn't want to bother her with my petty concerns about my own career." But, shortly thereafter, at a gathering of past and future Ginsburg clerks, the judge took Alisa and her other incoming clerks aside and said of their clerkships, "the question is not whether, it's when."

For Alisa, this cryptic assurance proved a gift. She clerked for a year with Louis H. Pollak, a judge on the Eastern District of Pennsylvania bench and former dean of Yale Law School, before she joined Justice Ginsburg at the Supreme Court. Alisa had a wonderful time with Pollak, a gifted storyteller famous for mentoring young lawyers. Since Pollak often sat by designation on appellate courts, Alisa had the chance to watch both trials and appellate arguments — an experience that showed Alisa her heart was in appellate work.

"When I sat in listening to the oral arguments in the Third Circuit, I could have sat for eight hours with fascination," she remembers. Conversely, the factual disputes of trial practice made Alisa's eyes glaze over. "I was less interested in disputes that didn't have any significance beyond the facts."

In court Alisa saw trial attorneys act rudely toward each other, further souring her on trial work. "I can't stand that kind of contentious litigation. And my guess is that is also true of a lot of people who do appellate work," she says. "I was able to confirm, having seen the trial practice, that temperamentally I was not suited for it."

By the time Alisa began her Supreme Court clerkship, she had already decided where she wanted to be afterwards: at the Justice Department, doing appellate litigation. She applied to the Justice Department's prestigious program for recent law school graduates, known as DOJ Honors, and around Thanksgiving 1994, she was accepted. "While other [Supreme Court clerks] were milling about talking to all kinds of law firms, I knew where I was going, and I went straight through."

Alisa spent a fascinating year clerking for Justice Ginsburg. Clerks typically are assigned a few cases to analyze and then draft an opinion for each one. Alisa recalls working on a civil procedure case — a favorite topic for both Alisa and Ginsburg — and, in a harbinger of her future work at the Justice Department, a case involving the Employee Retirement Income Security Act (ERISA), the complex federal law that regulates private pension plans.

You won't see ERISA cases being discussed on Court TV; Alisa recalls a fellow Ginsburg clerk was astonished that she liked them. But Alisa relished the intellectual challenge of parsing the statute. "It's true in law generally that issues that may not sound interesting at a cocktail party are often the most interesting," she says.

In September 1995 Alisa came to the Civil Division eager to litigate but not completely aware of the responsibilities that come with practicing at the Justice Department. As Uncle Sam's counsel, the Justice Department works for virtually every federal agency. Because legal challenges to a statute often implicate programs at different agencies, part of Alisa's job is to make sure that interested agencies get to weigh in on cases that affect them. "The Labor Department will have an interest in a case involving the Postal Service."

On matters of legal strategy, agencies generally defer to the Justice Department, a difference from private practice, where "the client generally has the last word on everything." But Justice Department attorneys still must write briefs that accommodate multiple actors. "An agency will say, 'can you change this description because we're afraid it might undercut us in a different context,'" says Alisa. "Usually you can just do it without undermining anything else that you're trying to say."

Alisa found she liked the discipline of working for multiple clients. She also noticed that attorneys at the Department seemed bound by an ethic of legal fairness; they litigated by the Queensbury rules. It reminded her of a favorite saying of Justice Ginsburg: "you can never knock the parties' chess pieces off the chessboard." Ginsburg was talking about the role of a judge and her belief that parties to a lawsuit should be made to feel that they have had their day in court even if the law clearly is against them. To Alisa, Ginsburg's adage of fairness rang true at the Justice Department as well.

"We have the obligation not to brush aside the other side's strong arguments," she says. "Sometimes in the private sector there is so much pressure to win that there might be a temptation to overstate the position, whereas, if anything, the pressure in the government is to understate the position."

In rare cases, the Justice Department will even forgo the defense of a statute. For example, in *ACLU v. Mineta*, a 2004 case on which Alisa worked, the issue was a federal law prohibiting mass transit authorities from displaying advertisements advocating the legalization or medical use of controlled substances such as marijuana. Transit systems that accepted such ads risked losing federal funding.

When the law was challenged in the DC District Court, the court held that it constituted viewpoint discrimination, a violation of the First Amendment, and promptly struck down the statute. This decision was debatable — in theory, the law might be constitutional if transit authorities implement it through viewpoint-neutral ad policies by banning anti-drug use ads along with pro-legalization ads. But because Congress clearly didn't intend to restrict anti-drug messages, the Justice Department gave up its defense of the law and opted not to appeal.

"The government does not have a viable argument to advance in the statute's defense," concluded Paul D. Clement, the acting Solicitor General, in a December 23, 2004, letter to House and Senate legal counsel. To Alisa, the decision not to appeal is emblematic of legal decision-making at the Justice Department. "It's not just a straightforward question of how do we win," she says. Instead, the Department tries to adopt a "responsible legal position" when it goes to court.

But don't think Justice attorneys are shrinking violets in the courtroom. In *Nebraska Beef, Ltd. v. Greening*, a 2004 case, Alisa defended a group of federal meat inspectors against Nebraska Beef, a meatpacking company that sued the inspectors personally after it received several citations for unsanitary conditions at its Omaha plant. "My view was that this large plant was trying to intimidate the inspectors," says Alisa.

Nonetheless, the district court allowed the lawsuit to proceed. If Nebraska Beef won, the inspectors faced the prospect of paying damages from their own wallets. On appeal before the Eighth Circuit, Alisa laid out a passionate argument for why the inspectors should be immune from suit. She pointed to strong Eighth Circuit precedent and even cited *The Jungle*, Upton Sinclair's 1905 exposé of the wretched conditions at Chicago slaughterhouses, which helped prompt federal meat inspection laws. "I was clear and I was vehement. And that's all you can do." The Eighth Circuit ruled for the inspectors, and the lawsuit was dismissed.

By late summer 2005, Alisa had presented more than forty-five appellate arguments and had appeared in all of the federal circuit courts of appeal. She has been part of the small team of attorneys to work on the key federalism cases heard by the Rehnquist Court. Alisa helped write the government's unsuccessful brief in *United States v. Morrison*, where the Supreme Court, by a 5 to 4 margin, struck down the Violence Against Women Act because it exceeded Congress's Commerce Clause powers.

In *Raich*, the High Court's most recent opinion on the Commerce Clause, Alisa and other Justice attorneys successfully distinguished *Morrison* and won. "Once a case is lost, we try quickly to make sense of the outcome so that we can distinguish the case in other settings," says Alisa. "So, even though we defended the [Violence Against Women Act] in *Morrison*, the point in *Raich* was to explain how very different that provision was from the Controlled Substances Act."

Alisa tries to impart this litigation savvy to her students at Georgetown. And with their help, Alisa uses the class to reflect on the wisdom of the decisions themselves.

Asked what career advice she has for current law students, Alisa urges them to look at the Justice Department but also to consider state agencies and other federal agencies, which offer their own opportunities for appellate litigation. "The Department of Labor, the Federal Communications Commission, the Equal Employment Opportunity Commission, and many other federal agencies have their own in-house appellate staffs," she notes. "If you are really interested in doing appellate work, I think there are a large number of options."

Alisa's road to the Civil Division was neither long nor winding. She found her dream job two years out of law school. While it is tempting to trace her job satisfaction to her impeccable credentials—a stellar résumé does open doors—it doesn't help pick the right one. Alisa found the Civil Division after examining the options available to a young lawyer—law firm or government, trial practice or appellate work—and choosing the best fit for her.

NICOLA GOREN

Federal Agency Counsel

By Craig Holt Segall

Through the window of her tenth floor office, behind Nicola Goren's desk, the District of Columbia hums. Leaning backward and forward as she talks, laughing easily, and gesturing despite a cast on her arm, she is in her element. Papers from a major rulemaking at the Corporation for National and Community Service, the federal agency for which she is Associate General Counsel, lie on the long desk. The final rule had been finished just the week before, and Nicola is feeling ebullient after a year and a half of hard work. She is looking forward to the next challenge. It's a great situation, especially when you find out that she had not even been certain she was going to be a lawyer.

Nicola did not enter the law because she dreamed of courtroom glory. As she explains, "In my head, a lawyer was a litigator, and it was never my personality to be that kind of lawyer." Instead, she had been drawn to law while at college at Brandeis through a legal studies course in her junior year. Delving into the cases, she found herself fascinated by legal thought. "I thought this kind of study and this kind of dissecting facts and applying them and coming out with these incredible opinions was so fascinating," she recalls. "I really enjoyed it, but I still wasn't convinced I wanted to be a lawyer." What mattered to her was not the thrust and parry of a courtroom argument, but the issues of structure and function that underlie systems of law.

Nicola decided that she was not looking for a particular job so much as a particular working experience. When, years later, she was leaving law school without a job lined up, she explained her criteria to the dean. "I want to like the people I work with; I want to feel good about getting up in the morning to go to work every day; and I want a life." The work also had to be intellectually challenging. With those principles guiding her, Nicola has made her way through the legal career thicket to find a place where she can be happy, accomplished, and balanced.

Born to two academics, an Israeli-born father and an Egyptian-born mother in Liverpool, England, and growing up in both Britain and the United States, Nicola had early on developed an interest in different modes of government. Her father had a Ph.D. in naval architecture and worked designing offshore oil rigs; her mother had earned a masters' degree in political science, an interest that Nicola developed. When she returned to this country for college, the chance to learn about how the government worked was particularly exciting. "Part of the reason I wanted to work in government was because I knew nothing about how the U.S. government worked," she says. By working on the inside of government, she could come to understand it and pursue her interest in law. With that perspective, law school made sense, even though she still did not necessarily plan to be a lawyer. After graduating from Brandeis with a degree in European Cultural Studies, Nicola headed for Cornell Law School in the fall of 1989.

Cornell University sits above Cayuga Lake in upstate New York, a lovely but isolated location that gives students plenty of time to focus on their legal studies. For Nicola, it was almost too much time. She had been thinking about joining the Peace Corps, but her father had convinced her that it was important to start her career immediately. Living alone for the first time and confronted with the challenge of law school, she felt daunted.

"First year had major ups and major downs," she recalls. The smartest people she had ever met sat in class with her. At times this was exhilarating; at other times, it was intimidating. The emotional and intellectual intensity built until, by November, as the sky in upstate New York turned gray, it was time to get out. The place was "like a pressure cooker" and, by two weeks before Thanksgiving, she "felt like if I spent another day in that town, I was going to explode." A spontaneous four-day weekend trip to sunny Los Angeles, where her grandmother lived, sent her back into finals feeling a new equilibrium. When she walked out, a semester of intense effort behind her, she felt like she was floating. Law school had become a livable reality.

Over the next few years, Nicola made her place at the law school. She participated in the Public Interest Law Union. She helped plan a conference on the then-new Americans with Disability Act, and, continuing her interest in government, helped launch the *Cornell Journal of Law & Public Policy*. She took classes that interested her without being overly concerned by future career plans. Surprisingly for a government lawyer, she never took administrative law.

It was her summers, more than her academic experience, that shaped Nicola's later career choices. Her first summer she interned with the Suffolk County District Attorney in Boston. The nitty-gritty life of the DAs was compelling, but there was one real problem: "They paid so badly," says Nicola. Budget problems made the position untenable. "They had DAs right out of law school who had to work as busboys at night just to make ends meet."

Nicola worked as a summer associate at a Boston law firm her second summer, with the hope of comparing her DA's experience with law firm life. It was one of the best decisions she ever made, but not for the usual reasons. Describing the experience, she recalls a summer spent feeling alienated, in an atmosphere that did not fulfill her basic criteria for a job. "As much as I thought the work was interesting, I did not like the atmosphere. That was a big part of it for me," she says. "Just little silly things — three quarters of the way through the summer I'm told that I've been doing my billable hours wrong the entire summer and they're coming down on me for it. And the fact that I had to do billable hours at all had annoyed me from the beginning." After her summer experience, she was almost certain that a law firm career was not for her.

Back at Cornell, though, the "chaos of job hunting while you're in school" and the pressure to find a job before graduation briefly made her reconsider. Firm interviews reminded her of her summer realization. "After the first few I said 'why am I doing this?' I mean, why? It doesn't make any sense." Nicola returned to her criteria — a friendly, meaningful, and interesting job that would allow her to have a life. "I quickly realized that the types of jobs I was interested in were not the types that were coming on campus to meet you," she said. "I really decided that my first choice would be some kind of government work." Glancing nervously at her debt, she decided to go to Washington after law school to find a job that would fit her criteria and her personality.

Although Nicola had expected to come to DC jobless, she got lucky. Because "networking is key" in government work, Nicola had called people she knew in the capital. Most small government agencies do not participate in job fairs or on-campus interviews; you have to find your way through research and the advice of friends and mentors. These "tiny agencies that nobody even knows about" are rewarding places to work because they are small enough to give significant responsibilities to those fresh out of law school.

Nicola didn't have the advantage of the Internet; she had to network for her jobs. While she emphasizes finding friends and taking their advice, she also points young lawyers to government websites, such as UsaJobs.opm.gov, which gather government jobs under one roof.

The Presidential Management Fellows program, a highly competitive program that places young professionals in government work, is also a great option for those who know they want to do government work. For many, though, it will come down to talking with people who have already found good careers.

One such person had pointed Nicola to an open assistant general counsel job at the Congressional Budget Office (CBO), the agency that assists Congress with the budgeting process. "This is the kind of job that, had I seen it advertised, I probably never would have applied for it. First of all, the word 'budget' was in the title, and I didn't do numbers," Nicola laughs. But after interviewing with the General Counsel, Nicola saw that the job would deal more broadly with challenging government legal work, leaving the numbers for the economists in the CBO. She took the job.

Along with the General Counsel, she would be one of only two lawyers for an agency of 220 people. Every legal issue that came up in the complex budget process, as well as every other CBO legal and ethics issue, would flow through their little office. And when the General Counsel was away, Nicola stepped into the role.

"It was the best experience, especially right out of law school," Nicola says. It wasn't an easy experience. "It was daunting at the beginning; there was a very steep learning curve because so much of the law they dealt with was something I'd never heard of." With no administrative law background and certainly no experience with the budgeting process, Nicola had to get comfortable with "just being able to say 'I'm going to get back to you on that.'" For Nicola, who had come to law because she was enthralled by its intricate patterns and structures, the intellectual challenge was ideal. Rather than working on small pieces of larger problems, as she might have done as an associate at a firm, or building a narrow practice area, as some Department of Justice lawyers must do, she handled every issue the small agency faced. In her first year out, she was a generalist with broad responsibilities and a full portfolio.

The job certainly met her criterion for a good work environment, but her other goal — "I want to have a life" — was a little harder. Although Nicola was never looking for money, lower pay did make life more stressful. Nicola is frank about the debt burden young public interest lawyers carry. She had between sixty and eighty thousand dollars of debt and was making roughly thirty thousand dollars a year. "The first three years were really hard. I moved into an apartment, and once my loan payments kicked in ($850-900 a month) I realized I couldn't afford my rent," she recalls. "There were weeks where literally all I was eating was rice." A pair of gray wool pants, bought at a steep markdown, served as her office attire three days a week. Despite being the number two lawyer in the CBO, Nicola's personal budget was tight.

She found ways to make it bearable. Loan forgiveness from Cornell during her first two years helped her jump some of the debt hurdles. To make ends meet, Nicola took a part-time job as an adult volleyball instructor and referee. The nights out on the courts helped balance her days on the Hill. And they provided just enough extra funds to squeak by. But while money was in short supply, happiness was plentiful. Nicola was dating the man who would become her husband and who, at the time, was working for a large firm. This gave her a chance to compare their lives. "He had much less debt than I did. Much less debt and much higher pay. So he, in a way, was living large, but he was so unhappy from virtually the first day. I was stressed because I wasn't making much money but I was enjoying what I was doing." The daily joy of her job compensated for fiscal woes. Nicola feels she made the right decision. "It's doable. I won't say that the first years aren't hard, because they are, but it's so worth it."

The money problems cleared up over the years. Because she was working at a smaller agency—and would take jobs at other smaller places over her next few years—Nicola was not locked into the government's restrictive general schedule of payments. That meant that she could negotiate her way to a higher salary. Her salary jumped twenty-five percent during her second year as a result. Talking about this, she looks around her neat office with its broad desk and smiles. If she worked full-time she would be making in the low one hundred thousand dollar range; working part-time still makes for a comfortable life. "Now, honestly, I'm at a point—I never expected to make this much money in government."

Although she was happy at the CBO, Nicola began to feel the walls closing in after three years. The passion she brought to her work had also led others to begin to think of her as a budget lawyer. This was "exactly what I didn't want to be." Offers were coming in to go to work at places like the Senate Budget Committee. It was time to either leave or be permanently committed. Nicola put her networking skills to work.

Luckily, even as she got ready to leave her first job, Congress was getting ready to create a new one for her. From her position at the CBO, Nicola had a good view of the Hill. Congress was creating a new Office of Compliance, which would work to apply labor laws to congressional employees who had previously not been protected by the laws. With her work on the Americans with Disabilities Act in law school and her three years of government work, Nicola was perfect for the job of counsel for the new office. She got it.

It was every bit as fascinating and challenging as her first months at CBO had been. Although other parts of the government had compliance offices, this was an entirely new concept for Congress. It had to be created from scratch, which meant writing all the regulations and setting up the procedures that the office would use. At first it was wonderful. The work was in the underlying structure and function of government, where she would try to make things better in the present, rather than spending time in adversarial litigation later. But once the office was up and running, things changed.

"The structural work was over." That meant that Nicola's job was largely in employment law itself, dealing with the day-to-day concerns of congressional employees. For her, the intellectual excitement had passed. "Once it was up and running, . . . it wasn't challenging at all," said Nicola. After a year and a half, Nicola started looking for a new job, sorting through positions to find one that would suit her better.

It was 1998. Five years earlier, President Clinton had helped to create the new Corporation for National and Community Service, set up to call a new generation of Americans into public service. Sponsoring the AmeriCorps program, Senior Corps, and the educational program called Learn and Serve America, the Corporation was doing good work. It was looking for a new Associate General Counsel to serve as a program attorney, help with its appropriations and budget work and with employment and personnel issues. A job placement professional Nicola had been working with spotted the help-wanted ad and gave her a call.

She said Nicola needed to give the Corporation a look. "They're very mission-driven, and the people there are fantastic," she told Nicola. Nicola called the next day and sent in her résumé. The Corporation hired her shortly thereafter. She would be one of only seven attorneys helping to manage its large national programs. As always, she was ready for the challenge but insistent on keeping her life balanced and happy.

Nicola was swept up in the work, guiding the appropriations process, supporting the AmeriCorps program with its myriad complicated statutory interpretation issues, and working on employment issues. The AmeriCorps work was fulfilling, as it helped program staff and grantees to achieve their national service goals within the bounds of the law. Even the appropriations work turned out to be fascinating. "If you had asked me in law school, so do you want to be an appropriations lawyer when you graduate, I would have said I don't even know what you're talking about and probably no. But as it turns out it's a very interesting and intricate area of law that I love and I never would have thought that I would end up doing this," Nicola said. By basing her choices on her personal and professional needs rather than on a particular topical area, she had once again found unexpected beauty in a new area of the law. It was a more familiar area of the law that came to trouble her.

The personnel side of her job grew and grew. Due in part to Nicola's own research, the Corporation's employees discovered that they had the right to appeal adverse employment decisions and began to do so. Two years into her job, in 2000, Nicola was spending nearly all of her time doing personnel work, much of it litigation. She was becoming the sort of lawyer that she had not wanted to be. She was defending the Corporation against employees who had been fired or otherwise disciplined, caught up in interpersonal disputes rather than designing ways to resolve them early. "I was doing mostly what I did not enjoy. I really did not like litigation, and I was getting ready to quit."

It was a draining year. Nicola had had her first child in April. When she returned from maternity leave in October, personnel litigation was heating up. In November her father died in London. Nicola had to spend the month flying back and forth across the Atlantic. She felt that she "was just not coping."

It was not that Nicola was doing a bad job; it was that the job did not fit her life. "For me, it's a personality thing, and I think that people need to understand that you have to be able to look at a situation and just say 'you know, it's not that I can't do this' — I could, I won every case that I did, but I did not want to do it, it did not fit with my personality, it was affecting my home life." During that year, with the joys of her preferred areas of law behind her and a bleak future stretching ahead, she remembers coming home filled with stress. "I would go home and I couldn't even hear my son talking to me, I was so lost in my head." It had to end. Litigation was "all-consuming, and I did not want to have an all-consuming job."

By then, Nicola had learned a central lesson: she would not continue in jobs where she could not be healthy. She would steer by the criteria that she had decided on in law school. But she did not want to leave the Corporation. She believed in its mission and thought she could do good work there. It was time to negotiate her way to a better life. With the help of the sympathetic General Counsel, Nicola arranged to work only four days a week unless a major deadline was at hand. She also pressed for — and won — the hiring of a dedicated employment lawyer. That ended the litigation nightmare. Nicola had already taken over employment alternative dispute resolution in 1999, helping settle cases before they turned bad. She returned to program, to appropriations and regulatory and legislative work. Her life was back on an even keel.

In the past few years, she has immersed herself in the structure of the Corporation and has helped to streamline it and make it more accountable through a major rulemaking that governs agency operations.

The rulemaking process involves achieving policy goals while being attentive to obscure bureaucratic requirements. Nicola was at the center of it. It was the most complex, absorbing, and fulfilling work of her career. Beginning with meetings with other lawyers and managers of the Corporation, the process grew into attending a number of public meetings around the country, negotiating with the Office of Budget and Management, and drafting a series of technical regulatory publications. It was "policymaking at the highest level which is so much fun." Piles of paper grew in Nicola's office. "We had entire-day sessions where we just worked through these issues one by one and tried to figure out all of the unintended consequences," she remembers. "And then I would go back with what we had discussed and try and capture it in the rule and in the preamble."

A week after the rulemaking had been finished, the paper piles are now largely gone. Nicola's sense of accomplishment is not—the process was just as challenging as "the first semester of law school." "It's been fantastic. It's been frustrating at times because of the bureaucracy and it's taken a lot longer than I had hoped. But at the end of the day I'm very pleased with where it ended up and I just feel it's such an achievement for the agency." She will be working on a second, far more ambitious rulemaking, which will incorporate all the informal guidance documents that the Corporation puts out into one coherent set of rules. The community organizations that it supports will have an unambiguous guide to the entire process of working with the Corporation. It will be an enormous task. Nicola is looking forward to it. She thrives on this sort of structural challenge, solving problems before they start.

Life is good outside of work too. By negotiating a more flexible schedule—something that is relatively easy to do with the "pretty accommodating" government—Nicola is able to spend plenty of time with her family in northwest Washington, commuting to work by public transportation. There are two sons now, ages two and five. Her husband, once so stressed by big-firm life, has taken a job at a small plaintiff's firm and is much happier. Nicola hasn't given up volleyball and has also taken up women's soccer, yet she still has time to volunteer in her children's schools. Her work and her life balance, complementing each other.

Each job Nicola took helped her hone that balance. "Every position I had gave me more insight into my strengths and weaknesses than the one before—both from a substantive and a personality perspective. I was able to determine what type of work I liked and what type of work appealed to me less. I was also able to get a better understanding of myself." During her hardest periods at work, Nicola had considered leaving the law to become a mediator or work as law school staff, but she ultimately "came to understand that I am actually most happy researching, analyzing, and writing—probably all of the things that drew me to law in the first place. And I only figured that out in my third job."

Washington flows past behind Nicola's desk. She is smiling now, leaning forward. She reflects on her life, guided as much by personality as by planning. "I couldn't have imagined that it would be like this. I don't think I even had a vision. I just had criteria and this job meets all of them. I work with phenomenal people, both in the office and in the agency, and it's very mission-driven. I feel good about coming to work in the morning; I feel good about what we do, about what we're supporting. The work is always interesting. I have a life outside of work. I have no plans to leave."

WILLIAM E. THRO

State Solicitor General

By Lisa Saltzburg

"Virtually everything I ever wanted to do involved working for the government, largely defined," says William Thro. He originally envisioned himself an astronaut, not an attorney. (The moon landing took place when he was in kindergarten and left a lasting impression.) By the time he reached the seventh or eighth grade, however, the Space Program had faded and he had discovered he disliked bumpy flights. He then set his sights firmly on the law and has since spent his entire career in public service. Now Bill serves as the chief appellate counsel for the Commonwealth of Virginia and all her state agencies as State Solicitor General.

Bill always had an interest in law and politics, in spite of not knowing any lawyers growing up. He was raised in Elizabethtown, Kentucky, a small town in the sense that everyone knew everyone else, but not, he stresses, "a small town in the middle of nowhere." Its location fifty miles south of Louisville made the opportunities of a larger city reasonably accessible. Fort Knox, fifteen miles away, drew families from across the map, and Highway I-65 brought tourists through town. This provided for "a huge contrast," in the sense that at school he could easily find himself sitting between a "military brat" who had lived all over the world and the child of a tobacco farmer who might never have left Kentucky and had visited Louisville only a half dozen times.

That diversity meant that his classmates included both children of multimillionaires and others who didn't even have indoor plumbing. His own circumstances were at neither end of the spectrum. His father was associate superintendent of schools, and his mother was a high school guidance counselor. Both were the first people in their families to go to college. "Teachers are notoriously underpaid," he notes, but when you have only one child and you combine two incomes in a small town where many people are tobacco farmers who make much less than teachers, "you're pretty far up the socioeconomic strata."

As a teenager, Bill anticipated that pursuing his long-time goal would require a long-term plan. He considered applying to law school, a process that began with choosing the right college. His parents, concerned that their son would be lost at a large state school, encouraged him to seek not only the best preparation for law school, but the environment in which he would most thrive. They worried that, although he might be academically prepared for the Ivy Leagues or the Ivy equivalent, he was not ready culturally or socially, and they steered him toward small liberal arts colleges. He selected Hanover College, in Hanover, Indiana, in part because a recent valedictorian had graduated from Harvard Law School and had been offered a Supreme Court clerkship. This made an impression on Bill that if he did well at college, he might have similar opportunities.

Bill excelled at Hanover, but cautions that other people might have been bored to tears at a small school with strict rules. He double-majored in Business Administration and Political Science, and earned departmental honors in the latter. He had planned to go to law school from the beginning, but considers his academic advisor influential in keeping him on that path. Also, in his senior year he took a two-semester course in Constitutional and Legal History. The professor "was an incredible scholar" who constantly challenged his students' assumptions about the Constitution. Bill remarks that "even today, basically twenty years afterwards, I can remember his lectures on particular cases as if it were yesterday." Bill received the Crowe Citation, which is awarded to the outstanding male in each graduating class, and became the college's first Harry S. Truman Scholar by winning a highly competitive scholarship designed for students committed to a career in public service.

Those experiences and accolades helped him earn acceptance to the University of Virginia School of Law, which he chose over several other institutions. Bill would have been prepared to begin immediately, but he had also received a Rotary Foundation Ambassadorial Scholarship for one year of study at the University of Melbourne in Australia. Because the Australian academic year began in the spring, he thought he might have to defer law school, but UVA proved surprisingly accommodating. The school permitted him to split his first year, attending the fall semester as planned and the spring semester the following year.

His advisor in Melbourne quickly realized that, although Bill was earning his masters in political science, his real interest was constitutional law, and he steered Bill toward thesis work comparing the United States' and

Australia's constitutions. The program was entirely by thesis, with no coursework required, and was, to his mind, a more scholarly endeavor. He learned to pace himself and to develop self-discipline; if he wanted to take off for the beach on a beautiful day, he could, but he could not spend five consecutive days by the ocean.

The experience also forced him to mature in other ways. Having come from a small town and having attended a thousand-person college in a town of three thousand, he felt that he had "been in small-town everything." Suddenly, he found himself literally on the other side of the world in a city of three million people, all of them strangers. He reflects that this caused a great deal of growing up and introspection that might not have occurred had he simply gone straight through law school.

When asked if he liked law school, Bill responded that he "absolutely adored" it. "Virginia is a very special place," he explained, describing the campus as beautiful and Charlottesville as fantastic. The school at the time was "not incredibly competitive" because "they did not rank people," and "it seemed to be that no matter how hard you worked, you really couldn't make a grade higher than some form of a B, a B or a B+, and really no matter how hard you didn't work, as long as you attended class and kept up with the reading, it was awfully hard to make a grade below some form of a B."

Overall, Bill believes "it was far and away the best law school for me at that particular time" and describes himself as "very happy" with the education he received. Softball played a key role in law school. He coached his small section team, a difficult task considering the group included "a number of brilliant people," yet "no one who seemed capable of throwing, catching, or hitting a ball." Other activities took a backseat to legal scholarship. For Bill, working as a research assistant to A.E. Dick Howard and being on the law review most defined his law school experience and influenced his career.

He counts his work with Professor Howard as among the most important he has ever done. His position as a research assistant spanned most of his law school career from the time he returned from Australia through his third year. The Berlin Wall fell at around that time, and Bill's final project for Howard involved an independent study intended to assist those drafting a constitution for what was then Czechoslovakia. His project examined the nation's short but rich history of constitutional democracy prior to Nazi rule with an aim toward enabling Professor Howard to draw from that heritage. Bill predicted in his paper that the country would fall apart and become Czech and Slovakia, which is what happened, but in some respects he still feels that winning a case pales in comparison to the opportunity to play "a very small role in Professor Howard's fairly significant role in bringing democracy to Czechoslovakia."

He explains that law review was "a big influence, because it got me into scholarship, writing, researching, and editing, which is basically what I do now." It also sparked an interest in understanding the policy underlying a particular law, not just the law itself, as well as an early realization of that knowledge as an asset in brief writing and oral argument. He wrote his law review note on school finance litigation, inspired by the Kentucky school finance case, which was decided while he was at Virginia. "This fit nicely with Professor Howard's emphasis on state constitutions," and the timing was perfect. He "caught a magic moment in time," with the note's publication occurring just as school finance litigation again burst onto the national scene.

Howard, who "was very much a mentor" to Bill, doubted that private practice would suit him. "I really don't see you in a big firm," he once commented. "You'll be successful at it, but I don't think you'll ever like it." Because Bill was contemplating the lure and excitement of a big firm, that seemed a strange thing to say. He remembers the remark, though he assumes the professor has long forgotten it, and now considers it entirely accurate. He had spent his first law school summer at a relatively small firm in Louisville that did a fair amount of high-powered litigation work and the next summer in the St. Louis office of the firm now called Bryan Cave, which he describes as "a fantastic legal practice." He found the work fascinating, but "it still seemed to involve moving money from one Fortune 500 company to another." This doubtless proved important to Fortune 500 corporations and their stockholders but was not the "changing the world" type of work that he had always envisioned.

He believes that he would have found his way into public service regardless of his preliminary career choices. Even when he found himself in the private sector, it was with a behind-the-scenes role in government. He imagined, for example, helping to elect a gubernatorial candidate, then transitioning into an appointment with the assumption that, "if we lose the next election, I'll go back to making money."

His legal career began with a clerkship for Judge Ronald E. Meredith of the U.S. District Court for the Western District of Kentucky. Judge Meredith had served as chairman of the Kentucky Republican Party before his appointment to the bench. Bill therefore assumed that had he remained in his home state and established the political connections getting a job in government would not have proven overly difficult, but it might have required some patience because the only people being hired at that time were Democrats.

Bill was determined and farsighted in pursuit of his career goals, but never single-minded. He married during his third year of law school, and family and quality of life played a major role in his choices. Many, if not most, second-year law students work their second summer at the law firm they hope to enter after graduation, and he decided to go to St. Louis primarily because it had developed a reputation as one of the most livable cities in the country. His now former wife, however, found St. Louis uninhabitable and wanted to move to Colorado, an appealing enough place that he required little convincing to agree.

Following his clerkship he found that openings at large private firms were somewhat scarce nationwide and even more scarce in Colorado, which had developed a surplus of lawyers. Still, for him the timing and location proved ideal. Recently elected Attorney General Gale Norton was seeking to fill her office with bright, young Republican lawyers, and he fit the bill. The office had two openings at the time and allowed him to choose between criminal appellate practice and litigation on behalf of the state's educational institutions. The latter seemed more interesting, and that division proved more eager to have him. He jokes that, because he had written his law review note on school finance, they thought he knew something about education law, and he "was not about to dissuade them of that notion."

Although he only found out later how worried some in the office had been, his hiring caused a good deal of consternation. Apparently, "it was highly unusual for them to hire anyone who had never signed a pleading." Most of the new hires had two or three years of experience, whereas he had had none. Although the senior people in the office believed in his potential, his department was concerned about his initial ability, though his supervisors later told him that he had learned quickly and they needn't have worried. "I think there is a constant tension in AG's offices between the need to hire somebody who can do the work instantly and somebody who has no experience but is a potential star or superstar," he reflects.

The job involved representing institutions of higher education and the state Department of Education in any litigation matters. His primary clients were the Department itself (K through 12), Colorado State University, and the Colorado School of Mines. The litigation fascinated him because it involved so many constitutional and what he terms "quasi-constitutional" issues. This proved great training for his current job, he says, explaining that schools function in some ways like mini-states, and universities like small cities, with constitutional law questions such as First Amendment and Due Process issues arising constantly.

The job offered him the opportunity to take on significant responsibility for interesting work at a young age. He laughs as he describes an exchange with a visiting law school classmate working for a private firm. The man was pleased the firm had recently begun allowing him to attend depositions, and Bill was very happy for him. Bill was lead counsel on a Title IX case, and his acquaintance was shocked. When Bill later filed a certiorari petition in that same case, he was technically ineligible for membership in the U.S. Supreme Court Bar, having been admitted to the bar too recently to qualify for the requisite three years.

Still, Bill's classmate could console himself with the fact that he was making a lot more money. Bill had entered with a starting salary that barely exceeded his income as a judicial clerk. Three months after he started, the office instituted a hiring freeze and a wage freeze. As a result, he did not receive another raise for four years, despite a salary schedule in which he ought to have received a raise of about ten percent a year, meaning that he was "literally stuck at the bottom of the pay scale."

Bill's career ambitions and his former wife's geographic preferences both played a role in the decision to leave Colorado, as they did in the move to Colorado. A casual friend from law school had become a senior advisor to Virginia's Attorney General and reestablished communication after reading an article Bill had written. A job offer soon followed. Bill had "great clients" and "wonderful work" in Denver, but felt his career plateau. As highly as he regarded the Colorado Attorney General's office, he saw little opportunity for advancement. Further, he was seriously considering becoming in-house counsel to a public university. "That seemed more remote in Colorado than it did in Virginia," because "the Virginia Attorney General's office had much more influence on who got those in-house positions." Meanwhile, his wife, from whom he is now divorced, had begun to consider Colorado too far from her family in Virginia and preferred to head back east.

Bill served as Assistant Attorney General in the Education Section of Virginia's office of the Attorney General for two years, representing institutions of higher education with a little more autonomy than he had enjoyed in Denver. He served as Chief Counsel for Christopher Newport University and Norfolk University, as well as constitutional litigation counsel for other public universities. Christopher Newport, a small liberal arts college, had no in-house counsel at the time and called on him often. The school's leadership then decided to create the position and asked Bill to fill it.

Technically, such in-house counsel are under the command of the Attorney General's office, and the office had no qualms about his accepting the offer. However, the Section still needed his constitutional expertise and asked him continue to work on some cases, so he willingly continued to work in that capacity. In 2002, a newly elected Attorney General made him Deputy State Solicitor General. This new post involved assisting the Solicitor General with cases but was essentially a part-time position for Bill, who remained at Christopher Newport.

In 2004, his predecessor as Solicitor General left for private practice, and the Attorney General asked Bill to serve full-time as Solicitor General. The office is responsible for any appeal on the civil side involving a serious challenge to the constitutionality of a statute or regulation. During the 2005 term Bill argued two cases before the U.S. Supreme Court. Bill describes this post as "one of the best jobs in the world." "I get to practice constitutional law," he says, elaborating that with the exception of the U.S. Solicitor General's office and his counterparts in other states, few people have that opportunity.

Because the Solicitor General handles all of Virginia's litigation in the U.S. Supreme Court (except death penalty cases), Bill regularly files petitions. The one-time wannabe astronaut describes arguing before the Court as the lawyer's equivalent of walking on the moon. Having been part of the preparation team and officially on brief for the two cases his predecessor argued before the Court, he has the sense of having traveled to the moon without leaving the spaceship and feels the oral argument to be a novel and exciting, but not completely foreign, experience.

Back on earth, the typical day for him would ideally involve writing a brief or preparing for oral argument, but realistically he has many more concerns to address, and no day is altogether typical. He may spend some days fully immersed in legal research and writing and other days entirely engaged in meetings with the Attorney General or other members of the office. He puts out various fires, makes sure that briefs are filed, decides which amicus briefs to join, and monitors the office's overall strategy. This requires constant interaction with the Attorney General and constant awareness of the legal world both inside and outside the office.

Bill describes all Attorney's General offices as having "something of an advocacy agenda," that requires the Solicitor to consider "where we want to be politically, legally, and constitutionally." Each attorney in the Attorney General's office is assigned to one or more agencies, whose interests might conflict with that of the state as a whole. Consequently, Bill reviews many more briefs than he writes in order to ensure consistency. He needs to be aware of which cases courts, particularly the U.S. Supreme Court and the Fourth Circuit Court, are considering and in what ways those decisions might affect his pending cases and the issues his office considers important. He plays a minor role in training young attorneys but has not had the opportunity to "give back" as much as he would like in that respect.

Despite all the activity, including the frequent telephone calls that interrupt his day, the environment of his office seems relatively calm. His executive assistant volunteered that she found it a very pleasant place to work. Despite the formality of the security and the dress code, the spacious office has a comfortable feel, with family photos lining the window sills and tree-lined streets visible from the windows.

Work in Bill's office requires "non-lawyer" as well as litigation skills. "What I do requires a sense of the politics of a situation," he explains. He is always cognizant that his boss is an elected official who must make decisions taking into consideration their political ramifications. Virginia is the only state that prohibits its governors from running for reelection. With this turnover every four years, the Attorney General often considers running for governor, creating "a sort of perpetual campaign" that might not otherwise occur.

As far as stress goes, he is doing work he loves and has few complaints. Deadlines can always prove stressful and bureaucracy frustrating. Booking a hotel, for example, becomes much more complicated when the government is involved. The main trade-off, however, is the salary. Although Bill feels financially comfortable, he knows how much more income he could generate in private practice. His three children are young now, but he wonders what will happen if they want to go to college at an elite private university and then pursue law school or graduate studies.

Still, he feels that, generally, "public-sector jobs offer a higher quality of life in terms of being able to spend time with your kids or have a family life." He typically arrives at the office around eight and leaves by five-thirty or quarter to six. He would come in earlier, but he commutes an hour and fifteen minutes from Yorktown, where his wife (he is remarried) is a minister at a Presbyterian church. Fortunately, Richmond has remarkably little traffic for a city its size, thus enabling him to reach his downtown office building without sitting in gridlock. He tries not to work weekends, particularly when his children visit, but he often finds himself obliged to put in a few hours over a weekend and has occasionally worked all weekend.

Bill still enjoys legal scholarship and writes and speaks extensively on constitutional law and education law topics, but it is mostly a hobby pursued almost entirely on his own time, of which he simply does not have enough to write long articles. He leaves those to law professors with research assistants and the pressure to publish but does feel that he probably has more opportunities to speak and write than he would if he were in private practice. He also teaches a constitutional law course for undergraduate students at Christopher Newport University and has taught in George Mason's pre-law seminar.

When asked about his most important or meaningful work, he lists three examples that, interestingly, span his entire career, beginning with the research he did for Professor Howard in law school. Two cases stand out as particularly rewarding. During his time in Colorado, the state's Supreme Court ended school busing in Denver. Bill had been frustrated by the situation, particularly in one school, which "literally had said that white children could transfer to magnet and special programs, but African-American and Hispanic children could not, because if they left, it would disturb the racial balance." He believed the decision restored these children's access to such opportunities and that "the Denver public schools improved when they went away from the race-based decision making."

He has been involved in four U.S. Supreme Court cases, but considers *Virginia v. Hicks* the most meaningful. The Court decided the case, which involved the constitutionality of a trespass policy at a public housing complex, in 2003. A series of apartment buildings had essentially become an open-air drug market in which the parents, mostly single mothers, feared letting their children outside to play. The public housing authority attempted to "exclude non-residents in much the same way as a private, gated apartment community," a strategy that had dramatically reduced crime in the area, and the Court upheld the constitutionality of the plan. Other public housing authorities have since followed Richmond's model, and Bill considers it "a landmark case" that had a real impact on "bettering those people's lives and making it possible for public housing to be safe and secure nationwide." It generated little publicity elsewhere, but exemplified the kind of work he always hoped to do.

KEVIN RYAN

Children's Rights Advocate

By Aron B. Goetzl with contributions by Monica Lewis

Ask Kevin Ryan why he left his self-proclaimed dream job as New Jersey's first-ever Child Advocate in the winter of 2006 to head the very same child welfare system he had criticized so publicly as Child Advocate and you may be surprised to hear his characteristic bluntness turn inward. "I'd talked the talk about keeping kids safe and families strong for a long time," Kevin said, five months after making the move. "So enough of the talk, already. It was time to lead or sit down. When the governor [newly elected Governor Jon Corzine] asked, I saw the door opening to reform the system, so I walked inside."

But leaving the Office of the Child Advocate was "bittersweet — a blue moment" for him. His appointment to the post in the summer of 2003 by then-Governor James E. McGreevey followed nearly a decade of legal aid work for homeless teenagers at Covenant House, a nonprofit agency that serves homeless and runaway youth in the South Bronx, Times Square, and eventually across the Hudson River in Newark and Atlantic City, two of New Jersey's largest cities. From his first day in the position, when he launched an investigation into conduct at the state's only children's psychiatric center (on his second day at work, he initiated probes into overcrowded juvenile detention centers), Kevin appeared intent on turning the new office into a formidable voice for children. Just days after Kevin took the reins as Child Advocate, New Jersey's largest newspaper, the *Newark Star-Ledger*, editorialized, "New Jersey's new children's advocate looks like the kind of watchdog who intends to attack and stay on the attack."

The position was designed precisely for someone to get off to a fast start. The bill that created the office — which Kevin helped draft — made it "one of the most independent child advocate's offices that one could imagine," he says. While the position is not a new one for state governments (about twenty other states have appointed Child Advocates), "the state legislature equipped this office with some uniquely progressive powers—the power to subpoena, the power to view otherwise confidential government records, the power to publicly report and bring public exposure to a series of problems," Kevin explains. "In this way, we could shine an antiseptic light in dark corners."

Furthermore, the legislature handed the Office of the Child Advocate a $2.25 million budget that enabled the office to go about its work with resources to back up its rhetoric. Within two years, Kevin had recruited a staff of approximately thirty, including thirteen lawyers, of whom he says: "All have had fascinating careers as public interest lawyers."

Looking back on his experience as Child Advocate, Kevin is introspective. "Many times," he pauses, "I think we made things better for kids, usually by drawing the system's failings into the open. But sometimes, frankly, we didn't. The thing is—effective advocacy is a lot like music. It's about hitting the right notes at the right volume. I think too many of us, myself included, forget that the decibel level and the tone should be set by what's necessary to create conditions for change—the volume shouldn't be set too low because we're afraid to make waves, or too high because we're in love with our own voices. Trust me—it can backfire if the people we need to help us create change don't hear us, or they stop listening because we're strident and shrill. Advocacy is really an art form."

Kevin had plenty of opportunities to practice that art form in his two and a half years at the helm, especially considering the broad powers and resources given to the Child Advocate. Those undoubtedly reflected the nature of the time at which the Office was created.

"Back in 2003, New Jersey's child welfare system was reeling," Kevin says.

Specifically, the death of seven-year-old Faheem Williams, whose body was discovered hidden in a Newark basement in January 2003 after state child protection workers failed to follow up on calls that he was in danger, served as the immediate catalyst for change in the state's child welfare system, including the creation of the Child Advocate post. When news of that story broke, according to Kevin, the major media outlets that cover the state, including those in New York and Philadelphia, immediately became interested in an ongoing lawsuit against New Jersey's child protection system. The lawsuit was initially filed in 1999 by the New York-based nonprofit group, Children's Rights Inc. The case detailed how broken the state's child welfare system had become, and the state's newspapers galvanized the attention of the public with "heartbreaking reports" during the first half of 2003, according to Kevin.

"Their outrage about the deficiency in the [child welfare] system fueled reform efforts and the work that we do [now]," he says.

In particular, the Department of Human Services, the state agency responsible for overseeing the child welfare system in New Jersey, had come under intense criticism for a lack of caseworkers, modernized technology, organization, and focus, which enabled children like Faheem Williams to slip through the system's widening cracks.

The legislature, with the governor's strong support, decided there should be a new Office of the Child Advocate. "Every child protection system can be the stronger for an independent advocate monitoring aggressively the conditions for kids in that system," Kevin says. "It just is the reality that when someone is looking critically at how kids, whose voices don't resonate in the political process, fare and how accountable government is or is not, that the system changes and can improve as a result."

That Kevin initially became that person for New Jersey's children and now leads the reform effort he once monitored as Commissioner of the Department of Human Services, seems almost preordained, given his considerable experience working on children's issues in the New Jersey area and, perhaps more important, his passion for public service.

The oldest of six sons, Kevin has deep connections to New Jersey. Born on a military base in Ohio, Kevin's mother moved to South Amboy, a small town in the central part of the Garden State, when he was not quite a year old, while his father was serving in Vietnam in 1967. Kevin's parents instilled in all their sons from an early age the virtues of community activism and "contributing to the civic good," he says. Two of his brothers are in law enforcement, one is in public health, one is in international human rights, and the fifth — the only businessman in the group — is an education activist recently elected to his local board of education.

While Kevin was growing up in South Amboy, his parents, befitting the lessons they sought to pass on to their children, each played significant roles in the local community. Kevin's father was a teacher and his mother was an education reformer, including a stint as the chair of the local board of education. Furthermore, Kevin's father to this day volunteers with the South Amboy First Aid Squad, a commitment that has spanned five decades.

As if his parents weren't enough of an influence on steering Kevin toward a life of public service and activism, Kevin's wife, Clare, whom he met in college, spent a year volunteering at Covenant House in New Orleans and a year staffing a group home for developmentally disabled adults before the couple married, while Kevin attended law school. Kevin calls her "the conscience of our family." They now have six children of their own: three boys and three girls. "We're the Brady Bunch in search of an Alice who's willing to work for free and sleep in a tent in the backyard. No takers yet."

A popular American novel also played a key role in Kevin's work. "I know this will sound completely corny," Kevin says, chuckling. "I read *To Kill a Mockingbird* in ninth grade. I remember chapter and verse the back and forth between Atticus and Scout about why he was representing Tom. Harper Lee conveyed [Atticus's] reasons for defending Tom simply, and it inspired me: 'The main one is that if I didn't, I couldn't hold my head up in town. I couldn't even tell you or Jem not to do somethin' again.' That spoke so powerfully to the obligation that we all have to each other, and it has even more meaning for me now that I have children of my own."

Kevin attended college at the Catholic University of America in Washington, DC, where he volunteered to work the overnight shift at a local women's shelter. Kevin graduated *summa cum laude* in 1989 and immediately headed for law school as the logical next step in his desire to give back to the community through public service. He entered law school at the Georgetown University Law Center in the fall of 1989. There, he discovered a way to channel his passion for public service into a concrete career path, but it didn't happen in the classroom. Rather, it came through Kevin's volunteer work for an outreach van that visited the poorest neighborhoods of Washington providing food and blankets to homeless adolescents.

"I was moved by their struggle," he says. "I think I began to see this could be my life's work. All of these kids [had] so much promise, and if they just had adults who believed in them and loved them, the world would open up for them. If their communities were courageous and strong enough to support them, they'd be making better choices and they'd be safer."

Having seen the problem firsthand, Kevin determined that he wanted to be part of the solution. After graduating from Georgetown in 1992, Kevin received a Skadden Fellowship, which enabled him to begin his career doing exactly the kind of work that he decided he wanted to do in law school. He spent two years representing poor and homeless young people in Manhattan and the Bronx as part of Covenant House, and then stayed for three more years to continue his work at the agency in the areas of housing and family law.

Kevin describes the work he was doing for Covenant House in New York as "all clinic 101." He spent considerable time representing children in family court and families facing eviction in housing court.

To this day, Kevin looks back on those five years spent in New York City, particularly in the Bronx, with a mixture of fondness and disappointment. It's clear that what troubled Kevin so much about the nature of the work he was doing was also what attracted him to it—working for the underserved and underrepresented.

"The days I spent in the Bronx housing court still shape my thinking," he says. "The level of injustice that is experienced on a daily basis [there] is extraordinary."

It was during the course of his work at the Bronx housing court in the mid-1990s that Kevin began to envision a future tackling these issues outside the courthouse. "Those years changed my approach to the work. I became more and more certain that the injustices were systemic and could only be tackled completely if there was a policy change and a systemic response. I wanted to do that policy work. I wanted to change the system," he says.

In late 1997, Covenant House approached Kevin with an offer to do just the kind of policy work that he now wanted to do—in his home state of New Jersey. The organization asked Kevin to design and run advocacy and legal aid programs for homeless and runaway youth in two of New Jersey's poorest communities, Newark and Atlantic City.

"By the time I came to New Jersey, I was doing almost all policy work," Kevin says. "I began to do less legal aid work over time."

Kevin spent nearly five years advancing the policy agenda for homeless youth through Covenant House in New Jersey. He worked on both federal and state legislation. In the late 1990s, he fought against a juvenile crime bill advanced in the U.S. Senate to detain nonviolent children in facilities with adults. At the state level, he cowrote the New Jersey Homeless Youth Act, enacted in 1999, which provides state funds for new programs for homeless teenagers. He also worked on the New Jersey Family Care Act, enacted in 2000, which expanded health insurance coverage for teens aging out of the foster care system.

When McGreevey assumed control of the executive branch in January 2002, Kevin, after nearly five years working at Covenant House New Jersey, decided to join the new administration as the chief of staff for the state's Department of Human Services, a ten billion dollar agency that oversees all of New Jersey's programs for the disabled, mentally ill, poor families, and at-risk children. Kevin had worked on McGreevey's successful gubernatorial campaign in 2001. After nine months at the Department of Human Services, Kevin moved into the governor's office and played a key role in settling the Children's Rights lawsuit and drafting the Child Advocate legislation.

Given his litany of experiences working on child welfare issues both inside and outside of state government, Kevin was well prepared in October 2003 to assume the challenges and responsibilities of serving as New Jersey's first watchdog over its children's programs. In fact, he embraced the programs with a passion that one would expect from someone who found himself with a "once-in-a-lifetime" opportunity, as Kevin puts it. In addition to the investigations that Kevin launched on his first and second days in office, he kept his staff quite busy in the succeeding months. Within two years, Richard Wexler, the executive director of the Virginia-based National Coalition for Child Protection Reform, described Kevin's office as "the best of its kind—by far—in the nation." Kevin launched additional probes into aspects of New Jersey's child protection systems; he also reached agreements with public and private organizations to improve conditions for developmentally disabled children and end overcrowding in juvenile detention centers.

He calls his "happiest moment" in the position the day in 2005 when the state legislature enacted a health care reform law, which Kevin's staff researched and codrafted, that expanded health care coverage for thousands of children and families.

In the summer of 2005, Kevin and his team of lawyers were preparing for litigation to end the detention of children for months at a time because of an inability to find child welfare and mental health placements for them. As an illustration of the problem, Kevin described a twelve-year-old boy who was held for more than seven months in a juvenile detention center for an act that would not have put him in jail for even a night had he been an adult. Because of a scarcity of mental health programs, the boy languished in juvenile jail for months longer than he should have. On the eve of the threatened filing in September 2005, the state removed all such children from the detention centers and placed them in more appropriate settings.

The leaders of the agencies he monitored and criticized didn't always respond positively to Kevin's evaluations. In one instance, in March 2005 the former state Human Services Commissioner, whose agency had been criticized in one of Kevin's reports, lashed out at Kevin when he served as Child Advocate for "throw[ing] bricks from the cheap seats," according to the *Newark Star-Ledger*.

The criticism Kevin endured was far from the toughest part of his job as advocate. On the wall next to his desk in his office in a standard office building just a stone's throw from the capitol building in Trenton, Kevin has taped pictures of two children who died while they were in the state's child welfare system. He is rueful when describing the circumstances that led to their deaths.

"We learn about every child fatality that is due to abuse or neglect," he says. "Each is heartbreaking."

But they are also, in part, what drive Kevin. "We can't be in every home in New Jersey, but we can make this system stronger for kids. That's reason for hope, and it's what keeps us all going," he says.

It is hard to overlook the irony that, less than a year after being called a brick-thrower by the former Human Services Commissioner, Kevin has replaced him. How does he feel about the fact that those bricks will now be coming his way? "I'm not looking forward to it," he chuckles. "It wasn't an easy decision, and I'm not saying there aren't days, many days, when I wonder what in God's name I was thinking when I said 'yes' to the Governor," he laughs. "But the thing is, the system really can improve for kids, and [Governor] Jon Corzine is going to move heaven and earth for that to happen — so I want to be in this."

Kevin is discursive about the problems he wants to fix in the child welfare agency. The system needs more caseworkers, better training, clearer policies, more services for families and, he says, more focus on prevention. "Preventing abuse and neglect is about supporting and shaping strong families," which Kevin says became central to his approach to child welfare while he pursued a Masters of Law Degree at New York University School of Law, which he obtained in 2000. There he studied under Martin Guggenheim and Peggy Cooper Davis, family law scholars Kevin calls "the teachers of my life." Kevin credits the pair with shaping his thinking about child welfare by reminding him that "strong, vital, protected families have to be the cornerstone."

He recalls an allegory Guggenheim included in a recent book about people in a village who spend days and nights rescuing thousands of babies from a river of rushing water. When a new person comes upon the scene and declines to help the villagers pull the babies from the water, the rescuers are incensed. "They protest 'how can you not help us save these babies'," Kevin recounts, "but she walks past them. 'I'm going up-river to see what is putting our babies in this river.' That's a big part of this — we have to move these systems and resources up-river and get to the issues that threaten families. We have to prevent neglect and abuse much more aggressively."

Kevin published a turnaround plan for the child welfare system in June 2006 that sets priorities for the next twelve months. In it, he was careful not to promise too much, but as he describes those plans he suddenly jumps to his feet and paces the floor with a mixture of anticipation and worry reminiscent of an expectant father.

"It's big — we'll flourish and stumble in ways I can't predict. There's a lot of work ahead of us — we have to offer more services to families.

We have to give our frontline workers the supervision, training, and tools they need to make good judgments, keep kids safe, build forever families. The stakes are so high for kids."

Kevin understands the stakes are high for him too. He left an irrevocable five-year term as Child Advocate to serve at the pleasure of the governor in a position where his last three predecessors lasted an average of two years each. If history is a teacher, his tenure could be brief.

"All the more reason to act quickly to reprioritize the reform and get it focused on the fundamentals. If we launch the effort in the right direction, it can endure beyond the tenure of any particular leader. I know all the risks, but if you want to cross the river, you have to be willing to get wet."

"Success isn't about staying dry. I stayed plenty dry in the advocate's office," Kevin says wistfully. "Success is getting to the other side without drowning."

Another first in Kevin's career presented itself in July 2006. As part of his plan to reform the New Jersey child welfare system, the governor proposed the creation of a new state agency—the Department of Children and Families—that would "carve out" the child welfare divisions in state government from the much larger Department of Human Services. By doing so, Governor Corzine pledged to "bring more focus to the needs of our children." Corzine announced that Kevin was to be the first commissioner of the new department.

"Human Services is such a big department. Twenty-two thousand employees, ten operating divisions—it's the largest agency in state government. That structure has made it difficult to give child welfare reform the focus it needs and deserves." Kevin does not believe structural change is a panacea, but he is hopeful that a smaller, more focused agency will allow him and his leadership team to hasten the pace of change. He tempers almost all of his comments with warnings about the difficulty in fixing a system as troubled as the one he now leads, but he is unabashed about two points: Corzine's commitment to child welfare reform—Kevin calls him "a serious man filled with conviction"—and the talent of the team he has recruited to lead the effort with him. "These are the smartest and most experienced child advocates and administrators in the state. It's all about leadership."

As he looks out his office window and watches the sun set on the Delaware River, Kevin describes how the river flooded one week earlier, forcing Trenton to shut down and thousands of New Jersey residents to flee their homes. It was the third such flood in eighteen months, and it devastated large parts of the state. Then Kevin speaks of a dinner conversation he had with Corzine days earlier about the causes of the flood.

"He said up-river development was a big part of the problem. I thought about all the effort that goes into rescuing the flood victims and recovering from the damage, over and over again."

He points out his window, up the Delaware to the fading sun. "It's all about getting up-river."

BOB SCHIFF

Senate Committee
Counsel

By Brandi Davis

When ten senators gathered around the Lyndon B. Johnson Room conference table to hammer out the final details of the 2001 campaign finance reform bill, Bob Schiff was in the room whispering in Senator Russ Feingold's ear. Campaign finance was his issue — an area of expertise that he developed through private practice and work at Public Citizen, an advocacy organization. When an opportunity arose to join Senator Feingold's staff to advise on the issue, he jumped at the chance. After working for years on the outside on what came to be known as the McCain-Feingold bill, his thinking was, "Now I have a chance to be inside the room when the deal is cut." Not long after joining the staff, he was in the room helping to set the new limits on soft money contributions.

When Bob is describing his career path, he makes it sound as if he reached his position due to a string of luck and happenstance, but his story reveals a clear course of development. He may have not begun with a plan, but his easy confidence, hard work, and passion for the issue certainly helped him attain his current job as Chief Counsel for Senator Feingold. As a lawyer who has always blended public service with legal practice, it was only a matter of time before Bob would be working for a nonprofit or the government. Now sitting in on the conference of the Senate Judiciary Committee, Subcommittee on the Constitution, at an office tucked away on the top floor of the Hart Senate office building, Bob is Democratic Chief Counsel to the subcommittee and Feingold's top legal aide. He is responsible not only for campaign finance but for a broad array of issues from bankruptcy to congressional ethics to judicial nominations.

Although actively involved in politics since childhood, Bob was not sure about what he would do as a lawyer. He was born in 1957 and raised in Pittsburgh, Pennsylvania, where his parents were involved in the local political scene. His father, a nuclear physicist, served as president of the Pittsburgh ACLU chapter but passed away when Bob was young. His father and his mother, a speech instructor for the deaf, had been big Lyndon Johnson supporters and involved Bob in campaign activities at an early age. Bob recalls going door to door for George McGovern at age fourteen. His early exposure to politics was also accompanied by an early exposure to law. One of his role models was his father's brother, an appellate lawyer who worked for the precursor to the Department of Energy, the Public Service Commission of New York State, and the state's Solicitor General Office.

Bob chose a politically active college. Originally attracted to Brown University because of its unstructured curriculum, the deal was sealed when on his visit to the campus he observed a student boycott of classes over divesture in South Africa. Thinking the student activism was "really cool," Bob chose to attend Brown. When he entered Brown, law school was in the back of his mind, but he had not yet set his sights on a particular type of legal career. At Brown he took advantage of the liberal arts curriculum to explore many options. Ultimately majoring in European History, Bob did have one course, Politics and the Law, taught by Professor Ed Beiser. The course applied law school pedagogy and confirmed in Bob's mind that he would enjoy law school. He took the LSAT before leaving Brown and, when he did well, saw law as an opportunity he could always pursue and decided to take some time off before deciding whether to go to law school.

Before applying to law school, Bob headed to Washington, DC, and worked in two law-related jobs—as an investigator at the public defender's office and as a researcher who obtained documents from government agencies for out-of-town law firms. (This was long before the Internet made such documents readily available.) After the break, he was more than ready for law school. Bob believes taking time to work before law school was valuable. "It was an advantage to have been out for a few years and know that my capabilities were not defined by what I scored on my first-year exams."

Entering University of Michigan Law School, Bob still had no idea what he planned to do with his legal career; he claims he only knew that he wanted to clerk after graduating. Nevertheless, while in law school, he began to blend public interest and private practice in ways that would be coupled together throughout his career. He was actively involved in what became the National Association of Public Interest Law (NAPIL), now named Equal Justice Works. The Michigan group raised money to fund public interest summer fellowships for students with summer associate positions at firms. He was the chairman in his third year and was involved in chartering the national organization of NAPIL. He also remained active in politics, participating in both local and state campaigns, and was in a group called the Reagan Busters during the 1984 election. He volunteered on Election Day for Walter Mondale and Senator Carl Levin.

Of all his law school experiences, one that stood out was a project where Bob and a colleague, now Office of Management and Budget Director Rob Portman, had the primary responsibility for hammering out a draft fundraising proposal for the fellowship program to be sent to alumni of the law school. Together they fielded comments from alumni and incorporated the advice into the document. Bob enjoyed the legislative aspect of the project, perhaps an early premonition of his unfolding career. He learned then that "the people who were willing to pick up the pen or get on the computer and write have a lot of control over the direction of things or make things happen. Being the original drafter of something and taking the changes from other people is a good place to be."

Getting a clerkship after graduation was an instance where Bob's luck may have come into play. Originally Bob applied for clerkships where he had spent his law school summers—in Washington, DC, and Seattle—with plans to start working at a firm in whichever city he obtained a clerkship. Although he received several interviews, he had no offers, so he accepted an offer to work in the Seattle firm where he had spent his first-year summer. In 1985, during the spring of his third year, long after clerkship hiring season was over, he received a call from one of the lawyers he had worked with while summering in DC. The lawyer asked if he would be interested in clerking for Judge Barrington D. Parker on the DC District Court, who had an unexpected opening that he needed to fill for a clerk for a one-year term. Bob had an interview and was hired.

Bob jokes that working as a clerk gave him two experiences that he will never have again. First, as an older lawyer had warned him, it was the last job in which his phone calls would be returned right away. When Bob later entered private practice as an associate, he found that definitely to be true. Second, it was the last job where he got in at 8:15 A.M. every morning for an entire year. In Judge Parker's chambers, it was the law clerk's job to fill the water pitchers in the courtroom, so each morning Bob would roll a tray with water and ice into the courtroom to do the glamorous work of a federal law clerk.

Bob was presented with a number of opportunities as his clerkship ended. He says he would have been happy to take a public interest job had one fallen into his lap, but he had no idea how to go about getting one at that point. Private firms, however, were knocking at his door. He accepted a job with a small firm, Wellford, Wegman & Hoff, which billed itself as a public policy law firm. It was there that he would get his first exposure to election law and the legislative process.

Bob had two experiences with election law: he worked for a public interest client filing comments on soft-money regulations, and later had a paying job with corporate clients on the law firm's political action committee's legal issues. However, this was not the majority of the firm's or Bob's work. The law firm concentrated on energy regulatory work, which was not as interesting as Bob had hoped. He soon moved on to another firm that did more traditional litigation.

Bob would spend seven years in the private sector, always at small firms or small offices of big firms. While in private practice, he became an active member of the Washington Council of Lawyers (WCL), a voluntary bar association of attorneys in firms, government, and public interest groups, all of whom share an interest in *pro bono* work and public interest practice. However, his primary focus was commercial litigation, and he honed his federal trial and appellate litigation skills working on cases arising out of the savings and loan crisis. During his time as a litigator, he jokes, the only course he had during law school that he used was his Civil Procedure course.

When his firm, Comey, Boyd & Luskin, began to show signs of an impending downfall as conflicts arose among the partners, Bob put his feelers out for a new position. He interviewed for another law firm job and for an in-house position, but he feared that he would quickly become bored with the work and would shortly be forced to look for another job. He then began to seriously entertain the idea of making the jump to public interest. He had made significant contacts through the WCL and simply started talking to people about his interest.

Once he decided to look for a public interest job, Bob wasn't inclined to wait until an appropriate position arose. A friend advised him to get as many credit cards as he could before he quit the law firm job so if it took a long time, at least he could borrow using the cards. Bob followed her advice and gave notice to the firm that he would be leaving at the end of the year.

While finishing out his time at the firm, Bob received a call from Kathleen Welch, then executive director of NAPIL with whom he had worked for many years in assisting that organization. Welch told him about an opening at Public Citizen, a public interest watchdog group founded by Ralph Nader that was looking for someone to work on a conference on campaign finance for the first few months of the year. Bob realized that this was a job he would like permanently rather than just for a short time. He told the Public Citizen people he would be interested in a more long-term position as the group's campaign finance lobbyist.

Although he knew he would like the job, Bob still faced a big hurdle — accepting that Public Citizen could pay him only $40,000 a year. Even though he was now in a place where he had had his fill of private practice, Bob was coming from a law firm associate's salary, and money therefore was a big issue. It took him some time to "get his head around that," but after crunching some numbers, he knew he could make the position and the salary work.

He recognizes that he was in a much different position at that point in his career than most students trying to make a decision between a public interest job and a law firm. "I had enough years of making money that I had a house and if I could make the mortgage payment, I would be okay. I was making the decision with my eyes open."

He also had enough years in private practice to recognize that his lifestyle involved a certain amount of excess. Bob notes, "You can waste a lot of money when you are in private practice, and I think most people do. If you just go out to dinner a little less or go to cheaper restaurants, you can really save a lot and make do on a lot less than most people think they can."

When hired at Public Citizen in 1994, the plan was for him to spend the first part of his time trying to get a campaign finance bill signed and then move on to another issue. At that time both the House and the Senate had passed a version of a reform bill, and everyone was hopeful that a bill would be completed that year. Bob's job was to try to get the bill through conference. He spent a year focusing on that bill, but it was never completed. The Democrats lost the mid-term elections and control of the House to the Gingrich revolution. Campaign finance reform was no longer a priority in Congress but still continued to be Bob's life work.

Bob's job at Public Citizen was to be part media guru, part policy wonk, and part lobbyist. He was a Public Citizen spokesperson and often appeared on cable news shows debating the issue of campaign finance. Other times local stations would come to the office looking for a sound bite on the latest scandal affecting their representative.

"I liked the public appearances, media, and coming up with sound bites. We did a lot of kooky things then, like protests. There was a big fundraiser at the Willard Hotel. We had a protest outside and we put together a tongue-in-cheek press release about what was on the menu. We made up these clever dishes about tax breaks. People going to the lunch to get their energy and tax breaks." Bob then was on a radio show pretending he snuck inside the event and reporting on what everyone was eating.

Bob also spent a significant amount of time sitting at a conference table with great constitutional minds trying to figure out what policies would be constitutional and still work. This is where his legal skill came into play: in the legislative drafting process it was helpful in figuring out what the law should do and how it would actually play out. He also spent a lot of time on the Hill trying to influence congressional thinking on the issues.

Describing the skills one needs to develop to do advocacy work, Bob explains, "Working for an advocacy group involves a lot of things, including lobbying. It's a lot of trying to get attention to what you are doing by coming up with innovative ideas. Also writing reports and doing empirical research to make a point and support your position. All of these are things that you can't really study in law school, but becoming very detail-oriented and really understanding different subject areas and being able to dig into them quickly are good skills to develop. Interpersonal skills are good too."

In his position at Public Citizen, Bob had a chance to influence public policy, but it was frustrating at times to work from the outside. So when he got a call from Feingold's legislative assistant in 1998 asking him to recommend someone to advise Feingold on campaign finance, he thought, "I always wanted to work on the Hill. Now here's an opening in the subject I know the most about with the senator who I respect the most in the Senate. Why wouldn't I see if it is something I could do?" He called back to say he was interested and was hired three days later as Legislative Counsel.

Today Bob's life is much different from his litigation days. "Lawyers that do legislation are a different breed in a way. . . . [Litigators] have a much more structured life. You are working on a case and you have the deadlines; you kind of know how it's going to happen; you have different motions that happen different[ly] at times; you have discovery; you get a decision; you are going to appeal it; you have a deadline; you know how a case progresses."

"Legislation is always different. Every bill, whether it is big or small, has its own path, and every issue that you work on has its own path, [which] is influenced by current events—what's in the news, what do people care about, how much pressure is there because it's in the news—and personalities—how different members are interacting, how different members are getting along, who wants to help who, someone else has some ulterior motive for being helpful because they have a debt they want to repay or a debt they want to extract."

The unpredictability is what makes working on legislation exciting for Bob. "Anyone who says they know exactly what's going to happen is lying to you. . . . No one really knows and that's what makes it fun."

This unpredictability bleeds over to what one does on a daily basis. Bob might come in planning to work on one issue and spend his entire day on another because of what is in the news headlines that day. Nevertheless, while the work may be unpredictable, his role is very clear. As part of the staff, he is there to serve the needs of his senator. The work involves preparing statements and speeches for Feingold to deliver and memos to brief him on particular issues or legislation. There is also a lot of work with the staffers of other offices. In every capacity, Bob is representing Feingold.

Bob is responsible for a subcommittee staff that is composed of one other lawyer and two non-lawyers. The office typically has two legal interns that are there for a semester or a summer. Bob and the staff prepare materials for Feingold on the issues within the Judiciary Committee's jurisdiction. As Bob explains, "Feingold's a brilliant guy, but there are so many issues he can't know everything about everything. So we educate him, and he goes forth."

When the senators are in town, Bob's schedule revolves completely around Feingold's. It may involve attending hearings or committee meetings with the Senator where Bob's role is to whisper information or advice in the senator's ear and help him formulate questions and make decisions. Bob also tracks legislation that he has worked on or that is important to the senator. There is always an end-of-the-day rush as the staff prepares a packet of material that Feingold must read for the next day.

If the piece of legislation Bob is working on goes to the Floor of the Senate, things can be even more hectic and time-consuming. "It was one of the really fun things when I first started; the campaign finance reform bill went to the Floor. It is a big deal as a staffer if you are working for a senator who is a central player. Then you are there all the time, with him or monitoring what's happening if he's not there. Your signoff is needed on a lot of things if it's your bill. People are coming to talk to you about their amendments."

Then there are times when the work becomes nonstop, such as when the Senate was faced with Clinton's impeachment, or working on the Patriot Act. High-profile issues like these lead to some unique opportunities. After the depositions were taken of the key players in Clinton's impeachment trial, such as Monica Lewinsky's, only the senators plus one staffer could go into a room in the Capitol to view the depositions. Bob was able to view these materials a week before they were released to the public. Bob was also on the floor when Senator Feingold was the sole dissenting voice on the Patriot Act.

Despite the hectic schedules, Bob thinks this can be a good job for people who are looking to have a life outside of work. He notes that the work is very compressed in the middle of the week, with the longest days being Tuesday, Wednesday, and sometimes Thursday. He notes, "you can make plans for Thursday night and you can most likely make it. And weekends I work some but certainly not all and that's because I've always got Monday."

Now that he is on Capitol Hill, Bob works on the issues most important to him. He oversees the drafting of proposed legislation and helps prepare Senator Feingold's press statements on the issues. Working with Feingold, whose politics match his own, Bob often hears his exact words coming out of Feingold's mouth. "However," he quips, "they sound much better when he delivers them."

Being on the Hill does have some downsides; one is the relative lack of job security. Bob recalls his first reelection experience. "The first time my job was on the line was a year after I came. It was a very unique, scary feeling. I woke up on Election Day. I was out in Wisconsin. I went to help out at the end of the campaign. I could wake up the next day and have a job or I might not. And it was not in my control. That's just something people have to accept about doing this kind of work."

Bob is careful not to overstate the instability. "Now, if you are a lawyer and you've been hired because of your substantive expertise, then you will be more likely to find another job on the Hill if you want it, rather than someone who was hired because they were from the home state or what have you. It's not completely unstable. Having my eighth year with [Senator Feingold], if he lost I would be able to find another job on the Hill if I wanted to. It is definitely true that those already on the Hill have an easier job having something else on the Hill."

Other downsides are the pay and the lack of time to just sit and think. Of course, Bob will never make as much money as he could in private practice. The fast pace of the work means Bob often has to produce materials for the very next day. Bob sometimes wishes he had time to read more, but quickly adds that major things do get a lot of time and consideration.

However, for Bob the positives of getting to influence national policy on the issues dear to him and work with someone he really respects far outweigh the downsides. He recommends both practicing in Washington, DC, and on the Hill to young lawyers. For him, DC is a livable city with lots of interesting work for a lawyer. In addition, of course, there is no other place in the country one can really do the type of work he is doing.

As far as getting your own place in the decision-making room, Bob feels his experience offers some lessons. "To be on the Hill, you don't have to come here right away. If this is what you want to do, then think about getting a summer position. We have two law students here this summer. By and large you have to volunteer to do that but that's what these fellowship programs exist for, to give people a chance to do this kind of thing. And then if you can't get a job on the Hill right away, then work for an advocacy group and develop an area of expertise — which is another good thing, especially for a lawyer. Having substantive expertise on an issue you care about is a good way to be someone who has something to offer when hired."

Section5

Other Paths to Social
Change, Conclusion,
and Resources

Advocacy by Any
Other Name

By Alan B. Morrison and Diane T. Chin

In this chapter, we briefly introduce you to a foundation program director, a nonprofit executive director, and an organizer-lobbyist, all of whom obtained law degrees and practiced law for a while before choosing to pursue social change efforts along other paths. What they each have in common, as is true for most of our chapter subjects, is their commitment to justice causes, which transcends any commitment to a particular kind of advocacy and has led them to discover new talents and new opportunities.

Ignatius Bau, Program Director, The California Endowment

Ignatius Bau is a 1984 UC Berkeley, Boalt Hall School of Law graduate who now controls close to twenty-five million dollars in grantmaking to increase health access among underserved communities. But when he graduated from law school, Ignatius certainly didn't think that philanthropy was the world in which he would be spending his time in his dedication to improving the lives of immigrants and refugees.

The California Endowment, a ten-year-old private foundation, funds nonprofits to increase health care access to underserved communities. Headquartered in Los Angeles, the Endowment has five regional offices, and Ignatius is a program director in their San Francisco office. The Endowment operates a little differently from other foundations in that while it does accept grantee-driven applications, it also establishes its own service, policy, and advocacy goals to initiate grantmaking that will promote the Endowment's objectives. It is this strategy that Ignatius believes is most benefited by his legal training and his background as a lawyer and advocate. As part of the leadership of the foundation, he brings his perspective and expertise in drafting legislation and helping establish government and administrative policies and regulations. But he also brings to his career the perspective of a client advocate who has seen firsthand how a lack of access to government services affects individual lives on a daily basis. He also provides his analysis of how systems can be improved to increase access.

He notes that there are several other former attorneys on the staff of the Endowment. They all have a background in legal services and advocacy organizations that the Endowment had previously funded and bring a breadth of experience and perspectives about different constituents that the Endowment seeks to serve.

Among Ignatius's first jobs after law school, and the one that provided the foundation for his accomplishments as a leading immigrants' rights advocate, was as a staff attorney at the Lawyers' Committee for Civil Rights of the San Francisco Bay Area (known as the San Francisco Lawyers' Committee for Urban Affairs when he first started). In this role, Ignatius engaged in impact litigation as well as advocacy and public education, focusing on public benefits, education and health and immigration law. He also staffed a weekly clinic that provided direct services to low-income immigrant clients. During this time, Ignatius also became a consulting lawyer for the Immigrant HIV Assistance Project.

After a decade at the Lawyers' Committee and a few stints as an adjunct teacher of Immigration Law at a local law school, Ignatius shifted into policy work. He explains that his decision to make this transition was fueled by an analysis of where his interests and passions could be better met in his professional life. "It was clear after ten years that it wasn't the legal work — litigation, supervising the immigration clinics, writing briefs, and the like — that was driving me. More, it was coalition work, policy work and advocacy, training, and more direct community interaction." After making his decision, he took the first of several positions at the Asian and Pacific Islander Health Forum, where after six years he ultimately became its director for policy and programs.

"I got to the point that, while believing in the law as an avenue for social change, I also recognized its limitations. I thought I could potentially achieve more through other mechanisms," he explained. "Oddly, it was also my understanding that we live in a society that is capitalist and driven by markets, by profit, that led me to look at the health care environment and try to see where I could fit in to make a difference about the issues and communities that mattered to me. Laws and regulations clearly drive some of that, but how do you understand and work with and alter those market forces to achieve the changes you're trying to get? In part, by being able to impact those market forces." This understanding led to Ignatius's shift into philanthropy.

An example of his ability to influence the health care market is his belief that to increase cultural competency and language access in hospitals, he needed to aggressively pursue the accreditation bodies that hold power over health care organizations. With the promise of funding in hand, he gathered key individuals (easier to do as a funder than as an advocate) and explained his strategy to impact the Joint Commission for the Accreditation of Health Care Organizations as well as the National Committee for Quality Assurance. These organizations can grant or deny accreditation to health providers. If accreditation is not granted, they cannot provide their services. Ignatius has opened up a conversation with these organizations to look at improving accreditation standards to include the Endowment's priorities. His intent is to increase cultural competency and diversity among health care professionals as well as language access within health care programs. By providing essential funding and being able to leverage leadership on these issues, Ignatius can improve minorities' access to health care. He describes this as "engaging individuals and organizations that matter on the issues we want to move through grantmaking."

In his role as a program director, Ignatius helps to set the foundation's goals and then determines how best to achieve them. This can be through grantmaking or by utilizing other tools, such as commissioning research and publications, hosting conferences, and, increasingly, looking at the development of communications strategies such as media work or buying "persuasion advertisements" to impact the field. In this work, what Ignatius appreciates and enjoys most is being able to use the Endowment's financial resources to assist small organizations that might not otherwise be able to do their work because of their representation of marginalized communities. One example of this is a relatively small grant he was able to provide to the Intersex Society of North America. It had been unsuccessful in locating funds elsewhere but with the Endowment's support, it produced educational materials and training manuals for physicians and families to better understand the health issues that arise for intersex individuals.

Ignatius acknowledges that his success as a grantmaker is in part because he comes from the world that comprises many of his grantees' universe—immigrants' rights, health access for underrepresented and poor communities, and civil rights. His experience as an attorney and an advocate helps him "understand at an operational level how to help legal organizations shape proposals, and also when their stated objective is futile or needs to be reshaped." His strong relationships with potential grantees also allows him to have discussions with organizations about how to find a better fit within the priorities of the Endowment or a more appropriate funder for what they want to accomplish.

Having so many former practicing attorneys on the staff has led the Endowment to decide to fund litigation as well as policy advocacy. Ignatius's background allows him to explain to individuals both within the foundation and in grantee organizations how lobbying and advocacy can be accomplished within the limits of the IRS rules. An additional "lawyerly" skill that is routinely an asset in his work as a program director: the ability to engage in persuasive communication, both through public speaking and in his written reports recommending grantees for funding. Unlike some of his peers in philanthropy, he finds it easy, and frequently enjoyable, to give presentations and to engage in written analysis of how an organization seeking funds could advance the foundation's goals.

For those who might want to keep philanthropy in their minds as a possible career, Ignatius advises that it is better to think about social change goals overall and to evaluate whether working within foundations can be a part of those goals. He also recommends that individuals in the advocacy world reach out to foundations and volunteer to serve on proposal review committees and on nonprofit institutions' boards to get a better sense of how these organizations work financially.

Ignatius is still relatively new at his career. He states, "Philanthropy was never the goal. Advocacy and social change have been. Where it goes from here, I don't know." He is another individual who looks for opportunities to be in environments that can use his skills wisely, where he will feel that he contributes to advancing social aims that meet his values and lifestyle goals. Fortunately for the Endowment and the organizations that benefit from wise and thoughtful grantmaking in the field of health care, Ignatius finds himself at the right place for now.

Jamienne S. Studley, President and CEO, Public Advocates

Jamienne Studley, known to most people as Jamie, has had the kind of public interest career that many of us could never imagine. Before joining Public Advocates in 2004 as its president and chief executive officer, she was a college president (Skidmore College in New York), worked in both the Carter and Clinton Administrations, was an associate dean at Yale Law School, served as the first executive director of the National Association for Law Placement, and served on a variety of commissions focusing on improving diversity and access to legal services. She also tried private firm practice twice before concluding with finality that it was not the world for her.

When asked about her eclectic career, Jamie says, "I didn't typically see my choices in terms of law practice or not. I saw a combination of things I wanted to work on, like civil rights, justice, and fairness issues, particularly in education and women's rights, and improving efficiency — making things run as well as they could — and evaluated where I could create the greatest impact. Sometimes that meant being a practicing lawyer, and sometimes it did not."

When she graduated from Harvard Law School in 1975, she was among a small group of women who were entering the profession who also felt a deep responsibility for "representing our gender." Since then she has continued to open doors for others and to analyze how to overcome obstacles to opportunity. For Jamie, currently in a reflective stage of her life, it is the client, the mission of an agency, and her vision of social justice that drive her career decisionmaking. At a crossroads in her life as an advocate, she found herself often making decisions based on questions like, "Is this kind of opportunity likely to come before me again? Is this a unique moment on this issue, historically or for me personally, that calls me?"

She recalls such a moment in 1992 when she had been discussing a possible position at Stanford Law School with then Dean Paul Brest. At the same time, an opportunity arose to lead California Abortion Rights Action League (CARAL-North). It was a time of advocacy for reproductive rights, and Jamie was attracted to the potential that she could work on very concrete projects for women's rights. There was also an element that felt like "now or never" because of unusual political circumstances (Boxer, Feinstein, and Clinton were all on the ballot), the chance to make a difference ("I'm a pushover for being needed") and where she was in her personal life.

Jamie does not minimize the impact one's personal life has on one's career, and she acknowledges that her long-time, supportive marriage as well as the decision she and her lawyer-husband made not to have children, have afforded her greater flexibility when doors have been opened for her. "I've moved for [my husband's] job, he for mine, so we can take on challenges and take the broad view."

She says, "you can have it all, but not necessarily all at once." Balance and being able to understand your priorities are key. For example, to have the professional choices and chance to serve that Jamie and her husband have wanted, they have paid a price in pulling up roots and investing energy in settling down in new communities. "Trade-offs shift over the years; you can accommodate but not avoid them."

Jamie is responsible for making sure that Public Advocates, a well-respected, decades-old nonprofit advocacy and impact litigation office runs effectively, has the resources its staff and work require, and is a workplace that makes sense to its employees. None of this is easy, especially not if you are as thoughtful as Jamie is about how to make it all fit together. Her personnel goals include "making a long-term investment in avoiding burn out, sustaining people's pride, making modest improvements in rewards for employees within the organization." Her goal is to get the job done, and one of her means is to assure that everyone's contributions are valued and recognized.

The week-to-week workday is likely to include fundraising, board relations, staff management, communications strategy, and reflection on where any issue is at any given moment that might need Public Advocates' attention. Noting that the substantive work is "hard enough," Jamie acknowledges that management is "even harder." There is a constant need to put one's self in someone else's shoes—a client's, a staff attorney's, your development staff person's. What do they need at any given moment? How can you get them what they need with limited time and resources? Why are they doing what they are doing? How can you have empathy for their needs? How do you factor in different styles of working, communicating, and living within a collaborative workplace framework?

Jamie's approach to all of this is informed by the breadth of her experiences, which have given her a bird's eye view of the legal profession. That can be a tremendous help in bringing a deep level of understanding to what those positions need to function effectively. Unlike many who manage, however, Jamie has also had the chance to look at management, organizational development, and the legal profession in her various jobs. From her experience at Yale Law School, she gained insight into the needs of young lawyers. From her work at NALP, she deepened her understanding of obstacles for minority, women, and LGBT lawyers. And as acting general counsel at the U.S. Department of Education, she was the bridge among career and political staff. In all of her work, she came to understand one thing about herself—she likes to run things and to run them well.

Many lawyers become directors of organizations without the benefit of Jamie's experience and maturity. Jamie advises them to try to "understand the impact you and your style and work will have on those you manage. Unlock your door and reach out. We all seem inherently to understand the importance of networking externally. But communicating within your organization is crucial as well. For public interest activists, our shared passion and commitment and mission can glue us together. But combined with work intensity and scarce resources, it is easy to let capacity and system building—let alone listening and reflection—slip in preference to serving clients or other substantive work."

In addition, Jamie is convinced that a good manager gains satisfaction from coaching and mentoring and from growing institutional capacity. She knows that these accomplishments and successes may feel abstract. Directors sometimes will be in the background engaging in activities that no one else can see. Understand what "leadership" really means, not just what it might look like from the outside. Directors must be comfortable with taking the limelight or giving it up when it makes sense for the office as a whole: "know when it is important for your lawyers to do the press conference, to step in front of the cameras." For Jamie, an organization can have many public faces, and good staff morale means lots of intangible rewards and public acknowledgment for hard work.

When asked about the challenges of finding life-work "balance," Jamie balks a bit and offers a different approach, acknowledging that the idea of balance may not be "all that important" to her. "I think about what is currently most energizing and rewarding to me. Some of my most rewarding times, personally and professionally, were incredibly intense. There was no balance between my personal life and my professional life, and that felt just right at the moment." Jamie explains this with a food metaphor. "I'm not a slow-simmer kind of person. It's either on the fire or off the fire, like barbecue."

Jamie gives high marks to social justice advocates who can reflect about their goals and their own styles of work (or cooking), as well as how to advance the social issues that inspire them along their paths. She believes doors often open when one least expects them and that it takes imagination, energy, and curiosity to exploit the opportunity beyond the door.

Lori Wallach — Trade Warrior

Lori Wallach is a Harvard-trained lawyer who doesn't practice law, but she uses her legal training every day. Lori directs Global Trade Watch at Public Citizen from her tiny cluttered office on Capitol Hill. Her main activities are organizing, lobbying, and educating the press and the public, both here and abroad, none of which requires a law degree.

But law is vital to Lori's enormous success as a major force in transforming the issue of "free trade" from what used to be seen by Congress and the elitists in our society as an unmitigated benefit to all into what is now recognized to be a far more complicated set of problems — with clear losers as well as winners. She credits her legal education with providing her the tools of rigorous analysis that enables her to understand what the trade agreements, rules, and opinions from the World Trade Organization (WTO) actually do to real people and how they transfer power from elected officials to multinational companies and their trade associations. It is this analysis and the meticulous gathering of facts to support her arguments that have enabled her to turn the tide of public opinion so that, as she put it, much of the public now agrees with her when she proclaims, "Nor did Moses bring a third tablet called WTO down from Mount Sinai direct from God." And she also acknowledges that being able to say she is a Harvard lawyer comes in handy overseas when her credentials are questioned, not only because of her gender, but because of the positions she is taking.

When Lori came to Washington DC in 1990, she first worked for the Litigation Group at Public Citizen, but her heart was on the legislative front. When a position doing food and environmental regulatory issues opened up at Public Citizen's Congress Watch in late 1989, she jumped at the opportunity. Quite quickly, in significant part based on what she heard from industry lobbyists about the impact of the new free trade rules on health and environmental regulations, she figured out that she needed to understand how the new world of free trade operated, and once she did, how to stop it. Opponents of free trade in those days were labeled as protectionists — and some of them were — but Ralph Nader, the founder of Public Citizen but who no longer had a direct role in its work, saw that free trade had enormous health implications. Lori credits him with both pushing her to see its impact and teaching her how to battle it.

Some trade agreements were already in effect, but many more were on the way. Lori's first job was to slow down what seemed to many to be an inevitable tide, which meant work in Congress, and that in turn meant finding supporters from wherever she could. Some segments of labor saw the problem in terms of lost jobs, but others did not — or at least not right away. Environmentalists began to see that some of these new rules were being used to override previous victories, but they and labor were not natural allies. Farmers, religious leaders, small businesses, and many other diverse interests had to be educated and convinced of her positions. To Lori, this meant both understanding all the legal language and being able to translate it into words and images that would persuade her would-be partners, and eventually the general public that there were real problems with unbounded free trade. Moreover, she needed her legal skills to figure out how to write provisions that would reduce, if not eliminate, the problems that the WTO was creating.

What actually takes place in Congress is the end point of massive campaigns that precede it. Getting others to join the Citizens Trade Campaign and to help support it was a big step, but what the campaign did, especially in Seattle in 1999, made an enormous difference. The Seattle meeting was supposed to kick off a new round of trade negotiations designed to push the agenda that the campaign strongly opposed, but that never happened. Instead, our government and the rest of the world learned that even in the United States, trade was no longer seen as an unmitigated good and that it was doing serious damage to people here and abroad. That happened because the campaign, with Lori as one of its prime movers, orchestrated massive demonstrations of ordinary folks who wanted to make their views known. Not exactly a job for a lawyer, but if one works on global trade issues the way Lori does, this is at least as important as keeping up with the latest WTO ruling or reviewing a proposed trade agreement.

How did Lori become a "guerilla trade warrior," as the National Journal dubbed her? Her parents were not "political," but, as a child of a holocaust survivor, she was instilled with a set of principles focused on helping others. She also had experience in television news, as a Capitol Hill staffer, and on national and state political campaigns. But she also had prestigious credentials, which caused a short-term breach in her family relations because her father, especially, could not understand how she "could 'throw away' my chances to become financially secure and instead take a 'low paying, work to the bone, thankless job.'"

The pay is better now, but well below government salaries, and the working conditions have gone from barely scraping by to tolerable. The long hours have continued, although somewhat moderated. Lori still has to spend too much time doing the part of her job that she likes least—raising money for her group—but she manages to sneak away from time to time to pursue her primary avocation: scuba diving.

Being a lawyer is both essential and unnecessary to Lori in her battles on global trade. If someone without a bar card took her job, the organized bar would not come swooping down and charge her with unauthorized practice of law. Many of those who lobby on trade issues on all sides are not lawyers, and the same is true for most of the active members of her coalition. But Lori embraces her legal training because she knows how vital it is to her ability to make her case not in a court of law but in the court of public opinion and in the halls of Congress, where lawyers and non-lawyers alike compete for votes on the issue of global trade.

Conclusion

By Diane T. Chin

In this book we have attempted to convey that no single path can lead you to a rewarding, successful, and meaningful legal career outside a traditional law firm. You have met lawyers in small private practices and others who work at large, well-established government agencies and nonprofits. For obvious reasons, they were selected because they could convey that they enjoy their work and their lives. Alan Morrison and I both believe, having lived in the world of law and having both selected careers outside traditional law practice, that you can find a meaningful career too. We have known too many young lawyers who have left the practice of law because they did not find satisfaction in law firm work. Our goal is to help you find a way to stay in the field of law, working on issues that have meaning to you, because we also believe that the world will be a better place if you do.

For as many "bad lawyer" jokes as there are in the world, there are more "good lawyer" stories out there. We hope you will write your own.

Most of the lawyers I know who are happy have had a number of different kinds of jobs in a number of different fields, although some had found their niche, frequently already decided upon before law school, and have stayed there. What I can say with utter certainty is that no doors will be closed to you that cannot be opened again.

Finding meaningful and financially satisfactory work outside of traditional law firms may take more creativity, patience, risk-taking, and resolve than some of your peers must expend. Based upon personal experience, the narratives of the lawyers showcased in this book, and the students I have been privileged to work with, I know that it is worth the effort. Lawyers who use their legal training in nontraditional settings help make this world a better place every day. They help people every day. Some of them make the air more breathable and the water more drinkable. They change entire systems based on discrimination and hierarchy. And, equally important, they find satisfaction in both their personal and professional lives because of the contributions they bring to the world and the time they can spend with family and friends. The co-editors, authors, and subjects of this book believe that you can too.

Do not give up on your dreams. Persevere!

Resources and Helpful Hints

By Diane T. Chin

As the preceding chapters indicate, there can be uncertainty in finding the right fit within the legal profession, especially for those whose goal is to help make the world a better place for communities and issues that continue to be underrepresented. In this chapter, we describe some resources you can turn to, as well as a few helpful hints that we have learned as educators within the legal academy and as public interest practitioners.

Selecting the Right Law School

For those of you who are thinking about applying to law schools and do not think that a big, corporate law firm will be what you want, there are several factors to consider in finding the right law school fit. You might want to start with looking at information available on the websites of Equal Justice Works (www.equaljusticeworks.org) or the American Bar Association (www.abanet.org), both of which produce publications that describe law school resources for public interest and *pro bono* programs.

Talk to your college and university faculty who might be familiar with the legal field, or your pre-law advisor, and ask their advice. Also ask them for referrals to public interest and government attorneys they know who might be willing to talk to you about their own law school experiences.

Choose a law school in which you will feel comfortable if you do not plan to join a traditional law firm. Visit the law school. Meet with students, evaluate what kinds of student organizations exist, and ask about the institutional support for the kind of law student and lawyer you want to be.

Questions you should ask include:

- Is the culture of the law school one that supports students who want to pursue public interest careers?
- What courses, clinics, and seminars may be available to you so you can explore different fields and types of practice?
- Are there staff dedicated to working with you to identify opportunities outside of the law firm track?
- What level of resources is dedicated at the law school for students who do not want to enter traditional law practice?

You should also speak with alumni who are not working at law firms and ask for their evaluation of their own experience. Do not feel uncomfortable doing this. You can get referrals from the law school, but also ask people in your own network if they know graduates from specific law schools.

It is also important that you evaluate how much debt you feel comfortable managing upon graduation. It can feel and sometimes is overwhelming to think about taking out loans in the six figures. It is almost unfathomable to most students to think about how they will repay those loans, which might enhance the attractiveness of big law firm salaries.

You do not need to go to the most expensive law school that you get into to get a great legal education. Explore all of your options. Also find out as much as you can about any scholarships that might be available and if the law school you are considering has a loan repayment or forgiveness program. Paying for law school is an investment in your future, but you cannot think about it only as an investment that has a monetary payout to be a good school. Many of you are also investing in achieving your vision of having a career that will allow you daily to benefit your community or advance broader social goals. That payout may seem more elusive, but it is just as important.

Selecting the Right Path(s) for Law Students

All of the lawyers in our book have taken various paths and have walked through previously unknown doors to find meaningful professional lives. It is easy to develop tunnel vision at law school. Perhaps unwittingly, fueled by magazine rankings and other unobjective criteria, law school career services offices may simply become funnels straight into law firms, which frequently pay law schools to allow them on-campus to recruit promising students. We encourage you to maintain your intellectual curiosity and your social justice commitments. Explore as many possible career options, legal fields, and types of employing organizations as you can while you are in law school.

What you should do:

(1) Make an effort to get to know one or two key faculty members who have practice experience in government or public interest. Ask them to put you in touch with lawyers in the field who would be open to an informational interview.

(2) Take advantage of any alumni mentoring at your university or law school. Meet with alumni attorneys and continue to expand your network of people by obtaining additional references.

(3) While in law school, research practice areas through clinics, externships, summer jobs, and career exploration programming. In seeking out experiences, broaden your horizons as wide as you are comfortable with. Be sure that your law school résumé reflects your commitment to public interest through participation in student groups, volunteer activities, and clinics. This will be particularly helpful to those of you who think you will join a traditional law firm for a few years directly after law school but want a career elsewhere.

(4) As you are learning about your options, pay attention to what you do and do not like about your varied experiences. What are the skills you like to use every day? What kinds of tasks frustrate you? What do you need to learn more about? What kind of work environment is best for you? How much client or community contact do you want or need to make you happy? What strategies are being used by which kinds of lawyers, and how do you evaluate their effectiveness? What kinds of issues do you like to think about? What kind of work makes you feel good about yourself?

(5) Even as you are exploring career paths, learn early on about non-firm options that you may have when you graduate from law school. These include judicial clerkships, postgraduate public interest fellowships (for example, find out about Skadden, Equal Justice Works, or Soros fellowships that fund you to work at a nonprofit organization on advocacy projects or to provide direct services), and government (local, state, and federal) programs for new lawyers.

(6) Locate a group of law school peers (at your law school as well as others you meet) who can provide support to you, especially during the on-campus interviewing time, when you may feel very

isolated. Many students have come into my office in the fall to ask if they are crazy because "everyone else" is applying to work at a large firm and they are not. Of course this is not true, but it can feel as if it is. There are other students at every law school who are in a similar situation. Finding them will provide solace and support as well as remind you of your purpose when temptation to stray from your path may arise.

(7) Learn about budgeting and develop the skills you need to lead a life that is comfortable and within your means. For many of you, law school will be the first time you will be in an adult setting, responsible for more of your own household finances and household tasks. This can be a confusing time, especially if some of your peers go to work at firms during the summer and make more in ten weeks than you have over the course of several years. It is also tempting, if you choose to go to a law firm during the summers with the intention to reduce your debt load, to shift into a law firm lifestyle, including the enjoyment of new material goods and fancy dinners. Act in moderation. If you become accustomed to this new lifestyle, you may find yourself held suddenly captive to what are not so lovingly called in the industry the "golden handcuffs."

(8) If you don't know how to cook, now would be a good time to learn. If you don't know how to create a budget for yourself and the skills you need to live within that budget, ask someone you trust for help. Learn to balance your checkbook and never become too dependent on your credit cards. There are many great cookbooks out there as well as simple and easy-to-understand books about managing personal finances. A plethora of information is available on the Internet for these purposes as well.

Making the Transition

Many of our chapters tell the stories of individuals who had explored traditional firms and, for any number of reasons, decided that they did not offer the type of work, workplace culture, or lifestyle that would suit these individuals' goals. For those of you who want to transition, we reiterate advice that you have likely already received from a number of sources.

(1) While still at your law firm, take on *pro bono* cases and projects. Whether you are handling a case as co-counsel with a legal services

organization or serving on the board of directors of a nonprofit advocacy organization, *pro bono* work offers you many benefits besides feeding your soul. Through these efforts, you will network with individuals who may be able to help you make the transition as well as develop valuable skills and knowledge that will make any shift easier. You will also learn about organizations — those in your legal community you would like to work with and those you do not; which organizations are run in ways that you like and which are not; individuals with whom you would like to work and those you do not think would mesh with your style or goals. All of this information is incredibly important as you begin to develop your transition plan to a happier and more meaningful legal career. Also, many groups will hire someone they know over an unknown quantity, which is another reason to get in the door and work with people who might be in a position to hire you or recommend you to a colleague or organization when a job opens up.

(2) Some firms also allow associates to volunteer full-time at local criminal prosecutor's or defender's offices, other government agencies, and even nonprofits. Talk to your firm's *pro bono* coordinator to identify options.

(3) If you choose to go to a firm directly out of law school but think that you are only going to be there for a brief number of years (as is the case with a large number of associates), don't let yourself become accustomed to the lifestyle that a six-figure income may foster. Budget wisely, get out of debt, and do not be tempted to incur new debt that will make it difficult for you to give up fifty to seventy-five percent of your salary if an opportunity arises to do work that you could love. And set a time, such as two or three years after you start, when you promise yourself that you will take stock and evaluate your life and not just continue where you are because of inertia. This is when a supportive peer group will also be helpful.

(4) If you have been at a firm and have become accustomed to a firm's lifestyle, start evaluating your finances. Create a budget that will make it feasible for you to leave the firm within a reasonable time. Downsize your lifestyle if you need to. Pay off student loans as quickly as possible and do not incur additional debt.

(5) Consider applying for a judicial clerkship or staff attorney position with a court as a transition out of the firm.

(6) Many U.S. Attorneys' and federal public defenders' offices as well as local public defender and district attorneys' offices hire associates from law firms, especially if they have had any litigation

experience. Consider this option or other government agencies after a few years.

(7) You must network to make a successful transition. By this I do not mean that in any transition you will rely on connections. Rather, to know where you want to end up, you will need to engage in some informational interviews and let people know that you want to move into nonprofit, government, or private public interest practice. Contact friends from law school, faculty members, your law school public interest advisors, and law school alumni as well as colleagues from firms who you know have been successful in their own transitions. Get referrals to public interest and government lawyers who would be willing to take a few minutes to talk with you about what they know about their field and to provide advice about how you can prepare for a transition. Always thank those individuals who make time for you. If you do not, it will not only reflect badly on you but also upon the friend, family member, or colleague who made the referral.

(8) Be realistic in planning how long it will take to make a transition. It will take at least six months to a year or more unless you have a stellar *pro bono* history and were active in public interest activities as a law student, although some government agencies may hire you directly from your firm in a shorter time. Your transition plan should begin with budgeting and networking. As you become more confident in your goal, identify organizations and government agencies to which you would like to apply. Network with individuals connected to those potential employers. Conduct more informational interviews. Research job openings on the Web and through legal newspapers, and use your law school's public interest advising resources. Begin to send out applications. Have patience and be kind to yourself throughout this endeavor.

(9) A special word of caution to those who graduated from top-tier law schools. With all due respect, some of you have been able to operate in a world where the status of your law school alone has opened doors. While your law school's reputation may continue to give you a small edge, that edge will be quickly erased if you approach your transition with an air of entitlement. For nonprofit, legal services, and advocacy organizations especially, you will be competing with individuals who have been consistent in their public interest work, and frequently that can trump any Ivy League credentials. Be honest about your experience and modest when approaching your transition.

Other Resources

There are also a number of written and electronic materials available to help you in your exploration. Harvard's *Serving the Public: A Job Search Guide* is the bible for law students who want to engage in job searches in advocacy, nonprofit, and government agencies. The Bernard Koteen Office of Public Interest Advising (OPIA) at Harvard Law School (www.law.harvard.edu/students/opia) also provides an excellent service by offering online numerous publications that can help individuals explore new areas of law as well as transitions from firms to nonprofit or government employment. OPIA's *The Great Firm Escape: From Making a Living to Making a Difference* as well as the ABA's handbook on changing jobs might also give you good ideas.

Deborah Arron's *What Can You Do with a Law Degree?* provides an overview of career alternatives. Lisa L. Abrams' *The Official Guide to Legal Specialties* describes a variety of major practice areas that will introduce you to the activities and legal issues you may expect to encounter. The National Association of Law Placement's www.PSLawNet.org is a rich resource for law students and lawyers looking for nonprofit, government, and academic positions. National Legal Aid and Defender Association (www.nlada.org), Opportunity Knocks (www.opportunityknocks.org), Idealist (www.idealist.org), and Craig's List (www.craigslist.org) all provide job postings for those of you who may be ready to make a transition. Federal, state, and local governments all maintain websites about attorney job openings or positions (frequently in the policy or investigation realms) where legal training is an asset. (For federal jobs, look at UsaJobs.opm.gov.) You should also routinely scan your local legal newspapers. Start with some "window shopping" just to see what is out there. You may be pleasantly surprised to learn about an opening that would be of interest to you.

A colleague of mine who transitioned from the private sector recently commented to me that the job search experience of public interest law school students mirrors the actual process of locating a job in the real world better than the on-campus interviewing experience where corporate law firm representatives waving large fistfuls of money show up to invite you to join them. She is absolutely correct. What we have outlined is not anything novel. The steps we recommend are simply the steps that everyone in almost any field would take to engage in an effort to locate a job they want. This is simply to say that you can do this, and you can do it successfully. We wish you luck, of course, but we also hope that you will find the field of law that will be a place where your aspirations for a better world can be fulfilled.